COLT TERRY, GREEN BERET

Joseph G. Dawson III, General Editor

Editorial Board:
Robert Doughty
Brian Linn
Craig Symonds
Robert Wooster

Colt Terry,

GREEN BERET

CHARLES D. PATTON

Texas A&M University Press
COLLEGE STATION

Copyright © 2005 by Charles D. Patton
Manufactured in the United States of America
All rights reserved
First edition

ISBN 1-58544-373-5 (cloth : alk. paper) —

Contents

Preface

THIS IS THE STORY OF CURTIS "COLT" TERRY, one of the original Green Berets.[1] The information for this story came primarily from Colt's personal recollections documented in taped interviews. Many facts were confirmed with fellow paratroopers, military historians, and Special Forces NCOs and officers who served with him. (See the endnotes for full details of our research methods.)[2]

Colt gave the interviews to leave a record of his experiences. After hearing Colt's story, the author felt that other people should know this man.

This story is a nonfiction account based on certain sources, not a full biography but rather a detailed look at Colt's military service career. Colt reconstructed most of the quoted passages from his recollections, depicting, in essence, what others said but not necessarily always exactly what they had said.

Some dates are approximate and some names have been changed to protect the innocent and the guilty. The use of personal names has been avoided in certain situations where the individuals or their families might feel embarrassed. When a name was changed, pseudonyms were used and enclosed in quotation marks at first mention. The author has made an extensive effort to verify all names, but some were difficult to determine. We apologize for any errors made, especially to anyone's name.

These incidents took place over thirty-five years ago, and even though memories can fade over time, Colt's recollections are extraordinarily lucid and have been verified in many instances by other people who were present at the time. Even though not all incidents could be crosschecked, the author believes that this story can be reasonably relied upon for a realistic description of one of the men who set the standards for the U.S. Army's Special Forces, also known as the Green Berets.

People of all origins fought and died in America's wars. It seems fitting to describe those who served with and knew Colt simply by their deeds and

by their names, when known, rather than by superficial descriptions such as ethnicity or color.

The author thanks Colt for his friendship; Pat Terry, his wife, for introducing me to Colt and for sharing her husband with the world; Jim Sadkovich, Kevin Brock, Yvonne Lorence, and Mark Gatlin for their encouragement, support, and guidance; and Terry Belanger, God rest her soul, for her guidance and professionalism in the daunting task of editing his writing. The author also thanks, above all, his wife, Estella, for her love and patience during all the time required completing this work.

COLT TERRY, GREEN BERET

Introduction

THIS IS THE STORY OF AN ORDINARY MAN who performed extraordinary deeds. Colt Terry enlisted in the U.S. Army at the end of World War II, a time when no more wars could be imagined. He rose from private to master sergeant and, after nearly two years in Korea, including one tour behind enemy lines, received a field commission to second lieutenant. This rarely bestowed honor instilled in Colt an undying loyalty to the noncommissioned officers who were later under his command. He never forgot his roots, even after advancing throughout his career to the permanent rank of lieutenant colonel.

Colt received two Bronze Stars for bravery, two combat infantry badges, and a Purple Heart. His story includes examples of how, in war, some men die while others live, without reason or rationale. For this man, however, the reason why he was so many times spared did have a rationale—to save him for one incredible defining moment. For his bravest deed, in the author's opinion, he received no medal, but then many brave deeds and brave men go unrecognized in every war.

Other books written about the U.S. Army's Special Forces tell the story of war from the perspectives of commanders and emphasize units, positions, tactics, and strategies. This book offers the perspective of a fighter who, even as an officer, fought side by side with his friends and fellow soldiers. It portrays a loyal comrade who saved many men from certain death and who was saved from certain death by others. Colt's story is the story of many soldiers, both those who lived and those who died, the latter often unnecessarily and almost always undeservedly.

Colt Terry was one of the most highly trained soldiers in the U.S. Army. He learned, and then taught, ambushing, underwater demolition, sabotage, silent killing, and much more. Many of his students became Special Forces instructors. From his training methods to his example in battle, Colt was influential in setting the standards of this elite corps. He mastered German and Czech and trained insurgents for secret airdrops into Czechoslovakia, Germany, Korea, Vietnam, and Cambodia. He hunted, and was hunted by, Chinese, North Korean, North Vietnamese, and Viet Cong soldiers, and he killed many of them.

His story is also the story of all Green Berets and how their unending spirit and vast daring have served our country since the inception of the 10th Special Forces Group (Airborne) on June 19, 1952.[1] The original group consisted of triple volunteers—men who volunteered to join the army, volunteered to be paratroopers, and then volunteered to join Special Forces. Most of them also volunteered for duty in Vietnam, many for more than one tour. The jaunty hat, the green beret, that would set Special Forces apart from other units at that time would be adopted later.

Special Forces train to be self-sufficient, to function alone in hostile territory and yet, equally, to work together like blood brothers. They are the first to volunteer for the most dangerous assignments. At the same time, they are caring. As career soldiers, they care deeply about the army. Under fire they care about their comrades more than they care about themselves. Even in the midst of battle, they care about innocent people and even animals caught up in the action. Above all, they care about their fallen colleagues and go to great extremes to avoid leaving their wounded or dead behind on the field of battle.

Not all men can repeatedly cheat death in combat before crossing the threshold themselves. Some heroes live to tell their children about their war experiences, but many heroes die and must rely on others to speak their praises. This book is dedicated to those who gave their lives so that others could live, those who never had the chance to tell their stories.

Indoctrination and Combat Jump into Korea

CURTIS "COLT" TERRY WAS ONLY SIXTEEN
years old when he enlisted in the U.S. Army on September 26, 1945.[1] Underage and naïve, he had no idea what he was facing or what the army would become to him. At the time he was five feet, seven inches tall, all of 126 pounds, with dark, dark brown hair and a front tooth that stood out at nearly a 45-degree angle. He was not an attractive teenager. Deprived as a child in many ways, Colt did not have stability in his early years.

Colt was born on February 8, 1929. His father left his mother when the boy was four years old and his sisters were two and six years old. His mother struggled to support herself and her children alone in Kissimmee, Florida, then just a tiny hamlet where two highways crossed. As Colt recalls, "She was so poor that the stock market crash didn't make any difference in her life." His clothes were hand-me-downs, and he got into fights occasionally when he was teased about them.

He was of Irish, English, and German descent, which may have contributed to a hotheaded and stubborn temperament that would later cause him trouble from time to time. His mother, born in Kentucky, raised Colt with Christian principles that would stay with him throughout his life.

Soon after Colt started high school, in 1944, his mother pulled him out, against his wishes, and moved the family to Daytona. Even with Colt working part time, his mother found it difficult to support three children there. After struggling for a time, she decided to move back to Kissimmee less than a year later. But she would return without Colt.

In Daytona Beach the family had met a World War II veteran, Earl Heist, who had been injured in battle. He was a six-foot-tall German and as tough as he needed to be. When Colt's mother decided to go back to Kissimmee, she asked Earl if he would allow Colt to live with him if she sent him a little money each month. Earl agreed. The teen thought that it would be great to stay with a male role model, especially one who had been in the army, but he was in for a surprise.

Earl lived in an apartment right off the beach. The first morning when Earl came to wake Colt for school, the boy did not get out of bed right away. The next thing Colt knew, he was on the floor with his bed upside down on top of him.

This kind of male influence at this time in his life was not exactly what Colt expected, but it did teach him just enough respect for authority to carry him into early adulthood. Also at this time, Colt handled his first gun: a combination over/under .22-caliber rifle, 410-gauge shotgun. He went hunting for rabbits and deer, never seeing either. But he did learn how to aim and accurately shoot at moving targets, tossing tin cans in the air.

A few months later his mother sent Earl a letter telling him that she could no longer continue to send him money. She asked him to send her boy back to Kissimmee.

Colt no longer wanted to go back to that wide spot in the road—a place with no jobs and no hope. He told Earl, "It would be the lowest, but I would rather quit school and join the army than go back to nothing but citrus trees and cattle."

Earl had to agree: "The army would be good for you and you could get an education there. You might even like it and stay. However, you're only sixteen years old and can't join up yet."

Colt had his answer ready, "I can, if you'll change my birth certificate year by one and sign for me, they'll let me in."

Because the boy really wanted to join the army, he agreed. Within a short year, Earl Heist had taught Colt to be a man—to take responsibility for his own destiny and not to start fights but not to run away either. This, he felt, was enough to get Colt through boot camp at least. Colt joined up.

The army shipped him first to Fort McPherson, Georgia, for swearing in and then briefly to Fort Bragg, North Carolina, for shots and to issue his Class A uniform (the more formal one) and other gear. He then got back onto a troop train and traveled to Fort Hood, Texas, and basic training. After Colt arrived at boot camp, he lay in his barracks bed each night and thought sadly about the school years he was missing. He thought of how stupid it was not to have stayed in school. After basic training, because he did well on army tests, he was sent to the Army Air Force Radar School in Boca Raton, Florida, and received training in the repair and operation of radar, still a secret technology at the time.[2]

Because so many men had recently returned from World War II, Colt progressed slowly in rank. In 1947, as a private first class, he volunteered

Colt training with Sergeant Perry on radio and radar repair.

and was shipped off to jump school at Fort Benning, Georgia. He scored the maximum five hundred points on the Army Physical Training Test and graduated first in his class.[3] He was growing up and getting tougher.

WHEN HE GRADUATED FROM JUMP SCHOOL, COLT WAS assigned to the 82d Airborne Division at Fort Bragg, North Carolina. (The 82d Airborne, still headquartered at Fort Bragg today, is known as America's Honor Guard—always ready to go, any time, any place.) He was assigned to the 82d Airborne Replacement Company and within a few days reassigned to the 82d Airborne Signal Company.[4] As a paratrooper, he began to think of himself as "one tough hombre." Two platoon sergeants, M.Sgt. Robert E. Taylor and M.Sgt. Walter Talkovich, were also tough—on him. Taylor was a tall prizefighter from Oklahoma. Talkovich, a former Pennsylvania coal miner, had been drafted during World War II and had seen action. Each had found a home in the army.

One day Taylor told Colt, who was still a private first class at the time, that Colt had embarrassed him at the NCO (noncommissioned officer) meeting earlier that day. This comment confused the private because he had not been at the meeting. Taylor explained that Colt was the only man in his unit who did not have a high school education. The two sergeants had conspired to force him to go back to school and get his diploma. Although it was a GED (general equivalency diploma), it counted and was essential if he was ever going to have a chance to move up the ranks. At the time, he did not appreciate what this could mean to his army career.

IN 1948 HE WAS PROMOTED TO CORPORAL. HE WAS forever thankful to Sergeants Taylor and Talkovich for caring enough to set him on the right track.

By their example, the sergeants gave Colt his first lessons in true leadership. He learned to try to be as good as, or better than, his men at every task he asked of them. Because of these men, he also gained an undying affection for NCOs. Sergeant Taylor was later killed in Korea. When Sergeant Talkovich left the army, he retired to his farm in Pennsylvania.

About this time, Colt's 45-degree-angled front tooth was broken off in a minor car accident. This fortunate occurrence suddenly improved his looks.

ON SEPTEMBER 15, 1949, COLT'S ENLISTMENT WAS UP.[5] He was discharged with the right to reenlist within ninety days and retain his rank. Within two months, on November 3, 1949, finding life as a construction worker in West Palm Beach unattractive, he reenlisted in the 82d Airborne Division, Pathfinder Platoon. Soon after, he was promoted to sergeant (three stripes).

After more than a year as an NCO at Fort Bragg, Colt was ready for the next challenge. He came in from training one day and saw a notice on the bulletin board. The army wanted two jump-qualified NCOs from his company to join the 187th Regimental Combat Team in Korea. The 187th was organized at Fort Campbell, Kentucky, from two other airborne divisions. It was actually a bit larger than a regiment, with the later addition of the 674th Artillery and several antiaircraft units.[6]

Colt had received a "Dear John" letter from a girl he had been dating, which put him in a reckless mood—a response tendency that would reoccur throughout his military life. He wanted to get into the action. Colt ma-

Colt just out of parachute school and about to ship out to Korea.

neuvered his name onto the list by forgiving a small debt owed to him by the company clerk.

During their conversation, the clerk reminded Colt, "Korea is a shooting war. You could get killed. They need NCOs to replace ones who had been killed." Then he said point-blank, "Korea isn't a place you should go and, if you do, you'll come back in a body bag." The sergeant insisted that Korea was where he wanted to go.

Colt's name appeared on the orders the next day. Within a couple of weeks, he had been assigned to the 187th Regimental Combat Team with the MOS (military occupational specialty) of radio repairman/rifle-squad leader, his second promotion at the sergeant level, and on September 6, 1950, he was on his way to Korea.[7]

The army sent Colt by train to California and then by troopship to Korea. The trip took eleven days, and he was seasick during the entire trip. In Korea he traveled by train to reach the regiment near Taegu. When he got there, he was assigned to G (George) Company's 3d Platoon. The platoon leader, 1st Lt. Herbert J. Hedrick, looked at Colt's orders and told him: "We need a radio repairman like we need an extra hole in our heads. Welcome to the

Colt had to leave his 1950 Mercury behind when he went to Korea.

toughest platoon in the 187th." Hedrick appointed him assistant squad leader for the 3d Squad, which, in typical army tradition, had nothing to do with his MOS of being a radar and radio repairman. This was Colt's first experience at leading other men, and he did not feel ready for the job despite the good role models he had known. But this was Korea, and many men stepped into their first leadership role during this war.

AS BACKGROUND: AT THE END OF WORLD WAR II ON September 23, 1945, during the surrender of Japan, a four-country trusteeship consisting of the United States, Russia, China, and the United Kingdom was envisioned to oversee a united Korea. But the Russians never cooperated because they believed that their influence over northern Korea, and the strong support for communism among many southern citizens, would eventually unite the entire country. The mountainous north-south Korean peninsula was then arbitrarily split east-west into two halves along the thirty-eighth parallel—creating two separate governments, North and South. The Russians

Pay jump into South Korea near Taegu. Men were pulled off the front line to do certification jumps for their increased pay rate when due and then sent back.

then helped North Korea build and train a large army, while the United States attempted to get South Korea on a democratic footing with financial aid.

After the election of South Korea's first president, Syngman Rhee, on July 20, 1948, the United States then began to withdraw its military resources and, by the end of the year, had only 7,500 troops present on the peninsula. On May 3, 1949, the North Koreans began a series of attacks across the thirty-eighth parallel. The South Koreans repulsed each one. The United States, meanwhile, began pouring troops back into Korea. In June, 1950, the North massed its entire army along the thirty-eighth parallel, and fighting began in earnest. In October, 1950, the Chinese sent in an estimated 80,000 troops to help the communist North. The ensuing Korean War raged for three years, through 1953.

Toward the end of the conflict, the United States and other U.N. countries had 550,000 troops committed to defend South Korea, and the Chinese and North Koreans had 456,000. During the war, the United States and other U.N countries lost 36,000 combatants; the Chinese and North Koreans more than 214,000; and South Korea 47,000. On both sides, hundreds of thousands of civilians were also killed or missing. Yet this high-level view of war does

not begin to describe what the regular soldier experienced on the ground in Korea.[8]

On MARCH 23, 1951, ALONG WITH 2,859 OTHER TROOPERS in his regiment, Colt parachuted into North Korea at a place called Munson-ni. The men were replacements for G Company, which had been in Korea since October, 1950, as part of the U.N. combined force meant to attack and push north, away from Seoul, the invading North Korean army and their Chinese reinforcements.[9]

Colt's platoon jumped, as did other platoons, from C-119 aircraft, a double-bay cargo plane with clamshell doors in the rear and known as the "flying boxcar."[10] C-46s, C-47s, and C-82s were also used in the airdrop. The men in Colt's platoon formed two lines along an open bay that ran from the cockpit to the tail. Hanging over the open bay was all of their equipment strapped to parachutes. The whole arrangement was called the monorail system: the equipment dropped first and then the men followed out side doors.

Each paratrooper was so loaded down with equipment that two men had to help each trooper onto the airplane. The soldiers looked like overloaded packhorses. Each one carried a parachute on his back, a reserve chute on his front, his steel helmet, his rifle, four bandoleers of M1 ammo, two bando-leers across his chest for the BAR (Browning automatic rifle) man, six hand grenades—three strapped to each thigh in pouches—a canteen, a first-aid pouch, a gas-mask container with four or five rifle grenades, and, between his legs, a combat pack containing a sleeping bag, rubber galoshes, three days of C-rations, a change of underwear, and socks, toothpaste, poncho, first-aid kit, and a safety razor. The army expected soldiers to shave every day except when they were fighting, and they did. Many paratroopers, including Colt, also wore a .45-caliber pistol in a military holster with several ammo clips.

As their C-119 approached the drop zone, a red warning light came on, which signaled the troopers that they had four minutes before the plane would reach the area. On this jump, the troopers' parachutes would open automatically. Each would be tethered by a nylon line, called a static line, to a cable attached along the ceiling of the aircraft. At the parachute end of the static line was the "break cord." This would sever due to the weight of the man and his equipment when the paratrooper jumped out of the airplane, opening the chute and allowing the jumper to drift away from the aircraft.

The troopers stood up and hooked their static line to the cable. When a green light came on, each man did a combination stagger-and-shuffle step along the one-foot–wide metal floor next to the open bay and got into place next to the door. As Colt moved toward the door, he smacked his shin on a fold-up nylon seat that had been left down by another trooper. It infuriated him, which made it easier to jump out of the airplane. He and the other twenty-five soldiers were so miserable in the old aircraft anyway that they were glad to get out of it. As soon as he was out the door, he began counting, "One thousand, two thousand, three thousand"—then the chute opened.

As Colt drifted down, he expected enemy gunfire, but none came. At 0800 on this Good Friday, he landed in a rice field that was ten miles square. The North Koreans and Chinese must have seen all the chutes in the sky and fled. His squad later found teakettles still on fires and rations sitting open and uneaten.

His parachute caught a side draft, which caused him to drift and swing. He floated over the edge of the rice paddy and into an apple orchard adjacent to the drop zone. With so much equipment on, he could not guide himself very well. The parachutes were the old style T-7, unlike the square style in use today, and could cause a jumper to swing back and forth like a pendulum. If the parachute swings up just as he lands, it can slam its wearer into the ground. This happened to Colt. His upper right arm hit a limb on one of the apple trees on the way down. After landing, he could not move his right arm to pull the quick release on his chute. Because of the position in which his equipment landed, he could not reach the release with his left hand either. As a whole, his squad had been very lucky, but he was lying defenseless on the cold ground of the orchard.

Colt managed to pull his .45 automatic from its holster with his left hand. If any Chinese came along, at least he could shoot them. Suddenly, a corporal from his squad, Hernandez, emerged from the trees at the top of a nearby rice paddy dike. With his BAR, he was herding six prisoners, their hands on top of their heads. Colt could tell from how ruffled they looked that the corporal had caught them sleeping. From their Mao-style hats, he could tell that the prisoners were members of the Chinese Army.

As Hernandez marched the Chinese toward Colt, he said, "It's no time for a nap, Sarge."

Colt was not in a mood for humor. "I need help—I think my arm's broken."

The corporal, who spoke in broken English, turned to the six Chinese and said, "You don't move a fuckin' muscle, or I shoot you ass," as if they could understand. In fact, they did not understand but still smiled and complied.

Colt kept the prisoners covered with his .45 while the corporal helped him up. When he was on his feet, the sergeant found that he was able to move. He and the corporal prodded the prisoners to march on, with one of them carrying Colt's pack and other equipment, and headed off to find the rest of the squad and their company. As they walked along, Colt marveled at how much equipment had been abandoned all over the drop zone: machine-gun barrels broken loose, hand grenades, cases of ammunition, and supplies everywhere.

The feeling slowly returned to Colt's arm, which was not broken. After turning over the prisoners to designated guards, Colt's company remained in the vicinity for a few hours. Then they moved up to the hill overlooking the drop zone and dug foxholes. This was Colt's first official combat jump for which he could, if he wanted, add a small star to the center of his airborne jump wings.

THE AMERICANS DEFENDED THE HILL UNTIL THE NEXT night, when a tank unit broke through from the south. Saturday night, they all started north. Colt and his entire unit fell in behind the tanks. The paratroopers marched at double time all night behind those tanks, a distance of over twenty-five miles. One could have followed the 187th Regimental Combat Team by what the men threw away.

Steel helmets and galoshes were the first to go. Soon after, the horseshoe backpack went. Colt had wanted to wear his standard-issue paratrooper boots, but the pair he had was too small; he wore them until they gave him blisters and the blisters broke. Wool socks and waterproofing did not help much. It is tradition that members of an airborne unit, unless they are seriously injured, must keep fighting, so Colt kept moving with only socks and plastic battery bags on his feet, which wore through. He then replaced the socks with pieces of wool cut from a blanket and more plastic battery bags.

The next morning, Easter Sunday, March 25, 1951, all hell broke loose. The road became too narrow for the tanks, so the troopers went on without them. The regiment pursued a force that was primarily Chinese, with some North Korean regulars and even some armed civilians, all night until they took a stand at a Korean graveyard among some small hills. The Chinese had set up a textbook "area ambush." This occurs when men are placed in a configuration where the enemy will be caught in crossfire. A typical layout would be in the shape of an "L," with soldiers along each leg. The area in the center, to the right of the long leg of the "L," is called the "killing zone." That morning, the men of the Second Battalion, after nearly jogging all night, ran right into the enemy trap. Soaking wet, covered with mud, and having had no food for eighteen hours, the troopers started their combat experience by fighting their way out of the ambush.

When the shooting began, Colt dove behind a tree and landed next to a sergeant from his platoon. Bullets were flying everywhere. In all of the confusion of the previous night, Colt had become separated from his squad. Besides being tired, wet, bootless, and in the line of fire, he was having trouble with his M1, the normally reliable standard-army-issue rifle. He struggled to get it working properly, but mud kept it from automatically ejecting the spent shell casing when fired. After each shot, Colt had to use his foot to slide the bolt back until it ejected the casing. He could then manually put another round into the chamber and push the bolt forward with his hand. This procedure took vital seconds and turned his rapid-fire semiautomatic into a slow single-shot rifle—a dangerous disadvantage in combat. Others in his platoon were having similar problems.

As the shooting intensified, Colt regretted that he and the others had thrown away their steel helmets during the night. If everyone had kept them, they could more easily tell the Americans from the Chinese and North Koreans. Colt saw a burst from a Chinese machine gun take down five paratroopers at once—each shot through the neck or head. He wondered why someone did not try to shut down that weapon.

Colt spotted a North Korean, in civilian clothes, firing a "burp" gun (a small submachine gun) at other soldiers in his company. He told Sergeant "Hiller", "I've got one in my sights. I'm gonna drop 'im."[11]

Hiller responded, "No, don't shoot. We don't know where Easy [E] Company is."

Colt tried to argue. "This isn't an American. He has hair down to his ass." Hiller held firm. Colt would later regret this decision and the consequences it had for his platoon.

The cemetery on a peaceful day would have been idyllic and beautiful. The graves rose from the ground as tall mounds, all covered with neatly trimmed grass, and small black pine trees dotted the area. It might have looked like someone's lawn if not for the battle now swirling through it.

Colt and the platoon moved to the base of one of the grave mounds, joining Lieutenant Hedrick, 3d Platoon leader.[12] When they told him about the Korean they had seen, Hedrick said that the man was the security for a Chinese machine gun that they needed to knock out. The term "security" refers to placing one or more soldiers in a position to protect the rear or flank of a larger group. It would improve the Americans' chances of knocking out the machine gun if this enemy soldier could be eliminated.

The lieutenant called up a two-man bazooka team. Colt knelt behind a tree to provide covering fire. The assistant gunner put a round in the bazooka, wired it up, and tapped the gunner on the head to signal that it was ready. While they waited a fraction of a second for the gunner to fire at a target no more than twenty-five yards away, the machine gun turned on them. Two bullets, crashing through the trunk of the small tree two feet in front of Colt, zinged right past his face.

Just as the bazooka fired, bullets from the machine gun crashed through the assistant gunner's jaw. He flipped over backward. Nevertheless, the bazooka round found its target, killing one of the enemy and shutting down the machine gun. Before anyone could move, Sgt. Norwood K. Oates, a freckled-faced platoon medic from Oklahoma, rushed to the wounded man, sat him down, and applied an olive-drab battle dressing to his face. Colt remembered the contrast between the man's black hair and the red blood all over his face. Oates gave the soldier a shot of morphine, got him on his feet, and pointed him toward the aid station in the rear.

Because the American troops were covered with mud and wore no helmets, it was hard to distinguish them from the enemy, even at close range. Before the assistant gunner had staggered twenty feet, a paratrooper from an adjacent company, who thought the man was a Chinese soldier with his head camouflaged, shot him in the back.

Colt yelled, "Don't shoot! He's one of ours!" But it was too late. They all watched in awe as the gunner again rose to his feet and, holding in his intestines with his hands, staggered toward the aid station. Amazingly, he lived.

LIEUTENANT HEDRICK TOLD THE 1ST SQUAD LEADER TO bring along his team and follow him to the top of the ridge on which the machine gun was positioned. For some unknown reason, perhaps not hearing the command, 1st Squad failed to follow Hedrick. He crawled up the mound, alone, to the small ridge. From this position he could see that the machine gun was protecting the flank of about eighty Chinese troops. The Chinese, spread out in plain view, were lying on a small slope and shooting down into E Company, shooting Americans by the dozens.

Hedrick, not looking backward, thought that 1st Squad was right behind him. Observing an entire Chinese outfit spread before him like a shooting gallery, he put his carbine on full automatic and shot about fifteen Chinese with a series of short, well-aimed bursts. Colt could hear the enemy screaming and jabbering in Chinese.

Just then, the North Korean with the long hair and the burp gun, the man Colt had wanted to shoot earlier, jumped out of his foxhole and ran along the ridge toward Hedrick. The lieutenant was so focused on shooting the Chinese in front of him that he did not hear or see the North Korean coming at him. Even though he was right on top of Hedrick and could have shot him in the head or chest, he shot the lieutenant in both legs, a total of six times with 9-mm rounds, and then ran back to his foxhole. Only when Hedrick started yelling for a medic did anyone know that he was up on the ridge alone and had been hit.

The assistant platoon sergeant, M.Sgt. Paul Doule, began relaying Hedrick's call for a medic and then gave the order, "They're gonna attack! Fix bayonets!"

Colt had never been so frightened as he was at that moment. He knew little about bayonet fighting—only from a few hours of classes during his basic training four years earlier and a few times during his advanced infantry training. Pulling his bayonet from its sheath, he was shaking so hard that he could not get the bayonet on the end of his M1. Three times the bayonet dropped to the ground. Not wanting others to think he was a coward, he then put the rifle between his legs and used both hands to set the bayonet. Although bullets were flying all around him, he stayed totally focused on this task. Finally, he locked it into the end of his M1, or so he thought, and lifted the rifle into position. The bayonet fell to the ground. He gave up and said to himself, "If a Chinese soldier comes down that slope, I'll just have to shoot his ass."

AS COLT INCHED AROUND ONE OF THE LARGE BURIAL mounds, a young sergeant from another paratrooper company joined him from nowhere. The young NCO was separated from and looking for his squad. Colt sensed that the trooper was a real "wild ass."

His impression was immediately confirmed when the young man told him, "You're the ones doing all the fighting so I came over here to get in on the action." Colt never knew his name, but the soldier soon found the fight he was seeking.

When paratroopers go into battle, cooks are members of platoons. When an engagement starts, the cooks become fighters. Sgt. 1/C Leo J. Jakaitis, a cook from Colt's adopted platoon, came up to Colt, Sergeant "Wild Ass," and Master Sergeant Doule and said that the platoon leader had been shot up on the ridge. Pointing to the location, Sergeant Jakaitis said that someone had to go up and get the lieutenant before he bled to death.

Colt feared that the Doule was about to tell him to do it when Jakaitis told him and Sergeant "Wild Ass" to move out from behind their protective mound and provide covering fire while he went up the ridge to get the lieutenant and bring him down.

Not wanting Jakaitis to think him a coward, Colt blurted out, "Hell yes, we'll cover ya."

Colt and Sergeant "Wild Ass" stepped out from behind the grave into the open and started firing. When Jakaitis started up the hill, the North Korean with the long hair jumped out of his hole and was about to shoot him. Together, Colt and Sergeant "Wild Ass" fired, and the North Korean tumbled backward down the slope. As he did, Jakaitis turned around and thanked his two-man security team.

Jakaitis reached the top of the knoll, threw Hedrick over his shoulder, and started back down. Bullets were hitting all around them. Colt remembers screaming silently to himself for Jakaitis to hurry up because, standing out in the open, they were all going to be killed. He was scared, but he did not move until Jakaitis reached the bottom of the mound. The lieutenant's blood was pouring all over his rescuer. According to Colt's recollection, Sergeant Jakaitis was later awarded the Bronze Star for gallantry in action, the fifth-highest award among the top individual medals given in the military for gallantry or heroic service.[13]

Doule then pulled the platoon out of the graveyard, sending the men to a little shed in the rear area where a detail had been assigned to clean the company's M1 rifles. On the way to the shed, Colt decided to get rid of his malfunctioning M1. He came across a dead trooper, a good NCO whom he had known. Gently, Colt rolled the man over—he had been carrying a BAR, a fully automatic, .30-caliber weapon that delivered rounds in rapid fire. Heavy and powerful, a soldier who carried one usually wore a harness. Colt grabbed some ammo pouches, put on the harness, slung the BAR onto his shoulder, pointed the gun toward the sky, and test fired it. Now he had a functioning rifle.

Colt was now qualified for the Combat Infantryman Badge, and his first day in combat was not even over.

HE DID NOT REACH THE CLEANING SHED RIGHT AWAY. At the top of the hill above the little house he saw the platoon sergeant, Sgt. 1/C Richard V. Goltra, and his assistant, Master Sergeant Doule, take cover behind a small mound of dirt. As he flopped down beside them, Goltra told Colt to stay down—a sniper in the trees ahead of them was shooting at anyone who stuck his head up. Colt said that he was just trying to find his squad and asked them if he could do anything for them. He soon regretted making this offer.

Goltra told him to go down the hill. Lt. Earl K. Woolley was down there with a bunch of dead paratroopers. Goltra heard that Woolley had been hit with shrapnel from a Chinese hand grenade and did not even know if he was alive. Colt was to give the lieutenant any help that he needed.

Colt's first thoughts were, "Why the hell didn't the sergeant go down there himself," and "Why did I volunteer to help?" After a moment's reflection, he left his cover and his BAR, picked up an abandoned M1, and started running down the hill. It was not very steep and was sparsely dotted with scrub pines. He zigzagged like he had been taught in basic training. The sniper and other Chinese were shooting at him when the best possible thing happened. Colt was so frightened that he ran smack into one of the small pine trees. The collision flipped him over to one side and onto the ground. The sniper fired at that moment and missed. As Colt rolled down the hill, the sniper stopped shooting. Later, he figured that the sniper probably stopped shooting because he thought he had hit him.

At the bottom of the hill, Colt was back in the green graveyard. He found Lieutenant Woolley, with blood running down his face, looking like the "walking dead." A cheap Chinese hand grenade had gone off near him, and the tin shrapnel had hit him in the face.

As young as Colt was and with this being his first day of combat, seeing one of his leaders bloodied nearly scared him to madness. He realized more than ever that the same thing could happen to him. He blurted out that the platoon sergeant had sent him down to help. Colt could see about six or eight paratroopers lying on a little embankment. Each one had tried to locate and kill the sniper, and all had failed; their bodies were stacked like cordwood. Colt's biggest fear was to appear to be a coward in the eyes of the lieutenant. He asked the officer, "Sir, d'ya want me to check and see if any of 'em are alive?"

He responded: "No, son. If you go up there, you'll be laying right there beside them. The sniper has that spot sighted in." He then added, "Pick up as many rifles as you can carry and get 'em back up that hill."

Colt mumbled under his breath, "Oh, shit."

He gathered up about eight or nine M1s; they were very heavy. In the meantime another NCO, Sgt. Norman L. Bell, a Canadian in Colt's outfit, had made it down the hill. Lieutenant Woolley gave him the same assignment. When Bell had loaded up with M1s, he and Colt started up the hill about ten yards apart. They both tried to run in zigzags, but carrying such heavy loads uphill slowed them down and limited their agility. The sniper and his comrades began shooting at them.

Out of the corner of his eye, Colt saw Bell go down when a round hit him in the back. As he fell, Bell screamed and threw the rifles over his head. Colt was certain he was dead. Seeing this happen threw his legs into high gear. He made it to the top with his armful of rifles and without a scratch, but his feeling of accomplishment was short-lived. Colt suddenly realized that he could have been the one shot by the sniper—he was still alive only because the sniper had chosen the other man as his target. He thought that Sergeant Goltra seemed irked because he had come back up the hill. But Colt was equally upset with Goltra. He wanted to tell him to "get off his lard ass" but held his anger. Instead, Colt told him that Lieutenant Woolley was okay and explained how the lieutenant had sent him and the other man back up the hill with the rifles to be cleaned, and how the Canadian sergeant had been shot in the back. Goltra told him to take the rifles over to the cleaning shed.

When he arrived, he was surprised to find his missing squad there, hard at work over a giant wok full of boiling water. Their break from the action would be a brief one, though.

That night Colt and his squad formed a perimeter in the yard around the shed and dug in. Rain had been falling for about twelve hours. The air was cold, and everything was wet. Colt's foxhole soon filled with rainwater. They were all miserable. Colt and his foxhole partner, Cpl. Hubert A. Meredith, wrapped in wet olive-drab blankets, sat on the edge of the foxhole. Ribbing the sergeant, Meredith told him to stop chattering his teeth—the Chinese would know where they were. But Colt could not keep his teeth from chattering; he would stay miserable in the same place for the entire night. They listened to a wounded Chinese soldier scream all night, obviously in great pain. He stopped just before daybreak, probably because he died. The fighting continued.

Two days later, when they had moved and were fighting up a mountain, Meredith was killed while trying to rescue Goltra, their platoon sergeant, after he had been shot. When Meredith reached up to pull him down off a ridge, two rounds struck the corporal in the head. He died instantly. Goltra lived.

AFTER TWO DAYS OF FIGHTING, THE CHINESE PULLED back, and it was quiet around Colt's company. His 3d Platoon went out on a reconnaissance patrol and found no enemy. G Company was then moved to the rear. Colt developed a severe cough along the way.

Colt finally took himself to their small aid station because his fellow soldiers were concerned that, if he were with them when they went back to the fighting, his cough would give away their position. He arrived there in the dark, and as he approached one of the squad tents, a doctor stepped out and saw him.[14] The doctor could hear Colt's cough, but the first thing he asked him about was what he was wearing on his feet. Colt told him that they were blankets and plastic bags, because of his blisters and bleeding sores, but that he was not there for that reason, he was there about his bad cold and cough. The doctor listened to Colt's chest with his stethoscope and in seconds diagnosed a severe case of pneumonia. He had two 55-gallon drums positioned and laid a stretcher across them. Orderlies put Colt on the stretcher, covered him with enough blankets to stop him from shivering, and told him that they would get him to the hospital first thing in the morning.

One of the medics gave him a shot of something and asked him if he needed a pill to help him sleep. Exhausted, Colt answered, "No. I'll sleep through the night ... even if the Chinese come."

The next morning he was shipped to a mobile army surgical hospital (MASH).[15] When he got out of the hospital, about ten days later, someone gave him a pair of boots that fit.

AFTER HIS RELEASE FROM THE HOSPITAL IN EARLY MAY, 1951, Colt returned by train to G Company, which was again in the apple orchard near Taegu. It was springtime, and the war was going better. The men were able to do some training. Colt was now sergeant first class, leading the 3d Squad, 3d Platoon. One of the troopers assigned to his squad was a World War II veteran of the 504th Airborne Infantry Regiment called "Leroy," a tall, thin man and known rogue from Arkansas. Each time he was promoted, the army soon demoted him for one infraction or another. In army lingo he was known as a "professional private." Colt assigned one of the BARs to Leroy, who reluctantly accepted it. He did not like the gun because it was too heavy, but he had no choice.

IN JUNE, 1951, G COMPANY, 187TH REGIMENTAL COMBAT Team, was soon reinforced from other units to bring it back to full strength and then went back into action, with ground transportation this time. As squad leader in the 3d Platoon, Colt served under Lt. Jones N. Epps Sr., an officer who had survived the previous battle and who, during Colt's entire first tour in Korea, survived a number of others. Lieutenant Epps, normally only a platoon leader, served several times as acting commander of G Company whenever the unit lost its commander, which apparently happened often. It seemed to Colt that every time his company went into battle, all of its officers were killed or wounded except Epps. This was not entirely true, for Epps, while a lieutenant, had been wounded on February 14, 1951, but soon after returned to duty. Yet amazingly the officer would emerge unscathed from a number of engagements that Colt witnessed. According to Colt, Epps did not hide behind his men in battle; he was no coward. In fact, Colt believed that few men were braver, and he would serve on the battlefield with him again.

Lieutenant Epps, again in his normal role as platoon leader, called for Colt's 3d Squad to report to the company commander's post near the front immediately. The commander, Capt. John D. "Jack" Miley, was, as Colt recalled, a short West Point graduate. Like Epps, Miley had been previously wounded, on March 28, 1951, and returned to duty.[16] The captain asked Colt if he could see a burned-out knoll in the distance, one that had been napalmed. The sergeant snappily confirmed that he did, even though he was not exactly sure to which hill the officer pointed. Miley read the uncertainty in his eyes. He pointed again and told him to get over next to him and look down his arm. The commander was not very polite, and he did not need to be. It was important that Colt know exactly which hill he meant.

Colt, not wanting to appear stupid, pointed in the same direction and told Miley that he had it. The commander ordered him to take his squad off the hill so the enemy would not see it, bring it around to the right, get into a skirmish line, and sweep up the target hill. The sergeant was to report as soon as he was on the top, hold his position, and protect the company's flank. Colt confirmed the order and left to brief his squad. But there were two burned-out knolls side by side.

3d Squad still included Leroy, the born killer. Colt told his men that the main force was going to attack straight up the hill they were on and explained how the main force would be running into all kinds of Chinese. All the Americans had to do was take the little napalmed knoll with no one on it and wait for the main unit to do the heavy fighting. The sergeant told his men that it should be a "piece of cake."

When the squad was off the main hill and in position to start up the knoll, Colt told the men to grab plenty of ammo and "lock and load." He directed them into a skirmish line that spread out across the bottom of the knoll before they moved up. He assigned a BAR man on each end of the line; Leroy was one of them. Riflemen filled in the space between the BARs. Colt led from the middle of the line; his final order was to shoot anything that moved. The Americans started up the knoll.

The summer heat and humidity pressed down on them. The knoll was longer and higher than it had appeared to Colt when he first saw it. And soon his men found it crawling with Chinese. The navy had dropped napalm on the top of the hill and driven the enemy down the sides, so the defenders had not completely dug in again. The squad fought their way up, one step at a time, and killed, by Colt's estimate, between thirty and thirty-five Chinese before reaching the top. His men did not get a scratch.

When they reached the top of the hill, Colt heard Leroy yell that he was out of ammunition. This upset Colt because at first he thought that Leroy had not taken his basic load of two hundred rounds. He was about to jump all over him when one of the other men said, "Sergeant Leroy must'a killed fifteen Chinks by himself." When Colt went over to give him some of the ammo that he carried, Leroy's BAR was still smoking and burning hot.

He told the men to dig in. As they began to do so, one of the men yelled back, "If this was a piece of cake, Sarge, I don't want to be with you when they give us a tough job!"

Colt called his platoon sergeant, Sergeant Miller, on the radio. Miller told him to set off some smoke to mark his position while he delivered Colt's message to Captain Miley. Miller was soon back on the radio with a message from

Miley: "Tell that stupid son-of-a-bitch that he's on the wrong hill and to get off it now because it's crawling with Chinese."

Colt responded that it was not crawling with Chinese anymore because his squad had killed them all on the way up, about thirty of them. He told Miller that his men were in their foxholes as he spoke. Colt could hear Captain Miley in the background telling his sergeant to order "that dumb ass" off that hill, that he was on the wrong knoll.

Just then, Second Battalion commander Lt. Col. John F. Conners walked up behind Miley and told him to wait. Over the radio Colt and his men could hear Miley telling Connors, "That stupid bastard didn't understand and took the wrong hill." Conners asked if the sergeant and his squad had taken the higher hill next to the target. Miley confirmed that he had and pointed to the signal smoke, telling the colonel, "They're holding it now."

Later Colt learned that Conners had told Miley not to scold the squad leader and not to move his men. The captain, as directed, told Colt to hold the knoll while the battalion swept around from the opposite side to reinforce his squad and knock the Chinese off the other hill. Taking the knoll was a job well done for Colt and his squad, but "no cigar," as the saying goes.

FROM FEBRUARY 20 THROUGH MARCH 6, 1951, MANY OF the paratroopers, including Leroy, had been involved in an offensive named Operation Killer, followed by campaigns called Operation Ripper and, the one that included the airdrop described earlier, Operation Courageous.[17] The mission of these operations was to drive the Communists north, which meant killing Chinese and North Koreans soldiers wherever encountered. The 187th Regimental Combat Team, including G Company, took a lot of casualties in all three. Troop replacements were being trucked in daily.

As the fighting began again for his unit that May, the company again lost so many men, killed and wounded, that it was pulled back for additional reinforcement. As the men moved into reserve, they were given a rest on the side of a hill near the front lines. Colt left his squad sitting there while he went to a platoon briefing. While his men rested, they watched events transpiring about fifty yards away.

Two captured Chinese were being brought in for questioning along the road at the bottom of the hill. The Americans had been trying to capture Chinese soldiers for interrogation. These two prisoners had voluntarily surrendered. Dressed in the quilted light tan uniforms and Mao-style hats of the Chinese Army, they stood with their hands on their heads next to a jeep parked near a small hut on a dirt road. Colt guessed later that they were not even combat troops but rather served in some support capacity.

The Chinese were smiling. Leroy did not like that. He told the squad to look at "the bastards" down there smiling. He was irritated that the "sons of bitches" were going back to the prison camp at Koje Do to enjoy three square meals a day and a nice warm bed. With winter coming on, he complained that they would be out of the "damned snow" and have it made. Leroy then announced that he was going to go down and shoot them.

The other men started egging him on, not believing that he would actually do it. They teased him with such comments as "Ah, you're full of shit. You wouldn't shoot 'em." Leroy got up, set down his BAR, and walked down the hill to the jeep. Four American officers were leaning over the hood looking at a map. Leroy walked around the jeep to avoid the officers, who did not notice him, and over to the two prisoners. The unarmed Chinese still had their hands on their heads.

As Leroy came up to them, he pulled his .45 from its holster and yelled, "Let's see ya smile now, you son-of-a-bitch!" Bam! He shot one of the soldiers in the face and killed him instantly. The other one started to back away. "Don't you run away!" Leroy shouted. Bam! He shot the second one in the face, also killing him instantly. It was cold-blooded murder, plain and simple.

Just as Leroy shot the second Chinese, the company's Regimental S-2 (intelligence officer), Major "Kohn," drove up in a jeep. With a reputation of being as mean as a snake, the major had seen what happened as he pulled up but was powerless to stop it. He had been counting on interrogating the two prisoners.

Jumping from his vehicle, the major yelled to the nearby officers to arrest Leroy. The four officers grabbed him, took away his weapon, and ripped off his gear. They tied his hands behind his back and threw him into the jeep. He was flown to Tokyo for a mental evaluation.

According to Colt's recollection, when Leroy first arrived in Tokyo, the army put him in a hospital ward for the insane and assigned a psychiatrist to evaluate him. He remained there all winter. The medical conclusion was that there was nothing wrong with Leroy except that he was a cold-blooded killer. But Colt already knew that.

OF COURSE, LEROY WAS NOT THE ONLY KILLER IN THE war.

Often, when an enemy soldier is killed, it is not clear who actually fired the lethal shot. At other times it is crystal clear. In late April, 1951, Colt clearly killed a Chinese soldier in an unavoidable situation. He thought about it often and wished that it had not been necessary.

His company had overrun a Chinese position. Most of the enemy had escaped or been killed; one was trapped, however, hiding in a storage cave. The sun was going down, and the Americans had to camp there for the night. The soldier refused to come out, and Colt could not leave him there, in the middle of their camp, in the dark.

Even though Colt was now the acting first sergeant, he consulted with another sergeant as to what should be done. They knew for sure that the soldier was in the cave. All that the other NCO could suggest was to order the man again to come out. Colt crawled halfway into the cave and yelled. He did not know any Chinese but thought that maybe the other man spoke Korean, the language of the country in which he was fighting. The only Korean Colt knew was the phrase "Come here!" He did not know how to tell the man that they would not shoot him if he came out. Finally, Colt had to put an end to the danger by lobbing a grenade into the cave.

He did not sleep well that night. The next morning, after heating up some cocoa (he lived on cocoa and crackers), Colt found that he could not eat or drink; his appetite was gone. He turned around just in time to see some men dragging the Chinese soldier's body out of the cave. Over by the road, next to a jeep, stood a chaplain and a soldier. The soldier pointed at Colt just as he happened to look over at them. He saw the chaplain's reaction and really felt bad.

This may not have been the first enemy soldier that Colt had killed, but it was the first one that he was certain of having done alone. For any soldier, the first kill is always the hardest. After that, numbness begins to set in.

IN MAY, 1951, THE HOSPITAL SENT LEROY BACK TO G Company's bivouac area for a general court-martial. Even though the men were living in tents, the trial proceeded quite formally. Throughout the history of the U.S. Army, not many soldiers have beaten a general court-martial. The army does not usually prosecute a soldier without solid evidence. In this case, an officer had witnessed the crime firsthand. There seemed to be no doubt about Leroy's guilt.

Leroy found a good defense officer to represent him. The defense officer subpoenaed the commanding general of the 187th Regimental Combat Team to testify to the court that the name of one of their recent operations was Killer. He had other officers testify that the general orders given to their men were "To move north and to kill Chinese and North Koreans." The men had been told at one point to take no prisoners.

Leroy beat the case. The army sent him back to Colt's squad.

As soon as he arrived back at camp, Leroy walked into Colt's tent and cockily greeted him. "Hey, Sarge, how the fuck are ya?"

Colt told him, "I haven't been doing so well, Leroy. I've been living in the mud, having Chinese shoot at my ass while you're cat napping in a padded cell back in Tokyo."

To which Leroy responded, "Well, some of us get the breaks."

Colt then ordered, "Pick up the BAR."

Leroy, still cocky, said, "I ain't carrying no BAR. It's too heavy and I'm too old."

Leroy was tough, but Colt was tougher. "You just got out of a general court-martial that you beat by a hair. If we hadn't been told to go north and kill Chinese, you'd be headed for a firing squad right now. Now that you beat one general court-martial, d'ya wanna try for another by disobeying my orders? I'm giving you a direct order to pick up that BAR and grease it up. We're going back into combat."

Leroy gave in. "Okay Sarge, you don't need to get all riled up. I was just testin' you."

Colt ended the conversation with, "Well, test it on someone else." Leroy picked up the BAR and left.

Replacements arrived to bring the battalion back up to strength, during which time Colt was promoted to first sergeant. Soon the unit moved to an area called Inje Pass.

In Korea with the 187th Regimental Combat Team

2

ON A DAY IN MAY, 1951, COLT, WITH PVT.
J. B. "Smith" driving, pulled up in a jeep full of ammunition for G Company, their unit. As they approached its position along the Soyang River at the Inje Pass, the Chinese, who were dug in on the hill across the river, started shooting at them. Smith pulled the jeep behind a small house until Colt could figure out what to do next. E Company had arrived here a few hours earlier and, catching the Chinese sleeping, had crossed the river before the enemy realized that U.S. troops were at the foot of their hill. The Chinese now had E Company pinned down at the riverbank with the Soyang behind them.

When the men of G Company arrived and waded into the river to join the other Americans on the opposite side, the enemy rained lead down on them. This ford was supposed to be shallow, but the river was swollen chest high from recent thunderstorms. The men carried their rifles over their heads, making them easy targets for the Chinese on the hill above. But the company successfully crossed with only a few casualties.

When Colt got to the river, the shooting had quieted down. He found two men from G Company there, both dead. They were Sgt. 1/C "Spook" Rydel and Pfc. Amato. There was nothing he could do for them, so he crossed the river. He could see the men from both companies positioned along the bank. Until Colt waded into the water, he had no idea what a mistake it would be and how many Chinese would be trying to shoot him. Bullets began hitting a foot in front of him, flying over his head and hitting behind him, and striking the water on both sides of him. He even watched the trail of one bullet in the water as it passed between his legs. The Chinese were so high up on a ridgeline that he could not see them to shoot back, but they could see him.

He prayed, "Lord, just let me get through this day."

Because of the height of the hill, which extended the distance that the bullets had to travel, combined with the poor aim of the Chinese, he made it unscathed.

As Colt neared the shore, he came upon one of his company's men lying face down in shallow water. He dragged the soldier up onto the beach. He did not know at the time that a bullet had ricocheted off the water and hit the man's dog tags—driving them into his chest and knocking him out. The wound bled a lot but was not life threatening. Colt learned later that two sergeants had seen the man go down in deep water and, thinking he was dead, had dragged him into shallow water and left him there, planning to recover his body later (they were under heavy fire at the time).

Two tanks, unable to cross at the designated fording point, had gone downstream about a half mile to a shallower spot. They soon arrived at the beach, buttoned up because they were taking a lot of machine-gun fire. One of Colt's paratroopers, lying on the sand behind a log for cover, was wounded just as the tanks arrived. The tankers did not see him, and one vehicle rolled right over his head and killed him. Colt was upset and fumed but realized that this unnecessary death was an accident.

Bullets were still flying everywhere. Colt crouched behind one tank and followed it along the beach as he looked for his company commander, Capt. Jones N. Epps, who apparently was somewhere farther down. Other tanks, spaced about fifty to sixty yards apart, were firing up the hill at the Chinese. Whenever Colt's tank stopped, he stopped too. Proceeding up the beach without cover would have been suicidal—or so Colt believed.

Suddenly he saw Lt. Col. "Poopy" Conners walk up to the tank that Colt had adopted and under which he was crouching. A big six-foot, two-inch Irishman, the colonel could talk a man's ears off and walk him to death too. He was nicknamed "Poopy" because, with the pace he kept, he "pooped" out all the younger men around him.

Connors squatted down to greet Colt. "Good morning, First Sergeant." When Colt looked up and saw the colonel, he jumped up and saluted him without thinking. Saluting an officer on the battlefield can be a death sentence for that man—alerting every enemy gun within range that he is a target worth shooting. Conners did not care; he returned the salute.

Conners asked Colt, "Where's Epps?"

Colt responded, "I think his command post is set up near the end of the beach under the last tank."

Conners invited Colt to accompany him, and they started walking down the beach, completely out in the open. The colonel had his radio operator with him, a tall, lanky NCO carrying a large radio on his back with a tall antenna. The Chinese had to know that a tall man with two escorts, one carrying a radio, had to be an important figure. Conners, Colt, and the radioman walked down the beach as though they were out for a Sunday stroll.

The lieutenant colonel quizzed Colt as they walked: "How's your company doing? How many men have we lost, so far?"

Colt told him, "I've seen five plus one that the last tank rolled over."

"Those damned tankers," Conners replied.

The lieutenant colonel continued talking with the sergeant as they walked, keeping the men's minds off the danger. The radioman walked close to Conners, on his right, trying to get what little cover he could from the officer's body. Colt walked on Conners's left, the side from which the gunfire was coming. In the military a soldier always walks to the left of someone more senior in rank so his right hand is free to salute. As they moved down the beach shoulder to shoulder, Colt thought that this would be his last day on earth.

It wasn't that the Chinese didn't try. They threw everything they had at the trio. Bullets were hitting the sand inches to the front, back, and sides of the men and flying over their heads into the river beyond. The three walked from tank to tank for three hundred yards, passing six vehicles and visiting briefly with the men hiding behind each one. Colt heard every bullet that missed them and struck the water nearby or the ground around them. He did not want Connors to think that he was a coward, so he tried hard to be calm while answering the officer's continuous questions.

The lieutenant colonel continued his quiz. "What's your ammunition situation?"

Colt told him: "The men are low on it. We need the ammo that's across the river."

Conners asked, "Who's gonna to do that?"

Colt was cornered; he had to answer that he would be the one, as soon as he reported to Captain Epps and let him know that it was here.

They finally reached the last tank. Epps had dug a big hole in the sand beneath the vehicle for his command post.

Conners got down on his hands and knees, looked into the hole, and hollered, "Jones, you in there?"

Epps replied, "Good morning, Colonel."

Conners asked Epps how things were going but added, almost in the same breath, that Epps had to get things together and get his men off the beach. The captain was glad to see his first sergeant and asked Colt if he knew that they were running out of ammunition. Colt told him about the load stashed across the river. Epps then asked him what he was going to do about it. Again, Colt had to admit that he was going back across the river right away, get the jeep, and bring up the ammo.

His commander smiled and told Conners, "That's my first sergeant."

Conners, looking at a map with the captain, told him, "Attack up the hill. Either wipe 'em out or drive 'em off the hill."

It was clear that his men would not last long there on the beach. The captain turned to Colt: "We're going to attack as soon as you get the ammunition here. We'll be getting the tanks ready while you're bringing the ammo."

Returning back down the beach to try to locate a safer crossing point, Colt passed a young trooper named "Antonio," someone he knew really well. Antonio was a wisecracker and warned the sergeant, "Don't get your ass shot off. The Chinese are waitin' for you!"

Colt had walked no more than ten feet past him when Antonio stood up to say something else. At that moment a sniper's bullet hit and killed the trooper. Even though Colt was nearby, with all the noise around him, he did not hear Antonio. Colt learned of his death the next day, from men who were with Antonio when he was hit, after the sergeant was asked to help identify bodies.

Colt often wondered why the sniper had chosen between him and Antonio, a fun-loving and generous man.

He walked farther down the river on the Chinese side before getting into the water to go back across. The riverbank was undercut where he decided to jump in. To his surprise, Colt almost landed on top of other paratroopers. An entire company, F (Fox), was lined up in the river under the overhanging bank, waiting for Colt's G Company and E Company to clear the beach and move up the hill.

A wounded man, lying on a stretcher on the bank, was waiting to be taken across the river. A medic asked Colt if he would take one end of the stretcher and help carry him across. He agreed. Colt had to quiet the wounded soldier several times, not only to avoid the Chinese hearing them but also for fear that his own men might shoot them accidentally. They made it across.

Colt returned to the jeep and its driver. They worked their way downriver until they found a shallow spot that was firm enough to drive the jeep across. After they delivered the ammunition to G Company, now joined by F Company, they and E Company attacked up the hill. No one in the paratrooper units knew that a company of marines was on the other side of the mountain, thus squeezing the Chinese in between two forces. For the Chinese, it became a fight to the death. The Americans prevailed but with heavy losses.

WITHIN DAYS, THE PARATROOPERS ENGAGED THE enemy in a tough fight for another hill, Hill 420, named for its height in meters.[1] The men dug foxholes on the attack side of the knoll and set up a 60-mm mortar behind the crest. G Company held the hill for about two weeks. The Chinese came down from higher ground into a saddle and attacked uphill against the unit's position. As Colt recalled, G Company alone killed three or four hundred Chinese. Here Colt received his first combat injury when a shrapnel fragment from a Chinese hand grenade penetrated his field jacket and lodged under his skin, over his ribs. With the fragment removed and the small wound patched up, he continued in the battle.

The fighting on Hill 420 became even more intense in the days that followed. On May 31 the Chinese overran G Company.[2] Colt was guarding the company XO (executive officer), Lieutenant "Hall," as he desperately spoke into the EE8 telephone to Lieutenant Colonel Conners. In a nervous voice Hall reported that his men could not hold the hill any longer. The company commander, Captain Epps, was up at the forward element of the defensive line, and the Chinese had obviously overrun that area. Colt was on his way forward when Lieutenant Hall asked him to provide security during his call.

As the lieutenant spoke to Lieutenant Colonel Conners, Colt noticed Chinese running past them about twenty yards farther down the hill. The enemy had broken through the company's front line after overrunning its machine-gun position and riflemen. Colt began picking off enemy soldiers as they ran through the Americans' CP (command post). He knew they were Chinese by their quilted uniforms. They were carrying rations and ammunition on their backs.[3]

Hall again told Conners that his company could not hold the hill: the enemy was running through their position, and his first sergeant was shooting them down right in front of him. Colt was aggravated at the lieutenant for sounding frightened over the phone, but he could not blame him. Neither of them knew what might be in store during the next few seconds. Colt later remembered that his tongue was so dry that he could have struck a match on it. He could hear Conners yelling back on the phone that reinforcements were coming up the hill. Hall kept repeating that they could not hold.

Conners kept yelling back at him. Colt heard him say that they had better still be on that "damn hill" when the reinforcements arrive. They had better hold it, or if not, they had better be dead.

So the lieutenant, Colt, and the other survivors stood their ground and fought back while under attack by superior forces using artillery, mortar, and machine-gun fire, which caused numerous casualties. Cpl. Rodolfo Hernandez was in a foxhole farther down the hill, below Colt and Hall's position. Hernandez, wounded in an exchange of grenades, continued firing at the onrushing enemy until a ruptured cartridge jammed his rifle. When that happened, the corporal rushed forward and engaged the enemy with only the bayonet on the end of his jammed rifle. He killed six of the enemy before falling unconscious from multiple wounds. His heroism in delaying the enemy's advance allowed Lieutenant Colonel Conners to counterattack with reinforcements and retake the lost ground. G Company held the hill. After the Chinese retreated, Corporal Hernandez was found lying under a number of the enemy he had killed. Although seriously wounded, Hernandez survived and was later awarded the Medal of Honor for his actions.[4]

In one year of combat, of 156 troopers in G Company, 72 were killed in action.[5] Jones N. Epps survived. But during this time, the regiment lost numerous other company commanders, dead or wounded.[6] One, a young captain, was shot in the face after being in the company all of one hour. Who was next on the list? Colt wondered when his turn would come, for he continued to see action.

STILL, IN EARLY JUNE, 1951, AFTER ONE OF THE BATTLES for Hill 420, it was one of Colt's duties as first sergeant to take a headcount of able-bodied men left to fight off the next attack. At about 1000 hours (10:00 A.M.) that morning, about four hours after they had repelled yet another Chinese attack, he was walking around a trail just below the crest of the hill, going from foxhole to foxhole to get a head count from each platoon. G Company had lost quite a few men, and the commander needed to know how many were left. Colt passed one foxhole occupied by two young troopers, Sergeant Richardson and Sgt. David N. White. He joked with them about cold milkshakes.

Right in front of their position was a North Korean lying face down. Although the man was not in uniform, Colt counted him as a North Korean because he was in the typical Korean civilian dress of white pants, white shirt, and black vest. He lay across the trail with a burp gun still in his outstretched hand. Colt stepped over him and walked on. When he had gone about six steps past the "dead" North Korean, the man jumped up and started shooting.

As Colt describes it, "That son of a bitch had been lying there for four hours faking being dead." He had been waiting for just the right time or until he could get up enough nerve. When he got to his feet, he sprayed Richardson and White with his burp gun. He turned to shoot Colt in the back. At that moment Colt slung his carbine down, but he was too late on the draw as he spun around.

Just then, ten to fifteen yards higher up the hill in the mortar section, Cpl. Jack H. Harvey from Jacksonville, Florida, had finished cleaning his M1 rifle. As the shooting started, he had just put in a clip of eight rounds and let the slide go forward. Harvey did not have time even to shoulder the weapon but shot from the hip. He hit the North Korean right in the side of the head with one or two of about four rounds. To Colt, the Korean looked like someone had snatched him by the hair on his head and yanked him down the hill. Colt looked up at Corporal Harvey and simply said, "Thanks, I owe you a beer."

Harvey replied, "First Sergeant, you owe me a case of beer."

Colt yelled for a medic for Richardson and White and ran to report to the company commander. Epps told him to get all of the men out of their foxholes and to shoot every enemy soldier again to make sure they were dead.[7]

Both Richardson and White survived. Richardson returned to the company after he recovered, but White never came back. Colt survived because of a fraction of a second in timing and the quickness, alertness, and skill of Corporal Harvey.

Now Colt and the others would get a break from the action.

IN EARLY JULY COLT WAS PROMOTED TO MASTER sergeant, and G Company was sent back to Japan until more replacements arrived from the States.[8] The men lived on the southern island of Kyushu in the small town of Beppu. It was a natural hot springs area with spas using water heated by volcanoes. To Colt, the contrast with the conditions of life in Japan compared to Korea seemed almost surreal. The respite from war was good for the men, but the rampant venereal disease and disciplinary problems that developed among them were not good. Colt was unhappy in Japan— too much action of the wrong kind and not enough of his kind.

He soon volunteered to take over the S-2 sergeant's job at regimental headquarters. The officer in charge of the S-2 section was Major Kohn, the same man who had arrested Leroy. Kohn did not get along with the headquarters' S-3 officer, which turned Colt into a political football. In addition, the major often intimidated Colt over petty matters, threatening more than once to reduce him in rank; the sergeant did not want to lose stripes that were so hard to get. Colt did not like the political pressure and wanted out.

Late one night he was reading Teletype messages and came across one that gave him hope. The army was seeking combat-experienced, airborne-qualified NCOs for a secret mission into North Korea. This was the kind of job Colt wanted and a way out of his situation. He maneuvered his name onto the top of the list of volunteers and was soon accepted. The mission was under the direction of Lt. Col. William C. Westmoreland. He had no idea what he was getting himself into.

When he received his orders, Colt dressed in his Class A uniform, grabbed his duffel bag, and headed for the railway station. While he was waiting for the train that would take him from Beppu to Sasebo, he heard its lonesome whistle and started to berate himself. He called himself names and berated himself for jumping into the line of fire. Remembering that he had done this sort of thing once before when he joined the army, he wondered why he had not learned the first time.

At Sasebo Colt caught the ferry to Korea. Colt's return to the peninsula marked the end of his time with the 187th Regimental Combat Team. He was now assigned to the Miscellaneous Group 8086th Army Unit.[9] But he never looked back or regretted the decision that again placed him in harm's way. He was off on a new adventure, or so he thought.

3 Behind Enemy Lines on Nan-do

"**A**LL OF OUR PLATOON LEADERS ARE DEAD. It's about time that they sent us a combat replacement." This was his greeting from Captain "Cassidy," adjutant for the 24th Infantry Division Replacement Company, when Colt arrived in Korea for his second tour on October 19, 1951.[1] For weeks the 24th Infantry Division had been attacking a Chinese-controlled hill and getting nowhere. Cassidy knew that Colt had earned his Combat Infantryman Badge on his first tour to Korea, which proved that he knew how to fight. He was just what the captain needed.

Colt responded, "No disrespect, sir, but I didn't volunteer to come here as a platoon leader. I'm here because I volunteered for a special assignment for Lt. Col. William C. Westmoreland."[2]

Cassidy did not believe him and said that he would send a telex to General Headquarters (GHQ) to confirm his story. The captain added that, if headquarters did not know what he was talking about, the sergeant would be missing a stripe. He told Colt to come back in two hours.

As a career soldier, this threat greatly concerned Colt and for good reason. He had worked hard to attain the rank of master sergeant and did not want to lose it. And he knew how the army could easily have lost track of him and his assignment. As he left the captain's office, he worried that the person who received the telex at GHQ would not know about the secret mission and would send Cassidy a negative response.

As he did in other crisis situations, Colt took immediate action. He went across the street from the captain's office and knocked on the door of the communications van parked there. A fellow master sergeant named "Hefflin" opened the door and invited him in. Colt explained the situation. They hit it off right away. Colt asked Hefflin, "Can you put me through to Lieutenant Colonel Westmoreland?"

After giving Colt a good look up and down, Hefflin told him: "Go to the phone on the telephone post in front of the trailer. When it rings, pick it up.

I'll be leaving for coffee. If you get caught, I wasn't here." Colt thanked him and walked to the pole and waited.

When the phone rang, he found himself talking directly to Lieutenant Colonel Westmoreland. Colt identified himself, and, to his amazement, Westmoreland remembered him from a minor encounter three years earlier: as a corporal back in late 1948, he had repaired an intercom box in the office of the lieutenant colonel, when he was a major, at the 82d Airborne Division Headquarters at Fort Bragg.[3] Colt reminded him that he had just transferred from the 187th Regimental Combat Team in Japan to volunteer for his secret mission but could not say any more on an open line. Westmoreland instructed him to say no more, that he knew what he meant, and asked him where he was. Colt explained his problem with the 24th Replacement adjutant and where that officer was located. The adjutant would receive the appropriate orders, Westmoreland said, and an aircraft would be down to pick up Colt that afternoon. Before he hung up, the colonel thanked Colt for volunteering for the mission and congratulated him on his promotion to master sergeant. Colt never ran across the communications sergeant again—to thank him.

When Colt reported to the adjutant at the appointed time, the captain had a new attitude. He told Colt that a jeep was waiting outside to take him to a nearby airfield and that an airplane would be there to pick him up in an hour. Colt saluted and thanked him. Within the hour the adjutant's driver dropped off the sergeant at a makeshift airfield that had steel matting for a runway—the type laid down by the navy's Seabees (construction battalion). In full combat uniform, including his pack and rifle, Colt sat down alone to wait.

Before long, a C-47 landed and taxied up. The C-47 is a very large aircraft. A captain welcomed Colt on board—as the only passenger and cargo. The army had sent a C-47, the workhorse of World War II, hundreds of miles to pick up a single sergeant, which today would be akin to sending a Boeing 747 to pick up one passenger.[4] The pilot had been told to ask no questions, just pick him up. This demonstrated to Colt the significance of his secret mission. He flew to Taegu, where U.S. Army Intelligence and the Central Intelligence Agency (CIA) ran a joint operation out of a large villa.[5] Thus began his involvement in a top-secret army mission with the code name Task Force Kirkland. As he disembarked from the C-47, Colt's entire life changed. It would never be the same again.

A MOST UNUSUAL CAPTAIN MET HIM AS HE GOT OFF the plane. He was young and ruggedly handsome, wearing riding britches, leather knee boots, a white scarf, and an Aussie hat, like a cowboy hat, only with the brim folded up on one side. He also carried a swagger stick. Colt snapped to attention and saluted. After quickly but casually returning the salute, the captain then put out his hand to shake Colt's hand—unheard of behavior in the army between an NCO and a captain. Then, of all things, he picked up Colt's duffel bag and carried it to a waiting jeep, which the captain himself drove. Officers do not carry an NCO's bags, do not drive jeeps themselves, and do not drive sergeants around, but this captain did all three. Thus began for Colt the process of developing a new attitude—one in which rank is respected but not overdone.

On a nearby beach Colt trained for six days on foreign weapons, including a number of older automatic weapons—the German Schmeisser, British Sten, and Swedish K as well as all types of demolitions. He had to know them all, for the CIA was providing obsolete, captured, and surplus World War II weapons to indigenous insurgents in North Korea, whom he would be training. He learned more about how he would be transported behind enemy lines to organize resistance.

After completing his training, Colt was transported by minesweeper to the island of Nan-do off the coast of North Korea.[6] Upon arrival, he found the island to be barren rock with no beach and no dock.[7] He literally stepped gingerly off the shifting boat onto a rock, where his new commander, Capt. Joseph Ulatoski, greeted him. The six-foot, two-inch officer had a reputation as a good leader. At the time, Ulatoski reported to Maj. Angelo R. Cocumelli; but soon after Colt arrived, Cocumelli was rotated back to the States.

In only six days Colt went from the comfort of the Japanese base to joining four other Americans on a tiny, barren island off North Korea—behind enemy lines. Although he had volunteered for this duty, he again began to question his own sanity. This rock was North Korean territory and was about ten to fifteen miles from the main coastline, near enough for Colt to spot a farmer on shore and to observe the movements of Chinese troops on the peninsula through high-power binoculars borrowed from the navy.[8] Likewise, the island's openness constantly exposed the Americans to the danger of discovery. It had no trees, water, or hiding places—only sparse grass, rocks, and rats as big as cats. The rats were so bad that the army would eventually allow the men to bring in two dogs to keep the rodents under control.

On Nan-do the Americans trained "indigenous mercenaries"—South Koreans, Mongolians, and even North Koreans and Chinese. Some displayed little if any loyalty to the political cause of Seoul; the army procured them from a prisoner of war stockade in South Korea. (Colt called them "indigenous" as well as "mercenaries" because most had their loyalties turned with the promise of food, weapons, and pay under the direction of the CIA.) As their chief instructor, Colt taught them how to use the foreign weapons as well as BARs, Thompson submachine guns, 60-mm mortars, explosive charges, and hand grenades. At times he took them on raids to blow up railroad tracks or bridges. He wore the same kind of CIA-provided uniform as was provided to the indigenous, a surplus World War II uniform, which he thought was provided in order to save money. The uniform that he selected for himself, because it did not fit any of his trainees, included an old Nazi camouflage jacket with swastikas still on the sleeves. Colt left the patches on because he thought they were "cool," but to relieve his concerns about wearing a Nazi relic, he sewed a small American flag inside the coat. Operating in North Korean territory, he was in constant danger of being captured and shot as a spy.

Colt's mission was dangerous in other ways. In addition to training the indigenous to perform sabotage, it included searching out and destroying enemy infrastructure, equipment, and troops as well as directing naval gunfire against targets in North Korea. Nan-do was the base for guerilla actions up and down the North Korean coast.

During their training, Colt led the insurgents in raids up and down the North Korean coast.[9] When a group of men completed training, they were transported to Sokchori, South Korea, on U.S. Navy ships for their final training, primarily in parachuting; they usually made one or two practice jumps.[10] When the indigenous were fully trained, Army Intelligence, 8240th Army Unit, under whose direction the army trainers functioned, dropped the mercenary teams from an A/B-26 bomber into North Korea.[11]

Captain Ulatoski's command was one of at least ten army units training mercenary teams to operate behind enemy lines, to perform sabotage, and to recruit North Koreans to assist the South Koreans in the war. Their mission was to keep the Chinese and North Korean armies continuously concerned about their rear to divert troops away from the front lines. The guerrilla teams were expendable and so were the training teams. Colt estimated that there were ten army units conducting operations behind enemy lines during the course of the Korean War, of which, to his knowledge, the members of only two teams survived, the one on Nan-do and another one on the west coast of North Korea—the other teams were captured or killed.[12] Of the trained guerrillas dropped into North Korea, many of them were also captured and killed and some immediately turned themselves in and joined the North Korean Army for food and shelter. Colt's experiences in this environment, naturally hostile because of the elements and unnaturally hostile because of the presence of the enemy, were all extreme.

For example, one hundred miles behind enemy lines in North Korea on a dark moonless night during November, 1951, he led a group of about thirty mercenary trainees up a dry riverbed on a mission to blow up a road bridge. The men carried, spread among them, several hundred pounds of explosives. Followed by his fourteen-year-old Korean interpreter, Kim, Colt felt his way carefully through the rocks, one quiet step at a time. The wind was blowing hard enough to keep him from hearing a Chinese soldier, only twenty yards away on the opposite riverbank, challenge him and his men.

Grabbing Colt's sleeve, Kim stopped him and whispered, "Sergeant, Chinese soldier challenge us."

"Tell 'im we're fishermen coming up from the beach," Colt whispered back.

Before Kim could utter a word, the enemy soldier opened up with his burp gun. The bullets snapped and cracked just above their heads and ricocheted off the rocks on the riverbank behind them. This was another one of Colt's lucky days. The Chinese sentry's aim was high and did not hit the charges he carried in the big pockets of his jump pants—two 2.5-pound blocks of C-3 plastic explosives, already primed with blasting caps, fuse, and fuse lighters. One stray bullet and Colt would have been blown into small pieces.

As he turned to tell Kim to call up the guerrilla leader to their position, Kim said, in the matter-of-fact manner of an old veteran, "Men run away." The indigenous had fled down the riverbed at the first shot. He and Kim were alone, and more Chinese sentries were now firing from other positions. Bullets were hitting the rocks all around them. Colt took the blocks of C-3 from his pockets, pulled the fuse lighters to ignite them, and quickly threw both in the direction of the nearest burp gun. Kim was kneeling next to him, holding a World War II–vintage carbine. Even though he was only fourteen years old, he knew that if he started shooting, the enemy would be able to zero in on him and Colt.

As soon as the blocks were in the air, Colt yelled to Kim, "Kap-su-da," which he meant as "Let's get the hell outta here."

He and Kim ran toward the beach as fast as the rocky riverbed and the dark allowed. When the C-3 exploded, all hell broke loose. Colt had not known until then that the Chinese had reinforced security on the bridge with several machine guns on the ridge above it. He could not worry about that now—they had to get to the beach before the indigenous left without them. The Chinese turned the machine guns on their retreat and raked the entire riverbed all the way to the beach. Apparently, the gunners could not see Colt and Kim under their cover of darkness, and the two miraculously made it to the beach without a scratch. They immediately realized that the two large sampans they had come in were already loaded with the indigenous and under way about fifty feet from shore—the guerrilla chief had panicked and wasted no time in getting the sampans away. When Kim yelled to them to come back and pick them up, they refused and yelled that it was too dangerous, too afraid of the machine-gun fire that was now zeroing in on the exchange of shouts and yelling. Colt told Kim, "Tell that son of a bitch that if he doesn't return now and pick us up, I will sink his sampan myself."

The indigenous started to return fire from the sampans. Colt told Kim to order them to stop shooting so as not to reveal their location. At that moment, a bullet ricocheted off the water and hit one of the guerrillas in the stomach. It lodged in his skin, and he started screaming that the bullet was burning him alive. To make matters worse, a full moon began to rise, and the sampans became visible to the Chinese.

To Colt's surprise, standing offshore were two World War II PT (patrol torpedo) boats, with dual 40-mm cannons, apparently operated by South Koreans working for the CIA.[13] From the gunfire, they knew that Colt and his group were in trouble, so they opened up on the Chinese. A full-fledged firefight ensued just over the heads of Colt and his men. Colt told Kim to tell the guerrilla chief to "shut the wounded man up. The Chinese are zeroing in on him. If he won't shut up, shoot the son of a bitch." The screaming stopped. Colt and Kim were still in the water, and the sergeant was getting even more furious. The sampan finally came in close enough to shore so that he and Kim, wading chest deep in icy water, could climb on board.

Once on deck, Colt noticed that the boat was not moving. When he asked why, the chief said that the pilot (the man who rows with a long oar in the stern) was hiding under the deck flooring and refused to come up.

"I've had enough of this bullshit," Colt said as he made his way to the stern. He pulled up the floorboard, reached into the hole, and pulled the man up by his hair. Shoving his .45 into the man's face, he said, "Row or die—it's your choice." Kim translated.

The bullets were now hitting the water all around the sampan. The pilot was terrified; however, when he heard Colt's message, he jumped up and started rowing. At that point Colt felt like killing, with his bare hands, the chief, the pilot, and the wounded man, who was again screaming in pain. Were it not for all the commotion that was making them a target, he said he would have shot them all.

When the sampan was out of range, Colt looked closely at the man's wound with a flashlight. The bullet had passed under the heavy skin over the man's stomach and was protruding slightly out of the other side. The wound was causing terrible pain. Immediately Colt took large tweezers from the first-aid kit and extracted the bullet. When he poured Merthiolate on the open wound, the man yelled even louder.

Now under the cover of the PT boats, Colt and his team headed back to Nan-do, though it was no safe haven. He felt that it was about as far from heaven as they could be without being in hell. The sergeant was angry that the mission had failed and, even worse, that it had turned into a fiasco. Yet he was still determined to blow up that bridge and decided that an aerial attack was needed.

The air force resisted flying into the Nan-do area, even to drop supplies to Colt and his men, because the pilots claimed that there were too many MIGs around. Colt and Captain Ulatoski knew that was not true. At Colt's suggestion, Ulatoski persuaded the captain of the destroyer USS *Higbee,* through the judicious use of souvenirs, to contact an aircraft carrier that was part of Task Force 77 for an air strike against the bridge (which would also complete Colt's mission for him).[14] When the navy flew the attack, their pilots saw no MIGs in the area.

Completing a mission would always be Colt's top priority. His determination and resourcefulness would later make him ideally qualified to be a Special Forces officer. These traits reflected the not-so-subtle changes taking place in Colt's character. He was becoming hardened from his constant exposure to dangerous assignments.

A U.S. NAVY BATTLESHIP, THE USS *IOWA*;[15] THREE heavy cruisers, the USS *Manchester,*[16] the USS *Rochester,*[17] and the USS *St. Paul;*[18] and a number of other ships patrolled North Korea's eastern coast.[19]

Their presence provided a degree of protection to the tiny island of Nan-do, but, of course, they were not always near the island. On one raid Captain Ula-toski received orders to capture some North Koreans for naval intelligence, which was seeking information about North Korean units operating near the Manchurian border. Ulatoski did not want to send Colt on a daylight raid with only his current group of indigenous trainees since he considered them possibly dangerous. He arranged for volunteers from the USS *Higbee* to ac-company Colt on the raid and gave them the use of a navy launch.

When the navy asked for three volunteers to attack a small harbor and village many miles north of Nan-do, literally everyone on the destroyer vol-unteered. The *Higbee*'s captain chose three men, a petty officer first class, an ensign, and a chief petty officer (CPO). Ulatoski returned to Nan-do, while Colt and the indigenous traveled north on the *Higbee* to the small harbor. The trainees were seasick during the entire voyage. The U.S. Navy was relieved when they finally disembarked with Colt onto the launch, near the North Korean port, which was close to the Manchurian border.

The raiding party headed toward a small village nestled at the rear of the anchorage. A Chinese junk was moored about two hundred yards offshore in the harbor. As the launch approached the vessel, two North Korean officers came out on the junk's fantail and, to their surprise, were face to face with the raiding party. Colt instructed the interpreter to tell the North Koreans to put their hands on their heads and not to move. One of them put his hands on his head, but the other dove over the side into the near freezing water.

When the launch was within fifty feet of the junk, the ensign, using a Thompson submachine gun, suddenly shot and killed the man in the wa-ter. The CPO exploded, "What the hell is wrong with you, sir? You lost your fuckin' mind? He wasn't goin' anywhere. Our launch goes faster than he could swim. All we had to do was pull alongside, grab him by the hair, and snatch him into the boat!"

Colt thought the CPO was going to hit the officer, but he obviously thought better of it. The other North Korean kept his hands on top of his head and did not move until he was captured. They found no one else on the junk. The Americans motored right up to the beach and moved into the village, which proved to be deserted. When the raiders were back on the launch and about one hundred yards offshore, a large-caliber machine gun, high on a hill above the village, opened up on them. One of the first rounds came through the launch's hull and shattered the petty officer's ankle. While the medic be-gan to give him first aid as he lay on the deck, the machine gunners on the hill fired another burst. Two bullets ricocheted off the water, crashed through the hull, and hit the same wounded man between his testicles and anus. One bullet lodged in his chest near his heart, and the other came to rest near his spine. Soon they pulled out of range.

As the launch headed toward the *Higbee*, the destroyer's captain sent a radio message to the *Manchester*, which had a hospital facility, for assistance. In less than an hour, the cruiser came alongside the launch and picked up the injured petty officer. Colt remained with the man until he was out of danger. The ship's doctors repaired his ankle and removed the .50-caliber bullet from his chest, but they left the other round next to his spine for fear of injuring his spinal cord. As soon as the sergeant heard that the petty officer would survive, he scheduled his return to Nan-do. But before he left the ship, Colt allowed himself to be talked into a little mischief that would have future consequences.

Aboard the *Manchester*, Colt bunked with the navy chiefs because of his rank. When a couple of the chiefs asked him what he drank, he told them water.

"No booze on your island?" one of them asked.

"We don't even have water—the navy ships that in," Colt explained.

So the chiefs built a still for Colt to take back with him. It was constructed from the lid of an old shell casing, some stopcocks, and twenty-five feet of copper tubing. Also, they gave him a supply of raisins, sugar, apricots, and yeast and showed him a recipe for moonshine. Everything fit nicely into a big cardboard box.

When the time came for him to return to Nan-do in the navy's launch, Colt climbed over the side with the box. Before he could step into the boat, an ensign walked up with a clipboard, the pages on it flapping violently in the stiff breeze, and insisted that the sergeant sign for the stuff in the box. Colt stopped breathing; he was in a pickle. Obviously, he did not want the ensign looking in the box, and he was not authorized to sign for anything.

With no choice left, Colt did the only logical thing, signing as "Douglas MacArthur, General, U.S. Army."

He folded over the sheet, handed it back to the ensign, and saluted him. The officer thanked him, turned, and left. With the strong breeze blowing, he did not lift the pages to look at the signature. Colt took his first breath only after the launch pulled away from the ship.

Colt's whiskey still, held by their cook and their chief interpreter.

Back on Nan-do, Colt succeeded at making moonshine, though he did not drink much himself. He would make one quart of clear liquor at a time. Three months later one of his radio operators showed him a message addressed to Captain Ulatoski. The operator suggested that the sergeant had better read it first.

The message stated: "Master Sergeant Terry is hereby reprimanded. Be advised that he is directed to never sign General MacArthur's name for anything, under any condition, ever again. He is hereby restricted to base for 60 days."

With Colt already restricted to Nan-do for nearly a year, the punishment meant little to him. Ulatoski could not believe what the sergeant had done. He called him into a hut they had built and gave the message to Colt to read, knowing full well that he had already read it. When the captain finished chewing out Colt, he told him, "You're not only restricted to base, all your privileges are suspended." Of course on Nan-do, he had no privileges. Ulatoski then added, "By the way, you're doing a hell of a job here. Keep it up."

But the two men would face a much more serious problem—mutiny.

TRAINING THE INDIGENOUS ON THIS ROCK ISLAND HAD meant that the Americans were in constant danger, not just from the Chinese and North Koreas on the nearby shore but also from the trainees. Neither Ulatoski nor Colt knew that their latest guerrilla chief, "Pak," had been a black marketer in South Korea. Given the choice between remaining in the stockade in South Korea or being released to go north as an insurgent leader, Pak had accepted the latter alternative as the more logical one. His choice, however, did not necessarily mean that he was a South Korean patriot. While listening to the radio after weeks of training on Nan-do, Pak became convinced that the Americans were losing the war and soon would be pushed off the peninsula. Being so far north, he concluded that his team's best course of action would be to capture the Americans and turn them over to the North Koreans. He and his men then would be on the winning side.

Pak did not know that Ulatoski had an informant working for him secretly on the chief's team. The agent warned the captain just before the rebellion began. When the showdown occurred, Pak told the Americans, "We intend to be on the winning side."

Ulatoski told the mutineers, "I'm afraid that we'll have to disappoint you." He showed them the navy's confirmation of receipt of a prearranged secret code from the commander. The code word instructed warships to converge on the island, target it, and blanket it with naval gunfire.

For emphasis, Ulatoski told them: "With deep water right up to our island, the navy ships will be able to come very, very close. The bombardment will be very, very intense. It'll begin before dawn." It was no bluff; the captain was telling the truth.

"Of course," Pak pointed out, "you Americans will die too."

"Unfortunately," Captain Ulatoski said, "the plan is set to work that way."

After discussing the situation further, the mutineers surrendered. The Americans took away their weapons and sent a coded message to call off the bombardment.

Captain Ulatoski did not want the Americans to mete out the necessary punishment because of possible ramifications after the war, so he asked the indigenous to determine the appropriate punishment for Pak. Their decision was execution. Ulatoski assigned Colt to witness it. The indigenous took their former leader to a tiny island, about the size of a football field, with a few pine trees and enough soil for a grave. After the men gave Pak a cigarette and a chance to say his last words, they shot and buried him there.

Ulatoski allowed the surviving mutineers to keep only their knives for self-defense until they again proved their trustworthiness. It took them three months to earn the return of their guns. During that time, armed only with their knives, they continued to carry out nightly missions against the North Koreans.

Meanwhile, another problem arose among the trainees on Nan-do. Not all the indigenous were men, for when the recruiting of potential guerrillas first started, a few women were inducted. The weather on Nan-do was too severe for most of them, and they were sent back to South Korea. Later, an incident occurred in which a woman goaded an indigenous leader, who was drunk on Colt's moonshine, into sitting on a hand grenade, which exploded and blew him to pieces. After that, women were no longer accepted as guerrilla fighters.

DISEASE WAS ANOTHER DANGER. COLT FOUND THAT the indigenous did not understand hygiene—the entire world was their toilet. Given the size of their little island, however, allowing this type of toilet behavior would soon bury them all in crap. Due to a serious bout with fever after drinking polluted stream water during his first tour in Korea, the sergeant understood the importance of hygiene. He instructed the Koreans to wash their hands in the ocean after urinating, even though they had a long walk down to the shore to do it; in addition, he explained that their practice of walking down a trail, getting the urge, stepping off to the side, and relieving themselves could also expose the men to disease. He then taught them how to build appropriate toilet facilities. They cut the ends off of fiberglass shell casings and dug them into the ground for urinals. Initially, they dug slit trenches for solid waste, but Colt eventually decided to show them how to build a portable latrine. With bars along the sides so that it could be picked up and carried, much like a sedan chair once used to transport East Indian royalty, the outhouse could be moved to a new trench when the old one filled up.

Colt had used the project more as a morale booster after a severe winter than as a serious endeavor. It turned out to be practical, however, though not for the Koreans. They refused to use it themselves but proudly showed it to all newcomers, telling them that it was "the sergeant's shithouse" and not to mess with it. The navy even provided a toilet seat. What really made the movable outhouse absurd was that each time they had to relocate it, the men had to pickax through almost solid rock to dig the next latrine. Colt was always

Colt's privy on Nan-do Island, with a guerilla trainee using the urinal.

concerned that the toilet seat would drop into the old hole whenever they lifted the outhouse to move it to a new location; it never did, though.

No one on Nan-do took baths. The weather was too severe for ocean bathing, and the limited amount of fresh water was reserved for drinking. The best Colt could hope for was to brush his teeth and change his clothes occasionally.

While the weather could be dangerous, the training was even more so. As part of their instruction in military weapons, Colt taught the men how to use the American hand grenade. They had to learn to pull the pin, release the safety lever, wait two seconds, and then toss the weapon. The error margin was only three seconds, for the grenades were set to explode five seconds after the safety lever was released.[20] After days of training—throwing grenades over a cliff for safety—they learned to throw enough grenades at one time to cover a sixty-foot radius with shrapnel. But while the weapons were dangerous, so was their drinking water.

For a time they had a cook, but he had little cooking to do since the only things that needed preparation were coffee and oatmeal. Everything else, such as C-rations and water, came in cans and only needed heating. Unfortunately, the water was shipped in used navy gunpowder cans. Even though the water had been treated, it still tasted like the can's previous contents. Consequently, the coffee always tasted bad. One can of water even poisoned a big,

Ranger-qualified lieutenant, who had to be evacuated. Replacing him took a long time.

Eventually, Lt. Albert W. C. Naylor-Foote arrived. Unknown to Colt, he was a CIA officer. Naylor-Foote told Colt that he had served as a British commando during World War II, but he had settled in the United States after the war, and was now nearly blind without his glasses. Even though he liked the lieutenant, Colt thought that he was too old, already over the age of forty, for the rigors of living on a rock island behind enemy lines. Colt had been through Ranger and parachute training, and at his young age of twenty-three, he could barely handle existence on Nan-do.

Naylor-Foote had a fondness for alcohol. He even resorted, when the output of Colt's still was exhausted, to drinking the medical alcohol from the first-aid kit. He ordered Colt to bring him a touch of alcohol in a glass each morning, mixed with anything. Captain Ulatoski tolerated the man's minor weaknesses because of his extensive knowledge; Naylor-Foote returned the favor by passing along to Colt a lot of what he knew.

The lieutenant had an unfortunate experience while he was on Nan-do.[21] It all started after the Darby team, one of the guerrilla teams that had "graduated" from Nan-do, jumped into North Korea. While it was hiding out there, one of its men radioed Nan-do to advise Captain Ulatoski that they had recovered a downed American pilot. Ulatoski, Colt, and Naylor-Foote went along with the story, though none of them believed it. The air force had been unable to drop supplies to Darby, which the Americans on Nan-do knew, and in the middle of winter, everyone in North Korea was starving. They also suspected that the guerrillas had surrendered to the North Koreans and traded information for food and shelter.

Perhaps the North Koreans had turned over an American pilot to the Darby team to use as bait in luring American rescuers into North Korea. If so, the North Koreans probably had convinced the pilot that they were going to let his fellow Americans come in and pick him up.

Naylor-Foote, though knowing the dangers, volunteered to be in charge of the rescue effort. He requested, from the navy, information about the pilot, including his grandmother's maiden name and any other facts that would be unknown to the North Koreans. The Darby team confirmed the pilot's dog-tag serial number and indicated that he had a broken leg. With this information, Ulatoski received permission from the navy to attempt a rescue or, at least, to get food to the pilot. The lieutenant knew he could be walking into a trap and would have to be very careful. Naylor-Foote insisted that Ulatoski allow Colt to go on the mission because he had trained the indigenous and knew them. They might be less likely to betray someone who had been close to them.

The Americans radioed the Darby team with instructions to take the pilot to a specific location, place him in the middle of a large circle carved in the snow, and then back off and leave him there. The mission was set for February 7, 1952.

On the day of the rescue operation, while Colt was waiting for a helicopter to arrive from the USS *Rochester*, he was describing to the chief of his indigenous trainees how to quickly draw his .45-caliber sidearm, cocking the hammer as the pistol emerged from the holster and firing it as soon as it was at eye level or even sooner if necessary. To make his point, he demonstrated the fast-draw technique. They walked a short distance to an area used for target practice. As Colt drew his pistol and brought it up to fire, it discharged prematurely, and the bullet went through his foot. Colt actually fired off several rounds at his target before the pain set in and he realized what he had done. The chief commented something to the effect of, "You might want to take care of that." Needless to say, Colt was embarrassed at doing something so stupid, and he feared that he might be accused of having done it on purpose.

The rescue mission was postponed for a day while the helicopter, originally sent to Nan-do to take part in the pilot's rescue, transported Colt to the USS *Manchester*'s sickbay. While well treated, he received a welcome different from what an injured soldier normally enjoys.

Colt had been on Nan-do for almost a year, without cutting his hair or shaving. His beard reached to his chest, and his mustache was as long as a Chinese philosopher's. His hair was almost as long. The helicopter landed on the fantail of the USS *Manchester*.[22] Since Colt could barely hobble, four sailors loaded him into a wire-basket stretcher, a type used for carrying injured men up and down stairs from deck to deck. As they loaded him, one, a navy chief, commented, "Man, is he ugly."

Another sailor responded, "You name it, I'll cage it."

Colt felt bad, not realizing before how unkempt he must have looked. When he arrived on board the cruiser, the captain, who did not want anyone on his ship with long hair, sent a barber to give him his first haircut in almost a year. Once in sickbay, many sailors visited him and asked about North Korea and the war. All the attention helped him feel better, though he felt more than a bit embarrassed. The doctor told the sergeant that he was very lucky: the bullet had missed all of the critical bones in his foot, and he would be able to walk normally when it healed.

The next day, the rescue operation from Nan-do proceeded without Colt, one of the ship's petty officers taking his place. Even with all of his suspicions that they were probably flying into a trap, Ulatoski and Naylor-Foote refused to scrub the mission.

As soon as the pilot set down the helicopter, the balance apparently was thrown off when some equipment and supplies reputedly were pushed off prematurely by Naylor-Foote, causing a rotor blade to hit ground, after which all of the blades disintegrated. Whatever the cause, the helicopter crashed and the North Koreans captured Naylor-Foote, the pilot, and the petty officer. The three spent the next two years in a prisoner of war camp. Colt heard later that the American pilot who was to be rescued was sent to the same camp. All of the captives eventually were liberated in a prisoner exchange.

Colt's hospital stay aboard the *Manchester* was only a brief respite from danger. He was back on Nan-do in two weeks.

ABOUT A MONTH AFTER THE ATTEMPTED RESCUE mission, "Big Stup," a Mongolian, was at the helm in the rear of a junk.[23] His feet were so large that the Americans could find no boots to fit him, instead wrapping them with strips of blankets and plastic battery bags to keep them warm and dry; he stayed on the boat during missions to keep his foot coverings dry. Stup was uneducated, but he had become proficient at piloting the "one-lunger," as the men called their single-engine junk. Behind it they usually towed a smaller sampan, with which they could slip in quietly through the breakers (much like those along the Florida Gulf Coast) and assassinate North Korean sentries on the beaches. Some nights, Colt and his guerrilla band went far up the coast in the direction of the Manchurian border. They could travel half the night, at a speed of about eight to ten mph, to get to a destination about thirty-five to forty miles away but always turned around in time to return to Nan-do before daybreak. Colt had tried using a thirty-four-foot navy launch on these patrols, but it was damaged in a storm. Also, it was noisy and not as effective as the junk-and-sampan combination.

On this particular patrol, Colt's men had left the sampan at Nan-do. The men had not found any enemy, but they did find a bull. Food on Nan-do was limited to C-rations and rice, so the indigenous wanted to take the animal back for food; taking it would also deprive the enemy of much-needed food.

The indigenous leader was a dangerous man. Captain Ulatoski had told Colt to be diplomatic with him or he might, as Ulatoski put it, "shoot your ass." Colt did not want the men to bother with the bull, so he told the chief that it was too big, would swamp the boat, and would die in the frigid water. But the chief was set on towing the bull and tied it to the back of the junk anyway. With the bull under tow, the junk slowed to about three miles per hour, making Colt seasick. He managed to check on the bull from time to time; it was soon dead.

As the junk chugged through the pitch-black night in total blackout and far from the coast, Colt began to hear an unfamiliar sound—something was swishing alongside them. He could also see a faint florescence—something was breaking the water. All of a sudden, a bright spotlight blinded everyone in the boat.[24] A heavy cruiser was directly alongside. Colt immediately knew that it must be a U.S. Navy vessel and that its crew would think that he and his men were North Koreans smuggling agents into South Korea, a common occurrence. The sea was calm, otherwise the huge cruiser would have swamped or crushed their boat.

His suspicion was soon confirmed when he heard, from somewhere behind the glaring light and about twenty feet above them, a command in English through a megaphone: "Hands up. Lay to and stand by." Colt raised his hands and the others followed his lead.

A U.S. Navy cruiser would not hesitate to blow a junk full of North Koreans out of the water just for the target practice. Its 8-inch guns could make toothpicks out of the junk in moments. Colt jumped up and yelled: "Don't shoot! We're Task Force Kirkland. Send a radio message! Tell 'em we're Kirkland." He then turned to his interpreter and told him to order the men not to move a muscle and to keep their hands high in the air. He did likewise.

Colt again yelled to the sailors not to fire. He knew the navy liked to shoot first and ask questions later. One wrong move and he and his men would be lying among the pieces floating in the water. Through his interpreter he told the indigenous to smile. Colt could see their toothy grins standing out in the bright light of the arc lamps, but he still did not think that was enough to protect them. He then told the sailors, invisible behind the blinding light, that he was going to take off his jacket and show them something. Slowly Colt pulled off his Nazi jacket and turned it inside out so they could see the American flag sewn inside. This was enough to prompt one of the officers to ask for his name. He replied with his name, rank, and serial number.

The only response from the officer was "Stand by." Men on the deck of the cruiser kept guns pointed at the junk. Of the men on the boat, only Colt understood the degree of danger. After minutes that seemed like hours, the officer finally responded that they had identified them and knew that they were headed for Nan-do. He asked if the navy could be of any help.

Colt breathed a huge sigh of relief. He replied that he would appreciate their guiding them back to Nan-do. The officer agreed to and they did so. If that particular navy crew had not been well disciplined—and Colt had known some that were not—Colt and his team would have been a footnote in history, and in the future others would have died.

With all the experience Colt had already accumulated, his career was just beginning. He was ready to move to the next stage, away from war but not away from danger.

4 Special Forces Is Formed

WHILE HE WAS ON NAN-DO, COLT WAS recognized for his willingness to assume responsibility. On Captain Ulatoski's recommendation, he was commissioned a second lieutenant on June 1, 1952.[1]

Promoting an NCO to commissioned officer through a field promotion happens very infrequently. Ulatoski recommended Colt because he had demonstrated the characteristics of an officer by teaching others, maintaining a high character, demonstrating initiative, making sound decisions, and setting an example by being an honorable soldier.[2] Colt felt that his contributions were more along the lines of making life easier for his trainees, keeping the men alert, and helping keep morale high.

In addition, he received the Bronze Star on July 7, 1952, also on Captain Ulatoski's recommendation, for his service on Nan-do and for leading guerrillas on raids into North Korea. The citation read, in part: "Displaying technical skill and mastery of military science, Lieutenant Terry directed a highly classified project in support of combat operations. Lieutenant Terry's aggressive actions and outstanding achievements contributed significantly to the overall intelligence mission and furthered the United Nation's first armed campaign for international peace. His exemplary conduct reflects credit on himself and the military service."[3]

He also received a U.S. Navy commendation for directing naval gunfire on the enemy.[4] Colt himself believed that enduring the winter weather was harder than earning either of these awards.

Along with his promotion to second lieutenant, he also received orders to fly to Tokyo, where a general would pin his bars on him. Colt traveled by ship and plane to the Japanese capital. He had not had R&R (rest-and-recreation leave) for more than two years.

In Tokyo he found it good to see Americans who were polished, clean, and having fun. After the general pinned lieutenant bars on him, Colt enjoyed three days of R&R as an officer. Then he traveled by plane and by ship to get back behind enemy lines. As soon as he arrived on Nan-do, the others harassed him by constantly saluting him so he would have to return their salutes.

SOON AFTER HIS PROMOTION, COLT RECEIVED ORDERS rotating him back to the States. While he was being processed at Camp Drake in Japan, a captain asked if he wanted to volunteer for Special Forces. Colt thought he meant Special Services, which handles the army's sports teams, so he declined.

The captain then explained that the army was organizing a new group at Fort Bragg, and it was looking for soldiers with his experience—men who could teach guerrilla warfare. It sounded like what he had been doing in North Korea, so Colt volunteered. He was assigned to the 10th Special Forces Group (Airborne) under Col. Aaron Bank and his adjutant, 2d Lt. Robert D. "Bugs Bunny" Anderson.

On June 19, 1952, the 10th Special Forces Group was activated at Fort Bragg.[5] Colt applied to Special Forces, which would become known as the Green Berets, on July 8, 1952, and was accepted effective July 24.[6] Colt had volunteered for a group that would become one of the most elite military forces in the world. He started his career in Special Forces as one of its officers.

Even though Colt had learned much of what it meant to be an officer from such men as Ulatoski and Naylor-Foote, he had not had any formal officer training. A few months after arriving at Fort Bragg, in early 1953, Colt was sent on temporary duty to the Fort Benning Officers Infantry Basic Course.[7] There he began building a foundation for his commission. During his early years as a soldier, Colt had regularly endangered his life. For the next few years, as a somewhat unorthodox officer in training, he would occasionally endanger his career.

WHILE AT FORT BENNING, HE WALKED INTO A drugstore in Columbus, Georgia, to drop off some film for development. He thought two men might have been following him, but he discounted that possibility because he knew of no reason why anyone would be interested in him. A week later Colt returned to the drugstore to pick up his prints. As he showed the clerk his ticket, the clerk pointed toward the back of the store and told him that two federal men were in the back and wanted to talk with him. Colt was mystified.

He confronted the two men, asking them, "What the hell's up?"

They showed him credentials identifying themselves as Counterintelligence Corps (CIC) agents, telling Colt, "We want you to come down to our office and make a statement about some of your activities in North Korea."

To that he responded: "That information is secret and can't be disclosed without my commander's permission. Besides, I'm late for school at Fort Benning."

The CIC man countered with, "We aren't after operational information." Colt still refused to respond, which was allowed under the Uniform Code of Military Justice.[8]

When Colt returned to base, he reported the incident to his company commander, who ordered Colt to visit the federal building downtown and answer the CIC's questions. The CIC wanted information about everything that Colt knew about a Lieutenant Naylor-Foote. They asked him if he knew that Naylor-Foote had been captured on a raid to save a downed pilot and was held as a prisoner of war in North Korea from February, 1952, to May, 1953.[9]

He replied, "Yeah, I should have been with him."

The navy men who had been captured and later released with Naylor-Foote, after recovering from their ordeal, were now attempting to file charges against the lieutenant and Captain Ulatoski for allegedly misrepresenting their ranks, lying and other issues related to initiating the rescue effort, the mission's failure, and the subsequent capture and imprisonment of Naylor-Foote, Chief Petty Officer Duane Thorin and the injured navy flier, Lieutenant Ettinger.[10]

Colt did not like the CIC investigators because he felt that they would not take all of the circumstances into account. He believed that Naylor-Foote would have had problems in a prison camp because of his age, poor physical condition, dependency on his glasses, and need for alcohol. The North Koreans would have worked on his weaknesses.

Colt had liked Naylor-Foote and knew the man was smart and good at heart. When he had been a young master sergeant, the lieutenant had taught him important lessons about identifying Russian tanks in the dark and being accurate in reporting intelligence; he felt indebted to Naylor-Foote. Now that he was learning to be an officer, Colt had loyalties to those who had trained him. He was sorry about the ruinous effect that the Korean War would have had on the old lieutenant. The CIC was out to strip Naylor-Foote of his rank, cancel his back pay, and send him to prison for a long time, which he felt would be unfair penalties.[11] Colt never learned the outcome of the investigation.

HE WOULD ALSO HAVE HIS OWN BRUSHES WITH MATTERS of discipline. Colt was never truly irresponsible, only a bit rebellious, rambunctious, and short tempered after having been in combat.

One of Colt's roles as a commissioned officer was officer of the guard, whose duties included checking the Enlisted Men's Club and the NCO Club each evening to make sure that everything was in order. Just recently a sergeant, he knew that NCOs did not like officers coming into their club, but he was obligated to check it at least once during his evening tour.

One night he went into the NCO Club as usual and confirmed with the NCO in charge that everything was okay. Colt wished him a good evening and started to leave. As he turned to walk out, someone threw a full can of beer at him. It whistled past his head and spattered against the wall.

As officer of the guard, he wore an armband similar to the Military Police (MP). His head was protected with only a helmet liner, not a metal helmet, and he wore a loaded .45 automatic. There was no doubt that everyone in the bar knew who he was and what his job was.

Colt had just returned from North Korea and was still in "combat mode." He spun around, snatched his .45 from its holster, and jacked a round into the chamber. In a microsecond everyone was on the floor and under tables. He asked no one in particular, "Who's the son of a bitch that threw the beer can?" Nobody moved. Turning to the manager, Colt told him, "Close down this fuckin' club, now." Turning to the patrons, he ordered, "Everyone in here, stand up and get out!" Then he added a few choice words for effect. None of the patrons moved until the manager started shooing them outside. He then locked up for the night.

Colt got in his jeep, and his driver took him back to the command post. Although he had not caught the man who threw the beer, he felt somewhat satisfied by closing the club. Because he was a brand-new lieutenant, however, he thought that he should report the incident to the officer of the day. He woke up Capt. Thomas Wantling and told him what had happened.

The captain jumped off his bunk, hollering, "You what?" Colt was slow to realize that he had done something stupid and was probably in trouble. Wantling told him to keep quiet and say nothing about what he did—to anybody. "We'll wait and see if anyone says anything."

The lieutenant followed his advice, and no one ever mentioned the incident. Colt could have been disciplined for his action; Captain Wantling had done him a big favor. After this incident, Colt tried to settle into the personal side of his life, including getting married for the first time.[12]

AS THE SPECIAL FORCES GROUPS WERE DEVELOPING IN 1955, so was Colt. He was entering a stage that would prepare him for another war yet to come. During the next few years, he would hone his versatility and determination to fine edges.

The first Special Forces group was small and quite selective—about five hundred men and fifty officers. The smallest unit was called an A-team.[13] Each A-team consisted of a commanding officer (CO), an executive officer (XO), and ten NCOs, including a team sergeant, two medics, an intelligence sergeant, two engineer/demolition NCOs, two radio operators, and two weapons experts. One of the men was trained as back up to the intelligence sergeant. The light- and heavy-weapons men were cross-trained. Every man on an A-team was instructed in Morse code, so that any one of them could operate the radio, as well as in intelligence gathering and in demolition. Team members learned the language of the country to which their team would be assigned. Colt recalls operating sometimes as a split team, with the XO, either the team sergeant or the intelligence sergeant, and one of each of the specialties making up one of the two six-man teams. With such intense training as a unit, loyalty and respect among the men were very strong.

The A-teams reported to the B-team CO at least once daily by radio. A-teams reported to B-teams, B-teams reported to C-teams, and C-teams reported to group headquarters. B-teams and C-teams were administrative in nature.

B-teams were supposed to have four officers and twenty NCOs and typically had from three to twenty-six A-teams under their control, depending on the country size and the number of indigenous to be organized and trained for resistance. The role of the B-team was to direct, supply, and support its assigned A-teams. They were usually set up in (relatively) large towns. The CO for B-teams was normally a major, and the XO normally a captain. B-teams could have officers for administration (S-1), intelligence (S-2), operations (S-3), logistics (S-4), and an XO, all reporting to the major. Often, one officer would serve as both S-1 and S-4, while another served as both S-2 and S-3. B-teams also had about eleven NCOs—administration, operations, logistics, weapons (two), intelligence, demolitions (two), radio operation (two), and medic. Sometimes the weapons and demolitions NCOs would also function as administration and logistics personnel.

C-teams were similarly organized, larger in size, and responsible for a larger territory. They normally covered a corps area and reported to the commander of a group, such as 10th Special Forces Group (Airborne). C-teams usually had three to four B-teams, but there was no set amount—Colt was aware of a C-team with ten B-teams. C-teams were led by lieutenant colonels, with majors for XO and adjutant (S-1). Captains oversaw intelligence, operations, communications, and logistics. They also had doctors (two), a senior medical NCO, a sergeant major, and a number of radio operators (four or five).[14]

A good Special Forces officer, first and foremost, has to be a good soldier. Before he is allowed to join Special Forces, he must learn basic army skills, which are the foundation for the more advanced Special Forces training. Also, he must be Airborne (a qualified paratrooper) and would often be Ranger (a qualification rating for troopers trained for long-range patrols behind enemy lines and in small-unit tactics). When Special Forces was first organized, men were selected from among NCOs and officers with combat experience.

Colt was accepted into the first Special Forces group, the 10th Special Forces Group (Airborne), as it was being activated because he had battlefield experience in North Korea and because he had lived, trained, and fought with indigenous guerrillas, the kind of duty Special Forces would be doing. The mission of Special Forces included infiltrating into enemy countries and organizing, training, and arming guerrilla forces. Additional duties included special reconnaissance, small-scale offensives (to capture, destroy, recover, or inflict damage), psychological operations, and assisting commanders in relationships with civil authorities.[15]

The men in Special Forces were individually selected. Over time, through a constant testing and weeding-out process, they progressed from "select" to "elite," meaning only that these men were picked from among the brightest and toughest soldiers in the army and trained to be the best at every military skill. Those who could not meet the high standards of Special Forces were then culled from those who could.

THE OFFICE OF STRATEGIC SERVICES (OSS) WAS THE military organization that oversaw saboteurs, secret radio operations, and intelligence activities during World War II. The CIA was the successor organization to OSS, though established as a civilian operation. When the CIA tried to take control when Special Forces was being created, the U.S. government, and probably Pres. Dwight D. Eisenhower himself, did not want the new organization to be part of a civilian organization since Special Forces was a large body of men and military in nature. Colt's recollection is that the generals did not initially want to take on Special Forces, possibly because they saw it as a re-creation of the OSS. When the army finally agreed to take on the responsibility, Special Forces was assigned to the XVIII Airborne Corps at Fort Bragg.[16]

At this time the men of Special Forces wore regular army caps rather than the green beret that later became their trademark. Also, they did not yet have the teal blue patch with three lightning strikes and arrows (or the later version without the arrows). Instead, the men wore the red army Airborne patch with parachute and glider until mid-1950s.

Special Forces troops first started wearing green berets unofficially during training missions, after Maj. Herbert Brucker originally designated the green beret in 1953. Later that year 1st Lt. Roger Pezelle adopted it as the unofficial headgear for his A-team, Operational Detachment FA-32.[17] His men carried them in their rucksacks and put them on only after they parachuted into their destinations. Pres. John F. Kennedy gave the service official permission to wear the berets during a visit to Fort Bragg on October 12, 1961. The entire Special Forces held a big celebration when the announcement was made.[18] Ten to fifteen years later, Ranger companies, the 82d Airborne Division, and the air force's air commandos and security teams also began to wear berets, though in different colors. Eventually, all army units would be given permission to wear the beret.

Special Forces did not immediately earn their reputation; they had a lot of training to receive and to give. Although Colt had all of the necessary qualifications to join, it was not clear to him, or probably to any of the men, what it would one day mean to be a member of Special Forces. In 1953 they knew only that it meant a lot more training. Colt's role, at this stage of his career, was to learn to become an instructor.

LEADING A NIGHT JUMP NEAR FAYETTEVILLE, NORTH Carolina, Colt stood at the head of a planeload (known as a "stick") of paratroopers in the back of a C-47. The troopers were supporting a 10th Special

Forces Group (Airborne) training mission. Colt and his first sergeant, M.Sgt. Joseph Mancuso, were the jumpmasters, leading new Green Berets on their first night jump. Although Colt wore his parachute, he was not jumping with them. Colt gave them the standard commands: "Stand-up. Hook-up. Check your equipment. Sound off for equipment check." The men all stood up and hooked their static lines into the cable running along the aircraft ceiling. The jumper farthest from the door, after checking his equipment, sounded off first ("Twelve okay!"), then the next trooper ("Eleven okay!"), and so on down the line, each man hitting the man in front of him on the butt. As they did so, they shuffled down to stand in the doorway. Then they jumped, one after the other, out the door.

As soon as the men were out, Colt began talking to his team sergeant. Suddenly, within minutes, they realized that they could hear a strange noise— bam, bam. They both looked out of the open jump door. Holding onto to his static line, part way down, was one of the young paratroopers. What they were hearing was the sound of the trooper's steel helmet hitting the side of the airplane as the wind bounced him around. The C-47 had cleared the drop zone, so Colt did not want the soldier to let go over an unknown location.[19] He hollered to him to hold on and sent the sergeant to tell the pilot to turn the plane and make another pass over the drop zone. The pilot wanted to know what the heck they were doing to his airplane back there.

The plane flew back to the zone. Colt would have to convince the trooper to let go of his static line so that he would drop and the parachute would open. The pilot could not land the plane with the man hanging on to it since he would be dragged to death along the runway. The trooper was Colt's respon- sibility, and it was his job to get the man safely through this jump. Because he would not let go by himself, Colt had only one option. He hooked up his own parachute to the static line. Master Sergeant Mancuso helped the lieutenant out the door slowly and carefully, Colt holding on to the trooper's static line. He moved hand over hand down the line until he was on top of the trooper. Colt yelled at him to let go, but he would not budge. Prying the man's fingers back and then pulling the trooper's hands off his line, Colt fell away with him. Both chutes opened without problem, and they landed safely.

On the ground, all that Colt said to the trooper was that the plane was surely beating him black and blue up there. He did not report the near acci- dent so that the man's career would not be jeopardized. The next time they went up, the trooper jumped cleanly. As an instructor, Colt had to be a judge

of character as well as a judge of the training results. He sensed that the man had what it took to succeed in Special Forces, that he would be all right.

Germany would be Colt's next stop as an instructor.

ON SEPTEMBER 25, 1953, THE COLD WAR WAS AT A PEAK, and concerns about Communism raged.[20] The original 10th Special Forces Group (Airborne) had been reorganized into two groups, the 10th and the 77th. The 10th, commanded by Colonel Bank, went to Germany, while the 77th remained at Fort Bragg under the command of Col. Jack "Blackjack" Shannon. Later, on June 24, 1957, a third unit, the 1st Special Forces Group (Airborne), was organized and sent to Okinawa.[21]

Colt sailed from Wilmington, North Carolina, on a troop ship on November 10, 1953. He would remain in Europe until July 10, 1956. Colt was assigned to the 10th Special Forces Demolition/Sabotage Committee as a sabotage instructor.[22] He was not happy—he wanted to be where the action was, not in a classroom. Colonel Bank insisted that Colt was going to be an instructor and assigned him to Capt. Pete Thompson and Capt. Hugh Mitchell.

In no uncertain terms, Colt told Captain Mitchell that he did not want to teach sabotage. The captain said that he did not care what the lieutenant wanted—he was to get some books and start reading because he was going to become their expert in simple and industrial sabotage.

So Colt did just that. He learned how to blow up cars, houses, factories, and people. He taught other soldiers how to make explosives and incendiary devices from household supplies, booby-trap doors, pick locks, crack safes, and set fire to factories—and how to make all of these actions look like accidents. The training was effective but dangerous. The commander stopped instruction in some subjects after several accidents occurred and his safe was cracked.

The training that Colt personally conducted included teaching the men what to look for as saboteurs and how to use silenced weapons, special forms of sabotage, and demolitions. Dressed in civilian clothes, he toured his trainees through West German machinery factories, searching the plants they visited for weak entry points and sabotage opportunities for practice. At railway lines, bridges, and stations, he showed them how to damage a railroad and keep it out of service for various time periods—two, ten, thirty, or sixty days. He took them to coal mines and taught them how to stop the flow of coal

Colt landing in Badtolz, West Germany, after test jumping from a modified B-29 bomber. He wears a football helmet with hand-painted skull and crossbones.

to power plants. They visited every hydroelectric power plant in West Germany, and he showed them how to shut them down.

Colt was helping build the skills and traditions of Special Forces and to produce the next generation of instructors. He was also developing his leadership skills and learning how to use his men's strengths, to poll them for ideas, and to get the best from each of them. His tendency to be dogmatic diminished except when emergencies called for decisiveness. All of these skills would later prove valuable to him in combat.

During his time in Europe, Colt attended language classes for fifty-two weeks in Oberammergau, West Germany, at the U.S. Army Intelligence School, where he learned to speak Bohemian, the principal language of Czechoslovakia.[23] He also trained Czechoslovakians to fight the Soviets. Assigned as a specialist on Czechoslovakia, he not only learned the language but also became familiar with every bridge, railroad station, highway, radio station, and power plant in the country. He knew more about his assigned country than his home state of Florida.

On July 27, 1955, Colt was promoted to first lieutenant.[24] He was leader of Team FA-56 during most of his time in Europe, and even while in language school, he and his men had to pass the Special Forces six-week fitness test every year. At that time, in 1955, the CIA was preparing to drop Special Forces A-teams into Czechoslovakia to assist the local resistance in its fight against the Soviets and communism, but President Eisenhower refused to approve the plan. Other teams were earmarked for Poland, Romania, and other Eastern European countries. Before his language training (and later for the above possible invasions), Colt led a number of field exercises, which would require hiding large numbers of men in hostile areas.[25]

Field, or test, exercises were not easy to pull off and were not without danger. When each twelve-man team was ready to go into the field for a six-week top-secret training exercise, the soldiers flew to a secure staging area at an air force base in Molesworth, England, referred to as the "Ice Box." For the next five days, they were briefed on the mission, which would require a jump into West Germany, where the training areas were located.

Each team was assigned a series of missions within a guerrilla-warfare operational area (GWOA)—an assigned space of about fifty square kilometers, in this case. The size of a GWOA varied based on ethnic boundaries, number of targets, terrain, and other factors. The team would have to find its targets, often "missing pilots," anywhere within the GWOA, which was like looking for a needle in many haystacks. Special Forces team members often played the parts of missing pilots, but more often the air force snatched actual pilots as they climbed into their cockpits without warning so that they could not "G2" the test—that is, load their pockets with money, cigarettes, their favorite foods, and other items. This allowed a more realistic situation for them on the ground that was as close as possible to being actually shot down. The pilots were taken by truck into the German countryside and dumped alongside a road. In other exercises, instead of recovering pilots, a team's mission was to organize groups of troopers, who had parachuted into a territory theoretically invaded by an enemy, to recruit and to train indigenous resistance fighters.

One such field exercise began with a radio message that ordered Colt and his team to parachute into Germany and locate a sixty-man "resistance group," American soldiers who had been turned loose somewhere in a fifty-square-mile GWOA. In this scenario the Soviets had invaded West Germany and the sixty Americans represented local citizens who would be trained and organized for resistance actions against the enemy. Staging out of the Ice Box at night, Colt and his men jumped into a mountainside cow pasture in Bavaria from a specially modified B-29.[26] A plywood platform had been built over the aft bomb bay of the aircraft. With the bay doors open, the first three men straddled the opening, with just their hands and heels balancing them over the hole. The plane sometimes had only ten seconds over the drop zone because the zones were small. When the green light came on, the first three men dropped. The remaining twelve men had just seven seconds to leave the plane through the bomb bay.

As soon as the team was on the ground, Colt's first priority, before he was scheduled to rendezvous with the sixty prospective insurgents, was to find a safe area for his men to hide out. The next thing was to notify group headquarters that the landing had been safe with no injuries and to request a supply drop. Even ordering the drop exposed them to capture. Acting as the "enemy," units of local police departments and the U.S. 4th Armored Division were scouring the countryside to find Colt's team and other Special Forces units. Using the radio would expose his men to immediate capture, so Colt dispatched a radioman away from their safe area to transmit his message. The first message was a request for the immediate airdrop of C-rations, standard military food rations, and other supplies. The next objective was to locate and rendezvous with the sixty-man resistance group. Once located, he would get them to a safe area; brief them on their mission; house, feed, organize, and train them; and successfully attack a target, all while earning their respect and trust.

FOR THIS TEST EXERCISE, COLT'S TEAM HAD TO FIND and retrieve about sixty paratroopers from the 11th Airborne Division trucked in by the army and dropped off in a small forest. The troopers had instructions to make his team's assignment as difficult and as real as possible. The scenario designated the sixty men as West Germans who had escaped from a prison camp in the Soviet Union and returned to their homeland to form a resistance group to kill occupying Soviet soldiers. They had intermediate targets to destroy, but in the final stage all of the troopers would link up with other "guerrillas" and attack a final objective together. The entire mission would take weeks.

Colt sent most of the team out to locate the mock guerillas and sent the rest to try to locate a safe area large enough to conceal them and his team. Once the guerillas were located, Colt and his team moved them quickly away from the small woods without anyone being seen. Forests in Germany are in small patches maintained by forest *meisters* and closely watched by nearby local villagers and therefore not good hiding places. They could not stay in the open either. Finding a place for both his team and the guerrillas to hide would not be easy.

Colt quickly found a suitable location, a large German farm with a big barn. By then he had learned enough German to converse fairly well with the local people. He woke up the farmer, "Herman Schulenburg," and told him about the exercise—how they had parachuted in and why they needed a place to hide out. Schulenburg was delighted at the idea of hiding American soldiers. He gave them permission to stay in the barn (with the stipulation that they not smoke there), invited them into the house, and even woke up his wife to make coffee. Then he kept Colt and his team up all night, talking about World War II. Schulenburg immediately fell into the spirit of the exercise and asked Colt if he wanted him and some of his friends to sabotage the tanks. Although he was tempted, Colt declined the offer.

His men had packed German civilian clothes so the entire band of men could dress as locals and freely move about the area. Colt dispatched reconnaissance teams to look for the next place to hide. Eventually they would need to get closer to their end-of-mission target, a railroad bridge that they would "blow up." It was twenty-five miles away, so transportation was a critical part of the exercise. Schulenburg volunteered to chauffeur them around in his Volkswagen van while they prepared for the operation, which they readily accepted.

The men were getting "stir crazy" from being confined in such a small area. Colt talked to them about having to sit tight for a couple more weeks. A few days later he got into a fight with one of the troopers. The man had sneaked off to a bar in the local village and gotten very drunk. Colt, riding a rented motorcycle, came upon the stray staggering along the road. When Colt approached him, offering him a ride back to their hideout, the trooper hit him in the face. Before the man could hit him again, Colt tripped him onto his back, and as they wrestled, they rolled into a ditch. The trooper was fighting viciously.

For the first time in his life, Colt lost complete control of his temper. Getting on top of the drunk, he began to beat him with every ounce of his strength. The ditch had about a foot of water in it. Every time the trooper picked up his head up, Colt hit him again and his head went underwater. Finally, while he was holding the trooper's head underwater, he felt someone pulling on his collar and heard a voice yelling in German. Colt did not realize that the person pulling on him was an elderly woman, and he turned and pushed her. The shock of realizing that he just shoved an old lady snapped him out of his rage and probably saved the trooper's life. He apologized to the woman.

Colt took the trooper to the local police station to be locked up for being drunk. Of course, Colt could not tell the police that the man had also assaulted a military officer. On the way back to the farm, he was angry with himself for losing control. When Colt reported himself to Capt. Jack "Blackjack" Streigel, an ex-Ranger from Korea, the captain thought that Colt had gotten the worse of it, though Colt knew differently. The trooper was planning to press charges against Colt until he learned from Streigel that the lieutenant would then file countercharges—after all, the trooper had hit Colt first.[27]

Still feeling bad about losing control, Colt wanted to apologize to the man, but he never saw him again. If Colt had killed the trooper, it would have meant the brig, a dishonorable discharge, and the end of a promising career. As it was, he might have been thrown out of Special Forces, but an officer with wisdom had intervened. Another superior, such as Colonel Bank, might not have been as generous.

Colonel Bank had served with the OSS during World War II and, dressed as a Nazi soldier, had worked behind German lines as a spy. He was tough and knew how the game should be played. His attitude toward the men in Special Forces was "be tough or get out." Bank had other teams in the Ice Box with men who were ready to replace anyone who could not handle the demands or who misbehaved. His high expectations added pressure to this exercise.

As the simulation intensified, the umpires began to send out additional police with dogs to look for Colt's team since the regular troops had not found them. Colt rode his motorcycle to the bridge and took some pictures of it. It was guarded, twenty-four hours a day, with umpires stationed nearby as observers. He developed the film and studied the pictures. Examining the pictures, none of his men could see how they would possibly get six hundred pounds of demolition onto the bridge without getting caught. Although they would not be carrying real explosives, they were required to carry the actual weight—six hundred pounds of sandbags—without being detected.[28]

Colt, however, had a plan. He had already learned to keep his men as far away as possible from the site of a mission until it was time for the attack. It was now time to close in. With the help of his German host, he moved his combined force to a farm closer to the target. Once there, the men could not leave the farmyard, and Colt found himself scrambling eggs for over seventy men each morning to help keep up morale.[29]

The target was a steel railroad bridge with a catwalk down the center. Over each abutment, a square steel trapdoor, held in place with bolts, covered a space through which a man could drop to place explosives. With the charges set off on top of the abutments, the entire bridge would be taken out. On his surveillance of the target, however, Colt had identified two related major problems: trains ran across the tracks every eleven minutes, and the bolts on the trapdoors would need to be loosened before the attack—if these were not loosened beforehand, the explosives could not be placed within the eleven-minute window of opportunity. He would have to sneak onto the bridge alone, at least once, before the attack.

Colt drilled the men in the barnyard to perfect their timing and left them to practice. After dark, he drove his motorcycle as close as he could to the bridge and crept up to it. Because the strike was not expected for several weeks, the guards were not on the bridge. He was able to get on it and loosen the four bolts on each trapdoor, though not daring to remove them completely because German inspectors, who patrolled the bridge from time to time, would notice that they were missing. His team would attack the bridge the following night.

Schulenburg, the farmer, again came to their aid. He hitched up his horse and wagon, and Colt hid the simulated explosives and some of the men under straw. The wagon followed a dirt road down to the bridge. The lieutenant went ahead of it with the men who would "do the kills." The "killing" team would sneak up on the guards, tap them hard on the shoulders, and tell them that they were dead—symbolic of having killed them. They would not actually hurt the guards. Each tapped man would then lie down. Umpires on the bridge ensured that the guards complied. The first men off the wagon would form a security perimeter around the site while the rest moved the sandbags into position.

Minutes after the attack began, the guards had been "killed," and Colt was standing on the bridge in the pitch dark, holding up one of the trapdoors. Except for Colt and a young private, "Anthony," who was standing in a hole that had been covered by a trapdoor, everyone else had planted their explosives and had gotten off the bridge. Suddenly a bright light illuminated them. The two were standing directly in the path of an oncoming train arriving two minutes ahead of schedule. Anthony, a big man from New York, was finishing the placement of the simulated charges under the bridge. All that was left to do was tying together the detonating cords—so that it looked like a professional job and would earn the team top marks.

It was too late to get off the bridge. Colt either had to do something to evade the train or die. The young trooper was trying to squeeze into the space below the bridge, but his shoulders were too broad, and he was stuck in the opening, his head and shoulders high enough that the train would cut him in half. Colt considered his options, which seemed to number only two: he could jump over the side, hold on to the steel railing, and leave the other man to die, an option that was not acceptable to him, or he could stay to the end. He chose the second—if the young private had to die, then so would he.

Over the noise of the screaming whistle of the rapidly approaching train, Colt yelled, "Hands over your head!"

Either Anthony did not hear him or did not understand him. The train was very near and still moving fast. The engineer saw them in the light of his headlight and began to apply his brakes, though he knew it was too late. The train's horn wailed.

Again Colt yelled, "Get your hands up!"

Just as the train arrived at the bridge, the man understood. As he put up his arms, Colt jumped on the trooper's shoulders with both feet and knocked him into the narrow space below the bridge tracks. Then Colt dropped the trapdoor over the man, grabbed the handrail that ran along the side of the bridge, and leaped over it. Gripping the handrail tightly, he dangled far above the river as the train roared by. He heard the engineer yelling curse words at them in German. Colt struggled to hang on until the last car passed. Both men survived without injury.

Despite this incident, Colt's team earned the highest possible marks for the simulation. Colt would continue to train Special Forces teams in West Germany for three years. Along with his men, he learned the skills needed for cold-weather survival, skiing, parachuting into snow, sabotage, and demolition.

WHEN COLONEL BANK ROTATED BACK TO THE STATES, his replacement was Col. William E. "Wild Bill" Ekman, who had a reputation of being a tough but good man. He had been highly decorated for his conduct during the invasion of Normandy in World War II.

Wild Bill came very close to bouncing Colt from Special Forces. Colt, returning from a skiing weekend, had stood up for a group of innocent German civilians against two large bullies and was beaten up. To make matters worse, a fellow Special Forces officer, Lt. Irwin K. Cockett Jr., who had come to his aid had his jaw broken. When Colt was summoned to Colonel Ekman's office the next morning, he was sure that he would be dismissed from Special Forces.

The colonel did not bounce Colt, but he did order him to park his white Cadillac convertible until spring. Colt was thankful that his punishment was that minor. Discipline in Special Forces could be strict. When mischief turned into trouble, and not even serious trouble, the culprit was usually removed from Special Forces: if he were lucky, he was transferred to another army unit; if not, he was discharged from the army altogether. It was remarkable that Colt's career did not end with this incident. Fortunately, his discipline did not interfere with his training exercises.

COLT OPERATED AN ESCAPE-AND-EVASION NET, CALLED a "ratline" (a term used to describe the movement one might see in a line of rats that move, fast, from one hole to the next, one hiding place after another). The ratline operated across the fields and forests of West Germany. The U.S. Air Force had overall responsibility for escape and evasion for Europe, which meant that they had to conduct regular training exercises in the theater. Here, the 10th Special Forces also had the responsibility for the escape and evasion of downed pilots as well as training civilians to form resistance throughout all of Western and Eastern Europe in the event of a war. Each Special Forces team had a sector. The mission of Colt's team was to scour an area within a radius of fifty miles from southern Bavaria to the Rhine River. The team was part of a network of successive handoffs to freedom, with the mission to secretly move downed pilots to the next team in the network.

Handoffs occurred without any of the teams coming into contact with each other. To communicate, they used a series of drop points, secret markings in the forest, and passwords. Keeping the teams apart prevented the enemy from "rolling up the whole line" during a single operation. In such exercises, the "enemy" was portrayed by the 4th Armored Division, thousands of troops patrolling the countryside to look for Special Forces teams and to round up "downed pilots" and members of the ratlines.

As an example of how the system worked, Colt alerted the NCOs and their guerrilla trainees along his ratline to be on the lookout for a downed pilot. The airmen were given directions in advance that would put them on a course intersecting with the ratline. They were to look for certain items tied to tree limbs and bushes along a stream, remove them, and hide nearby. The items could be anything and were selected in advance so that pilots could be briefed at their airport before they flew.

In one case Colt's team and his trained guerrillas hung German beer bottle caps, the old-fashioned kind with wire bails, by string. In the designated area his team would hang dozens of them, each in an inconspicuous place; the pilots had to look carefully to find them. His men would go out several times per day and count the bottle caps. When a ratline found one or more missing, the soldiers looked for a pilot hiding in the immediate area. When they found him, they had a signal and exchanged passwords. They then took him to a special hiding area, where they would take his fingerprints and hold him until he was confirmed as a genuine American pilot.

The air force had a system to verify a pilot's identity by his name, rank, serial number, thumbprint, and index-finger print. The Federal Bureau of Investigation (FBI) trained the Special Forces teams in reading fingerprints. Within twenty-four hours, the air force confirmed or denied a pilot's identity, and the ratline brought the real pilots into the net and its series of safe houses. This system required considerable training and oversight.

A female air force officer was in charge of escape and evasion for Europe. During an exercise in November, 1955, Colt received a radio message that the officer, Lt. Col. Barbara Shimkus, wanted to inspect his ratline to determine if it met the proper standards.[30] At first he tried to object. Colt sent radio messages to 10th Special Forces Headquarters that the colonel's visit would jeopardize security and that they could not risk it. He requested that she be kept away from his net.

The answer came back that the group field coordinator, Lt. Col. William Ewald, did not care about the lieutenant's concerns; the lieutenant colonel would arrive the next day. Colt sent back a message suggesting that she dress in German clothes, arrive in a car with German plates, and bring nothing that would identify her affiliation with the U.S. Air Force. For the most part, she complied.

Colt was surprised to find the senior officer young, attractive, and quite intelligent. He briefed her on the operation. She wanted to go along that night to watch five pilots pass through one of the transfer points. Colt agreed to take her with him on his motorcycle. They would leave early, hide in the woods, and watch the handoff.

They arrived at dusk. As the October sun went down, the air turned cold.

After they were settled in their hiding place, a ditch full of leaves, they had to wait for some time. It was getting colder and colder, and they both started to shiver.

"What do Special Forces do when they're cold?" Shimkus asked.

"We huddle together and pile leaves over us," Colt replied.

"Let's do it," she said.

They gathered a big pile of leaves and piled them on top of themselves. Shimkus sat in front of Colt and snuggled her back up to his chest. She was a very attractive woman, and he was a young all-American male. With her perfume drifting back toward him, Colt started to get excited. He said to himself that he had better get out from under those leaves because he still had a long way to go in this army; if he came on to a lieutenant colonel, he would find himself in the stockade. Colt said that it was getting too warm for him, and he would have to step outside. He covered her again with leaves and stayed away from her until the ratline team and the pilots finally showed up. By then Colt was nearly frozen. As the colonel made mental notes, she and Colt watched one team arrive with the pilots and leave them. The airmen were not sitting alone more than a minute or two before the next ratline team arrived and exchanged a password for its countersign. The team picked up the pilots smooth as clockwork and was gone almost before the colonel knew it.

Getting back on the motorcycle, Colt and the colonel returned to the farmhouse. She remained in the area about a week. When she was back at headquarters, she wrote an efficiency report that gave Colt's team very high marks. The group commander showed the report to Colt. It read, in part: "This is an outstanding officer. He knows his job. Very professional but is too hard on his men." Colt read it to his men, and they all laughed.

In June, 1956, a month earlier than his adjusted rotation date, Colt returned to the United States, assigned as leader of FB-1 team at the 77th Special Forces Group at Fort Bragg.[31]

The Dangers of Maintaining Prowess

ON AUGUST 13, 1956, COLT ARRIVED AT Edward Gary Air Force Base in San Marcos, Texas, to attend an eighteen-week army aviation-tactics course—Army Primary Flight Training Class 57-3. After a brief altercation with one of the flight instructors, he was dropped from the class, and returned to the 535th Military Intelligence Group at Fort Bragg, where he was appointed as FA team leader under FB-4 in the 77th Special Forces Group.[1] Colt ran this and other teams through various training exercises during the next four years.

ONE DAY DURING THE WINTER OF 1956, COLT WALKED into the railroad station in Ogden, Utah, thirty-seven miles north of Salt Lake City; brushed the snow off his civilian clothes; and asked to speak with the stationmaster. A secretary showed him into the office of the stationmaster, who was an imposing figure behind his big mahogany desk.

Colt introduced himself, "Sir, we're having some Special Forces war games in the area, and I've come to ask you a favor."

The stationmaster, who had not seen a car pull up, looked at Colt and asked, "Where'd you come from?"

Colt answered, "We're staying at Como Park up at Morgan. It's closed for the season."

Morgan, Utah, is twenty-seven miles southeast of Ogden. Colt and his team had parachuted into southwestern Wyoming. As they skied toward Morgan, they had been living out in the elements, performing missions in rough and wide-open terrain for more than a week before they found Como Park.[2] With little shelter from the blowing snow and few places to hide, they knew they needed to find a better location. A two-man reconnaissance team found the closed amusement park. When they talked to the owner, he invited the soldiers to hide out in his site.

The stationmaster continued, "I know that place. How did you get here?"

Colt answered, "Walked."

The trainman was surprised, "Son, that's over twenty-five miles."

Colt joked, "I know, and I had to stay off the highway because people are looking for us."

The stationmaster returned to the original subject, "So, what favor can I do for Special Forces?"

The team's primary mission—to "blow up" the double railroad bridge at Devil's Slide—was a tough one, Colt decided after making a personal reconnaissance. The span was out in the open, with no ditches or gullies for his men to crawl along at night and no other means of concealment. The only solution was to take out the guards from a moving train.

Colt told the stationmaster: "In about a week a group of us want to ride one of your freight trains up to the double bridge at Devils Slide. When we get there, we'll have to jump off the train onto the bridge to take out the guards. We'll also be throwing off about six hundred pounds of sandbags, to simulate our explosives."

The stationmaster thought for a minute. "I think I can help you, but you've got to understand something. Trains are dangerous. We will only be able to slow the train down to 15 mph there. When that train slows down, your men have got to jump way out. If they land near the wheels, they could get killed or have their legs or arms cut off."

Colt countered, "If there's an accident, the army will accept full responsibility."

"That may be, son, but it's still our railroad." The stationmaster continued, "Get your men down here the night before and you can load your men and sandbags on a boxcar.

Colt said, "That'll be great, sir."

The two men sealed the deal with a handshake. The stationmaster then called to his secretary. "This young man walked here all the way from Como Park. I'm leaving to drive him back out there. I don't think he should have to walk another twenty-five miles today."

When Colt told the men that the stationmaster had agreed to let them board a boxcar, they were ecstatic. He quickly cooled their enthusiasm, however, by reminding them that they still had to find transportation from Como Park to Ogden without being seen, and they had to plan how to "kill" the guards. He had fifteen men on his team, and they had trained about twenty-five "simulated guerrillas," enlisted men from the Utah National Guard, as part of this exercise.

WHILE HIS TEAM LOCATED TRUCKS, WAGONS, AND other conveyances, Colt went out alone to arrange some extra "insurance"— one of his trademarks. He hiked over to Morgan High School and made a proposal to the principal after telling him who he was and what he and his team were doing. The lieutenant asked the principal if he thought that some parents would let a couple of carloads of their teenage daughters drive under the bridge at a certain time and stall their cars as a diversion. The principal thought it was an intriguing idea and agreed to ask around.

Colt went back the next day, and the principal announced that some parents had agreed to his proposal. The girls were waiting in his office for a briefing. Colt showed them on a map where to go and told them what to do. He sent one of his youngest and best-looking NCOs to go with them and to make sure that they found exactly the right place and arrived at the designated time. The girls' role was to divert the guards' attention and lure them off the bridge.

A few days later Colt's team arrived in the Ogden train yard in relays of two old cars, a van, and a station wagon.[3] The Utah State Highway Patrol, state police reserves, the county sheriff deputies (some mounted), and a Special Forces unit from Fort Bragg were looking for Colt's team as well as eight other teams operating in the area at that time. In transit, the men had to duck down so that the people searching for them would not detect and try to capture them. They filled bags with more than six hundred pounds of sand and gravel from the train yard and loaded them onto a boxcar—real explosives in that quantity, according to Colt, would have been enough to put the bridge out of commission for about thirty days. Colt briefed his "killers" on how to tap "killed" soldiers on the shoulder.

The mission went exactly as planned. The high school girls distracted the guards. The designated killers jumped off the train and tapped the guards before any of them knew what was happening, while the rest of the men dumped the sandbags off the train. The hardest part was to get past patrolling aggressors and back into the hills after they "blew" the bridge. But the team succeeded and received a perfect A+ rating from the army for accomplishing the mission without being caught.

Colt's commander later asked him what he would have done if one of his men had been run over by the train. Jokingly, the lieutenant responded that they would have completed the mission and then gone back to pick up the pieces. Colt's initiative and high marks on his training missions were recognized in the normal army fashion—eventually.

On June 17, 1957, Colt left this team and was transferred to Little Creek, Virginia, for underwater demolition training (UDT) with the navy. This included approximately forty-two days of top-secret instruction at the U.S. Naval School in Key West, Florida.[4]

This extremely strenuous conditioning program included all aspects of underwater demolitions, swimming, diving, conditioning, small-boat operations, and more. Toward the end of the initial conditioning portion of the course, Colt and his men had to swim two miles out to sea and back through ten-foot waves during a bad storm with lightning striking all around them.[5] They returned safely on that day, but not every swimming exercise went smoothly.

Two A-teams operated from a submarine during a nighttime sabotage-training exercise along the North Carolina coast. First Lt. William J. Eisenbraun led one of these groups. The teams had the mission to swim to an abandoned pier, destroy it with high explosives, and get away without being seen. During their swim to the target, Eisenbraun and his team were joined by a school of playful porpoises that soon became dangerous. The animals kept steering the men off course and getting tangled in their equipment. The team leader decided to abort the mission and directed his team toward the beach.

At that time, many people had never seen SCUBA equipment, especially in its quite primitive and formidable state during 1957. The men came onto the beach, out of the dark, where two elderly women were night fishing. When they saw the frogmen emerge from the sea in their rubber suits, big fins, facemasks, tanks, and double-hose regulators, the women tossed their fishing poles in the air, screamed, and fled toward town.

Colt, who was on shore to monitor the exercise, received a message by radio that the mission had been aborted. He was driving in his jeep toward the landing site when he heard police sirens. The men must be in trouble, he thought—Lieutenant Eisenbraun had a knack for that. When he arrived on the scene, state troopers had the frogmen surrounded, one of them telling Eisenbraun that he and his men should not be out scaring the locals. Colt intervened in the discussion and apologized to the women for everyone. He

Special Forces training in silent kills for Gene Hunt (right) and another trainee in North Carolina. They would later use poison-tipped arrows.

Colt doing a "free ascent," rising from depth on one breath, during underwater demolition training.

Training in high-speed pickups at Key West. Colt and his team volunteered to learn this in one day from U.S. Navy instructors.

then radioed the navy to advise them, "No pick-up. Mission aborted." Back at training headquarters, all of the men had a good laugh.

SPECIAL FORCES TEAMS NORMALLY WERE NOT ENGAGED directly in sabotage. Rather, they taught such tactics to the natives of countries in which they operated. But to be able to instruct others, they had to learn how to perform sabotage themselves.

During this time, around September, 1957, in Wilmington's harbor, the closest seaport to Fort Bragg, Colt and some of his team taught other Special Forces what they had learned at UDT school, including how to plant mines on the bottom of ship hulls and how to remove them.

A life-or-death decision for any diving mission is choosing the right diving partner. Before leaving for Wilmington, Colt received word that a new instructor was being assigned to his team. M.Sgt. Gene Hunt had broken his leg on a parachute jump. After a long hospitalization, he had gained a lot of weight and was still overweight when he returned to active duty. The army assigned him to Colt's team because, before joining Special Forces, Hunt had been an army hardhat diver doing underwater welding.

Their Special Forces team was like a family, and Colt consulted with his men on any changes in the unit's composition. Some of the instructors had met Hunt and thought that he was too fat to be in their elite underwater-instructors group. They did not think that he would be able to run for five miles and swim for five miles every day, as they had been doing. Colt said that he would think about their objections, which he did for a full day.

The next evening he gathered his instructors together and told them that he had decided to take Hunt. It was not the sergeant's fault that he had broken his leg on a jump. The men were to accept the sergeant and help him get back into shape. Colt said that he did not want to hear anymore about it. He knew that his men would abide by his decision, and they did. The team allowed Hunt to get back into shape gradually.

Meanwhile, Colt had located a moored U.S. Coast Guard cutter in the Wilmington harbor that was perfect for their training needs and had obtained the commander's permission to use his ship. Colt insisted on checking out the vessel himself before letting any of his students dive under it. He invited Sergeant Hunt to make the reconnaissance swim with him. While he and the sergeant were out, Colt told the other instructors to have the students don their wet suits, get the dummy mines ready to plant, and be ready to dive as soon as he and Hunt returned.

The two then left the dock. Tied together with a buddy line, a safety rule learned in the navy school, they followed the curve of the cutter's hull down toward the keel. To their surprise, the bottom leveled off and was flat. Since the harbor water was murky, it was so dark under the ship that Colt and Hunt could not see the luminous dials on their compasses or watches.[6]

The hull felt clean and smooth. The tide turned slack, and they suddenly ran smack into a radar dome hanging beneath the vessel. About the size of a small bedroom, the dome was round, smooth, and covered with rubberized plastic. They felt relieved to have a reference point and followed it around. They tried to swim to the other side but ran into the dome again. Within a few minutes of swimming away a second time, the two came right back to the dome. They were swimming in circles. With no visible reference point and each having one leg naturally stronger than the other, no matter what they did, the men kept swimming in circles.

After almost an hour had passed, Colt and Hunt realized that they were not finding their way out. Their first instinct was just to lie still and let the current take them out, but the water was still. Colt was at a loss as to what to do, and he knew their air was about gone. Hunt had a double-tank setup, but Colt, being smaller in size, wore only a single tank. He then felt Hunt take his hand in the dark. Wondering what the sergeant wanted with his hand, he went along with him. He placed Colt's hand on the ship's hull and ran it along a welding seam. They began to follow the seam. First, the seam went straight, then it went off at a right angle. Fortunately, it then went straight again. This jagged line pointed their way to the surface. As soon as the idea sunk in, Colt followed the seam so fast that he was dragging Hunt behind him. When they broke the surface, Hunt took out his mouthpiece and asked Colt, "Didn't scare ya, did it, sir?"

Half-kidding, Colt said: "Like hell it didn't. I gotta go change my shorts!"

When they were back on shore, Colt told the instructors, for this training exercise, not to let any students down without a hogging line—a line that runs under the ship and is tied-off to the railings on each side. As each two-man team carried its dummy mines down, they hooked on to the hogging line, following it down and back.

Colt thought how fortunate it was that he had decided to accept Sergeant Hunt on his team. It took an underwater welder to think of following a welding seam. Without Hunt as his partner that day, the lieutenant would have died. He thought through this experience for many years but could never devise any other way to have escaped from that dive. Colt made this lesson part of his training program.

Colt personally instructed eight A-teams for underwater-demolition missions while at Wilmington. Swimming almost every day put him in top condition.

IN APRIL AND MAY, 1957, COLT RECEIVED ORDERS TO serve as defense counsel in the courts-martial of different NCOs, an assignment that he did not want. He did not have the education in law to serve as anyone's lawyer, having only taken an army course on the Uniform Code of Military Justice. But he could not be excused from the assignment. Under the code, military personnel can choose any officer to defend them in court-martial proceedings. Usually a defendant requests a lawyer from the Judge Advocate General's Office or chooses a officer from a roster of those with

Colt, with M.Sgt. Skip Langston and Sergeant Rudolph, rehearse demonstrating closed-circuit rebreather during Armed Forces Day at Fort Myer, Virginia.

defense experience, either of whom is provided without charge by the army. Military personnel can also hire civilian lawyers at their own expense. The men who chose Colt as their defense counsel bypassed all of these options.

To everyone's surprise, including the defendant's, Colt won his couple of cases. The news spread. Before he knew what was happening, the word was out: "If you are in trouble, ask for Captain Terry."[7]

After another high-profile win in April, 1958, the demand became too much for him to handle. Even NCOs from other branches of the services were seeking him out. Colt asked for and was given relief from further assignments so that he could concentrate on training his men.

AT THIS POINT IN HIS CAREER, COLT WAS AT THE PEAK of his skills and was the kind of soldier the army likes to showcase. Often, when one reaches a pinnacle, something happens that brings the individual back to level ground.

For the celebration of Armed Forces Day on May 15, 1958, two Special Forces A-teams were assigned to parachute jump as part of the air show in Washington, D.C., in front of huge crowds.[8] Between training and teaching assignments, Colt was assigned to participate in the demonstrations. He and one of his team sergeants jumped out of a C-130 at twelve hundred feet, planning to make a spectacular landing in front of the hundreds of thousands of spectators. With favorable wind conditions at the drop zone, they had decided that, after leaving the plane and checking their chutes, they would get out of their harnesses and hang by their leg straps, a dangerous but showy display. As they landed on the runway, they could just let go of the leg straps, releasing their chutes to the wind and take their bows with no chance of being dragged.[9]

On this day, as soon as Colt was out of his harness and before he landed, a wind gust blew him sideways. He could hear a marine sergeant yelling "Jump! Jump!" But Colt knew that to release his chute at eighty to one hundred feet in the air would result in at least two broken legs. He could see that he was being blown into a display of navy aircraft arresting gear—the machinery that brings an aircraft to a quick-stop landing on an aircraft carrier. Colt did not think that he would get hurt if he hit the machinery, but he was wrong, slamming backward into two carbon dioxide bottles. The valve on one bottle hit him in the lower back, and the other bottle broke his leg. He was knocked unconscious for at least a few seconds. When he came to, an air force surgeon was standing over him, holding up Colt's middle by grasping his belt and telling him to not move. He told the lieutenant that if he did not move, they could save him.

They gently put him on a stretcher and into an ambulance. Within a matter of three to five minutes, Colt was in the air force hospital adjacent to the airfield. He would not have received faster and better medical assistance anywhere else in the world.

One of his vertebrae was broken as well as his leg; fortunately, his spinal cord was not severed. His hospital stay was only six weeks because knowledgeable doctors were available to treat his injury immediately. Colt was out of action for about another six weeks after his release. It would be a year before he was back to jumping. As soon as he was able, he shipped back to Fort Bragg.[10]

On August 1, 1958, Colt was assigned to the U.S. Army Special Warfare School for the purpose of presenting instructional support to the Personnel Testing Research Project.[11] On August 26 Colt was promoted to captain.[12] One NCO told Colt that his men had been worried that he was going to stay a first lieutenant for the rest of his life. As often happens in the army, along with a promotion came a new assignment.

THE FOLLOWING YEAR, IN MAY, 1959, COLT RETURNED to Washington for Armed Forces Day. Arriving late the night before, he checked into the BOQ (bachelor officers' quarters) at Fort Myer and asked where he might get a bite to eat. After receiving directions to the local snack bar, he changed into civilian clothes and went there for a hamburger. An extremely attractive blond came over to his table, sat down, and asked, "Are you here for Armed Forces Days?" Colt introduced himself, and she responded, "I'm Heidi."

Heidi was a young WAC sergeant stationed at Fort Myer. After they talked for a while, she asked him, "Have you ever seen the Tomb of the Unknown Soldier?"

Colt answered, "No, I'm ashamed to say."

Heidi asked, "Would you like to go see it now?"

A bit confused, Colt responded: "Sure, but it's late. How could we see it now?"

"I know a way, down through the graveyard," she said. "I'll show ya."

They drove to Arlington National Cemetery and left Colt's car in a parking lot. (The cemetery is inside Fort Myer and therefore had no entry gates or guards.) It was after midnight. They walked along a path through the cemetery. Even before they reached the tomb, Colt could hear the "click, click, click" of the guard's heels.[13]

When they were within earshot, Heidi whistled, and the guard whistled back; this signaled that no officers were around and that it was clear to approach. They waited for the guard to return to their side of the tomb. He knew Heidi, and it was obvious to Colt that he liked her. When she introduced them, the guard brought his rifle up and saluted, even though Colt was in civilian clothes. He returned the salute.

The guard asked Colt, "Sir, have you ever walked the post of the Tomb of the Unknown Soldier?"

Colt responded, "No, I never was fortunate enough. I wasn't tall enough to even be in your detachment." All of the guards must be at least six feet tall.

The guard offered, "Well, h w'd you like to walk this post one time tonight."

Colt answered, "You bet your sweet ass!"

He gave Colt his rifle and instructed: "Here's what you do. First, take this to Right Shoulder Arms. Then take twenty-two steps across. It's got to take you thirty seconds each way; count 1001, 1002, and so forth. Do an about face, and march back."

When Colt—in civilian clothes and borrowing the guard's rifle—walked the post that night, it was one of his proudest moments as a professional soldier. He felt that he had received a tremendous honor. Of course, he should have realized that he was showing disrespect to the detachment that had the responsibility to guard the tomb. In addition, all three of them could have been court-martialed and dishonorably discharged for violating regulations, if they had been caught. But Colt was focused more on having the opportunity to honor those with whom he had served and who had been with him when they were killed in action. He was appreciative of what Heidi and the guard had done for him.[14]

Colt continued to date Heidi while he was in Washington. When his Armed Forces Day duties were done, he returned to his training responsibilities.

ON MAY 20 HE ATTENDED THE U.S. ARMY INTELLIGENCE School at Fort Holabird, Maryland, for a special-intelligence course requiring top-secret clearance.[15] The next winter, 1959–60, his instruction shifted to cold-weather training. His supposedly quiet life of being stateside continued to be fraught with danger as a Special Forces veteran instructor.

Colt and his team bailed out at twelve hundred feet over their landing zone, high in the Rocky Mountains in Wyoming near the Utah border. They wore the white winter-combat uniforms of cold-weather fighters. Their mission was to practice survival techniques and to conduct simulated raids and sabotage against enemy communications under adverse weather conditions. Blizzard conditions in the Rockies had held up their exercise for ten days. Weather reports finally had forecast a good snow base, and the men expected easy skiing to their target destination in Utah. The troopers pushed their rucksacks out of the plane in a single bundle, followed by their skis in bundles, before they jumped. It was a beautiful, clear moonlit night over the Rockies, with no wind and unlimited visibility.

Because the weather had been so cold, the snow had piled up as light powder and stayed that way. As they landed, the men sank into the deep snow, so deep, in fact, that it was well over their heads, possibly by as much as eight feet, when they stopped sinking.[16] As they tried to climb out, more snow fell down on them. Only Sgt. 1/C Daniel Holloway could get out by himself. If Colt had not told Holloway to strap a pair of snowshoes to his leg, they would still be buried there today. When he landed, Colt's parachute was lying on top of the snow, and he tried to pull himself up using its lines. But his efforts just pulled the parachute and more snow in on top of him. He then yelled to Holloway to get his snowshoes on, climb out of his hole, get the skis, and use them to help the others. None of the team could get out until Holloway did. The sergeant managed to climb out, retrieved the skis, and used them to free Colt. Then, together, they helped two more men out; those two helped more out and so on until they were all free and up on their skis.

Pulling everyone out of the snow was extremely taxing on all of the men. They laughed about it later, but it was a serious matter at the time. No one had told Colt to bring the snowshoes; he just thought it was a good idea to have a pair with them. Also, if they had bundled them with the skis instead of strapping them to Holloway's leg, the snowshoes would have been completely out of their reach.

After the men recovered their breath and their equipment, they skied downhill to a sheep ranch. They were now in Utah. As night faded into dawn, they knocked on the door of the first ranch house they found. Colt introduced himself and the team to the owner and asked him if they could use his barn to rest. The rancher instead invited them into his house. He and his family were nice people. When Colt told them where he and the team had landed, the rancher did not believe him. He argued that if they had jumped into the Wyoming mountain area that they claimed, they would still be there. Colt could not convince him otherwise. His host explained that a bomber had crashed there during World War II, and it still had not been found.

The team spent one day at the ranch, rested up, organized their gear, and disposed of the heavier items; they found that they could not carry an eighty-pound pack full of equipment and make good time. They gave most of their C-rations to the rancher's family. When they left, the rancher, still in disbelief, told them that he believed them to be honest people, but they must be mistaken about where they had landed.

Colt's first radio message from their operations base instructed him of the time, location, and password with which to contact a local agent who would guide them to a safe area. The team skied down the mountain to meet up with the agent, a local Utah resident. After pushing hard to arrive at the contact point at the designated time, the agent never showed. Special Forces are trained to wait only a few minutes and then leave quickly if no contact is made to await further instructions at their next radio contact.

Being a Special Forces officer demands good judgment, which Colt demonstrated in his decision to bring snowshoes. Another officer conceived what he thought was a good plan, but he used bad judgment in deciding to put up his team at a motel behind a truck stop. If his men had remained in their rooms, they might not have been discovered, but they decided to patronize the restaurant. The group commander of the exercise, Col. Noble L. "Rusty" Riggs, figured that someone would be dumb enough to try that trick, so he checked out the truck stop. When he found them, he elevated the team's XO to CO on the spot, instructed him to move his men into the mountains, and transferred the CO, a West Point graduate who should have known better, back to the regular army.

Colt said later that he and his team might have tried a creative stunt like that too if there had been a truck stop in their guerrilla-warfare operational area. He and his team received high marks on the exercise. Colt continued to alternate between being the trainer and being the trainee.

AS A LEADER OF SPECIAL FORCES TEAMS, COLT CONTINUED to learn how to tackle impossible missions under the harshest conditions, to stay out of trouble, and to get the job done.

6 Okinawa

AFTER SOME TIME IN GEORGIA AND A
short leave, in February, 1960, Colt was assigned to the 1st Special Forces
Group (Airborne) in Okinawa.[1] When he reported for duty, the commander,
Col. Francis B. "Frank" Mills, assigned him to command Detachment A-33,
known as one of the toughest and best Special Forces teams in the group. He
told Colt that he considered him to be one of the few officers who were tough
enough to handle that team. The men were all bachelors with no ties back
home and were not only tough but also borderline reckless.

Oddly enough, Detachment A-33 was designated a cold-weather-survival
training team, and its members assigned to receive ski instruction—in tropical Okinawa, where there was never any snow and no mountains. Nevertheless, the assignment fit Colt's experience. In addition to having been a ski instructor in West Germany and a cold-weather-survival instructor, he had
taken regular skiing trips to Utah while he had been stationed at Fort Bragg.

Yet with no place to ski anywhere near Okinawa, Colt faced a challenge in
carrying out his teaching assignments. During the summer, he accomplished
the initial training by creatively using rice straw spread on a grass-covered
ammunition bunker; this way the men could practice sidestepping and sliding down it. The men were clumsy at first and looked odd in their shorts and
T-shirts, but they learned the rudiments of skiing. During the winter, he flew
them to Japan or Korea. Then, in the middle of his training assignment, Colt
was suddenly redirected into something unexpected.

ONE VERY COLD NIGHT IN 1961, THE TEAM FLEW TO A
drop zone in South Korea just northwest of Seoul. The men played pinochle
during the four-hour flight from Okinawa. When the city lights came into
view, they all got down to business. On this particular night, they were dropping onto a sandy beach along the Han River. The jump was considered a
"Hollywood jump" (that is, safer as compared to those in other drop zones)

because of the sandy beach on which they would land, though a trooper was occasionally blown into the river.

Maj. John Todd, the group S-4 (logistics officer) for the 1st Special Forces Group (Airborne), came along as a "strap hanger," a paratrooper who needed to make a pay jump. To remain qualified for the extra pay given for the dangers of jumping from airplanes, a paratrooper had to make at least one jump every ninety days. They often jumped at least every month. As a strap hanger, he was not normally part of the training mission, but at six feet, two inches tall and weighing 240 pounds, the major was not about to be denied participation. Colt told Major Todd that, as the ranking officer on board, he should be the first one out the left door; the captain planned to be the first one out the right door.

The major responded with a simple "Okay," but that was enough to elicit a few muffled chuckles, at their own risk, from the other men. Todd had a squeaky voice at a pitch higher than most men could even imitate, but he was so big and strong that no one would dare comment about it.

As the aircraft approached the drop zone, the red light came on. Colt went down the line to check his men, make sure their parachutes were on right, and tighten up their straps a bit. Everyone was hooked up with safety pins in place. Paratroopers can be a bit nervous before they jump—they know all the things that can go wrong.

When Colt reached the front of the line, he hollered to Todd, "Major, are you ready?"

Todd snapped back, "Yeah, I'm ready! Why the hell are you questioning me?"

Colt should have known better, but as jumpmaster of the aircraft, it was his responsibility to check everyone who was dropping. Obviously, Todd was no novice. Colt backpedaled, "Sorry, major, just doin' my job."

Todd glared at him as he stood at the open door on the left and Colt stood at the door on the right. Each was watching out of the corner of his eye for the light to turn from red to green. The instant that the light changed color, they were out the door. In rapid succession the rest of the men followed.

Todd got a slight head start. When his chute opened, it popped open right under Colt's butt. The captain was literally sitting on the top of the major's canopy, a dangerous situation for both of them. His own chute, only partially open, was beginning to collapse. The moonlit night was cold, crisp, and beautiful—and so quiet that everyone could hear anything that was said.

The major's squeaky voice vibrated across the air, "Get off my parachute, you son of a bitch!" Colt could hear the other men, all strung out behind them, laughing like hyenas.

At parachute school, a trooper learns not to try to walk off a parachute. It is like deep snow—he will just sink lower and lower. He is told to roll off and fall. As he rolls off, his own parachute is supposed to open up. Despite the danger to himself, Colt was worried about what he was doing to the major's chute. He rolled off and went sailing past Todd. Colt noticed that the major's chute had collapsed a bit and, as he went by, heard Todd yelling. "I hope you bust your ass!"

The captain fell about one hundred feet before his chute opened into a big beautiful mushroom. At that moment he released his rucksack and equipment. (A paratrooper carries his rucksack and other gear on a line and releases them to drop and hang about fifteen feet below him so that they will hit the ground before he does.) Colt landed softly. After gathering his chute and gear, he carried the chute to a waiting truck. As he approached the vehicle, he heard Major Todd talking loudly to some of the men and wanting to know who had landed on his chute. Colt turned in his chute to the parachute rigger and crossed his name off the list. Then he walked over to the major.

"What d'ya want, ya little fucker?" Todd yelled at him in his squeaky voice.

Despite Todd's way of addressing him, Colt believed that the major liked him. He said, "I don't know what happened, sir, but the minute my chute opened I found myself sitting on top of your canopy. I rolled off as quickly as I could. I was lucky my chute opened at all."

The man had arms as big as Colt's thighs. He threw them out and gave Colt a big bear hug and laughed heartily. "If it had been anyone else, I would have kicked his ass!" Todd said. "If I live to be a hundred, I'll never forget this jump." As training jumps go, this one was routine compared to some others.

The toughest jumps were the high altitude, low opening (HALO) jumps, in which the troopers jump from altitudes so high (25,000–34,000 feet) that they have to wear oxygen masks and a portable oxygen bottle (six inches by two inches, sewn into the harness) but open their chutes only a few thousand (2,000–3,500) feet above the ground. HALO jumps are used for clandestine infiltration operations and are very dangerous.[2] If a trooper stares too long at something on the ground, he can become hypnotized and be killed by failing to deploy his parachute. Colt really cared about his men and went to great extremes to make sure that they received thorough training in all forms of jumping.

AS COLT RAN HIS MEN THROUGH A WIDE VARIETY OF training exercises, he was preparing them for war. None of them could know that the next war would be unlike any that Americans had ever fought before. It would not have clear battle lines; it would not have a clear mission or a clear exit strategy; the enemy would be hard to distinguish from civilians; and their own country's resolve would be lacking. Despite the difficulties to be faced, the men were gaining important skills in ingenuity, camaraderie, and leadership, all of which would stand them in good stead when the time came. The leadership skills Colt had started learning back on the island of Nan-do came together on a training mission run out of Okinawa in 1962.

His team had not looked forward to leaving the tropical atmosphere of Okinawa to jump into the snowy Korean mountains, but this last mission was very important. It would test each man and determine his proficiency in his designated military occupational specialty. The exercise was going to be a hard six weeks of hiking and living in the snow. For these reasons and more, Colt had not looked forward to this mission either. The men jumped with heavy loads—fifty-five-pound rucksacks. Colt's pack weighed about eighty pounds because he carried extra items.

The captain had secretly arranged a hideout site before they left, but he purposely did not tell his men. After they parachuted into the drop zone and organized their gear, they faced a march of twenty miles into the mountains. They also joined up with a unit of Korean Special Forces, serving as the guerrillas who would be trained. All the way up the mountain trail, Colt struggled with his heavy pack. He was the only officer on the team, but his NCOs had been in the army a long time. NCOs tend to take a liking to some officers and a strong disliking to others. Fortunately, Colt's NCOs liked him and kidded him about his struggle with the heavy pack.

"Goddamn, sir. We thought you were smarter than to bring so much stuff," Sgt. 1/C Bert Smith said.

"Whaddya got in that rucksack, sir, bricks?" another asked.

The captain did not say anything. He just bent over a little more and shifted the load higher on his back.

Near the top of the mountain, Colt found his Korean contact. He had arranged to rent a house where the team would hide. Located at the peak in a valley so small that it was almost unnoticed on land maps, the place was beautiful—terraces, little streams running downhill through hundreds of small rice fields, and no access by road, only trails and, luckily, no snow. The house even had floors that were heated in a crude but effective way by a wood fur-nace underneath. It was in a perfect location as a base for the team's planned operations during the next six weeks.

When the men entered the house, which had no furniture, they removed their boots, left them by the door, and settled down on warm four-by-six-foot straw mats. Everyone started talking about the jump.

Sgt. 1/C Bert Millhouse Smith, the team's intelligence specialist, asked Colt, "How'd ya find this place?"

Colt needled him. "A good intelligence man gets out and beats the bushes to learn what's going on."

Bert, feeling the effects of their long uphill hike, wished aloud, "What we really need is a small shot to help us sleep."

Colt reached in his rucksack, pulled out a bottle of Wild Turkey, and said, "Funny you should mention it." Colt poured himself a capful. It was against regulations to have booze on a mission, but he had felt it justified for maintaining morale.

Another man asked him if he was going to share it with his team. Colt had not touched the shot yet. He then asked mischievously for the men to remind him who was making fun of him coming up the trail. In chorus, they responded that it was none of them; they never said a word. He poured every-one a drink.

Afterward, they set up a security detail—one man was to be awake at all times—and the rest of them crawled into their sleeping bags. Colt took the first watch.

As the days went by, the hideout became crucial. It had to be kept se-cret at all costs. One of the indigenous asked Colt if he would help a child in a nearby village who had been sick for several weeks. The captain agreed to do so. While he and one of his guerilla trainees were giving first aid to the young Korean, a security force that had been sweeping through all the surrounding villages captured them. They had been turned in for a reward.

Colt feigned a broken ankle and told his captors that his men had brought him to the village because of his injury. He tricked them into carrying him to the jail. When they simply locked him and his trainee in the cell, Colt knew that the situation was not like it was in real war. If the North Koreans or the Chinese had captured them, they would have been stripped naked. He would not have resisted. It was part of the game.

When the umpires arrived, Colt took them aside and asked, "If we make an escape attempt, will you back us up?"

They laughed, knowing Colt for a long time. "You're not gettin' out of this captain. You're here and you're sittin' out the rest of the maneuvers."

Colt pressed them. "If we make a successful play here, are you going to back us up?"

They discussed his question, then agreed, "Yeah, we'll back you up." They saw no way that he could succeed.

By not searching him, Colt's captors did not find his pistol, a German Luger that he kept in place by a string around his waist and hung below his waistline inside his pants. He waited for the senior Korean official, a lieutenant colonel named "Kim," to come in and sit down. As one of Kim's men started to interrogate the prisoners, Colt edged as close to the colonel as he could without raising suspicion. Then he spun around, grabbed Kim by the throat, put his own face up to the colonel's, jerked the Luger out of his pants, and stuck it right in the colonel's ear. Colt demanded a jeep, an escort out of the jail, and directions for the way out of the city.

The umpires never expected this kind of scenario. The opposing forces objected, claimed that he could not do that, and demanded to know where he got the gun. He told them how they had failed to search him and warned them, for emphasis, that "the son of a bitch" was loaded too. The umpires felt that it was quite irregular, but they decided to stick with their agreement and brought the jeep.

As they walked out the door, Colt's trainee just kept shaking his head and repeating, "Sir, you're beautiful."

The umpires drove Colt and his fellow trooper far out into the countryside and dropped them off. They waited for the umpires to drive off before heading up into the mountains through the snow. The village was far from their hideout, and the opposition never discovered its location. Colt's team accomplished all of its missions successfully.

When the men returned to Okinawa, their commander gave the men an A rating for outstanding performance. While Colt continued to train men on Okinawa, American involvement in Vietnam was escalating, and the need for his trainees was growing.

AS BACKGROUND: THE VIETNAM WAR WAS FOUGHT from 1961 through 1975. It started in 1961 as a countermeasure against communism in Southeast Asia when Pres. John F. Kennedy sent in 900 Special Operations forces to train and support South Vietnam's army and to

Colt standing on one ski, holding a cup of coffee, and talking to Colonel Browne about a problem with skis without metal edges during ski training at Hokkaido, Japan (temporary duty from Okinawa).

Class ready for initial jump at the 1st Special Forces Group parachute school when Colt (not pictured) was commandant at Okinawa.

counteract guerilla activities. In 1963 Kennedy sent in another 5,000 U.S. troops and authorized the first air attack. Then in March, 1965, Lyndon B. Johnson, Kennedy's successor, sent in 3,500 U.S. Marines. By that time, over 100 U.S. soldiers had already been killed in Vietnam.

By the end of 1965, the number of U.S. troops there had reached 125,000; air raids were steady; and the war raged. Vietnam was an agricultural country and had few factories and little infrastructure to bomb. The jungle was thick, making mechanized military ground equipment ineffective. As a result, the warfare was unconventional—guerilla warfare.

Between 1967 and 1969, demonstrations about the war's futility peaked in the United States, and Pres. Richard Nixon began to slowly withdraw forces. In 1973 a ceasefire was declared, and in April, 1975, the last Americans left Vietnam. Well over 1,000,000 military and civilians were killed during this war; the United States lost 58,000. Of course, the experiences of the men fighting on the ground tell a story different from most of the history books.[3]

IN 1961, BEFORE THE UNITED STATES WAS OFFICIALLY involved in the war in Vietnam, Maj. John S. "Jack" Warren and Capt. Harold J. Rose took two Special Forces teams into the country under the CIA's direction. The Special Forces units were not "advisors," nor were they working with the South Vietnamese Army, as described in the press. They were there to train indigenous to fight as guerrillas. Working for the CIA differed from working for the army. Despite the agency's reputation for spending lots of cash money, supplies were catch-as-catch-can; mail was irregular; the rules were different.

The Special Forces teams were dispatched to the Da Nang area, later called the I Corps area. They worked with Montagnards and Nungs (a Vietnamese minority of ethnic Chinese ancestry).[4]

As part of their training, in 1962 four Special Forces NCOs took a team of these indigenous on a reconnaissance mission in search of Viet Cong (VC) as part of their counterguerrilla "on-the-job" training. Two of the men were S.Sgt. Wayne E. Marchand and Sgt. James Gabriel Jr.[5] Colt recalls that the other two men were Sgt. Francis Quinn and Sgt. George Groom. He heard at the time that the patrol had stopped in a village to make radio contact with headquarters when the VC ambushed it. Gabriel, the radioman, was shot in the back as he was transmitting a message that they were under attack. His wound was not immediately fatal. Marchand, the weapons man, while attempting to help Gabriel, was also wounded. A turncoat among the indigenous trainees had shot both men. After capturing the other two NCOs, the VC killed Gabriel and Marchand because they could not travel. The two captured men were released a month later at a May Day propaganda event.

Colt knew Marchand well. He had been in Colt's Detachment A-33 when they were based on Okinawa. Everyone in Special Forces, including Colt, took the loss of these men hard and realized that it was not an exercise now but war. They also rallied around the men's families.

When the first two Special Forces teams returned to Okinawa, they were replaced with two other teams. CIA officials soon learned how efficient these units were and requested Special Forces to send ten more teams into Vietnam.

WHEN THE SPECIAL FORCES TEAMS FIRST STARTED going into Vietnam, Colt was still on Okinawa, training South Vietnamese, Thai, Lao, and Malaysian officers. For four to six weeks, he trained each group in land mines, personnel mines, and antitank mines. He also taught ambush techniques, using both classroom and field-training methods.

During field training, he had his students take up ambush positions and observe a man, dressed in black pajamas and rubber sandals and carrying an AK-47, walk out of the woods and down to the water's edge as if he were going to cross the stream. As previously instructed by Colt, the man stopped, looked around, hesitated, and then walked back into the woods. He did not return. The man left when he did because he could smell the trainees. This lesson illustrated that a soldier who has been living like an animal in the jungle for a time easily notices human scents.

Colt instructed the men not to use perfumed soap, cologne, shaving lotions, tobacco, or anything else that a heightened sense of smell could pick up in the jungle. The man then came out of the jungle a second time. Colt walked him through the ambush positions until the man picked out the trainee whose scent he had noticed.

Movement was another key to ambushes. Once established, no one can move until the trap is sprung or called off. Colt excelled at teaching ambushes, and he was always ready to put his skills to use.

Special Forces teams steadily left the 1st Special Forces Group (Airborne) on Okinawa for six-month Vietnam tours under the direction of the CIA before returning to the island.[6] Soon, teams were turning right around and going back again. Colt became uncomfortable about not being part of the action, about feeling like a shirker. The returning men even began to ask him why he had not been to Vietnam. He worried that his men might begin to think that he was afraid to go. At that time he was married. The couple had no children, and his wife worked. Colt felt that he could go.

The captain told the group's XO that he wanted to volunteer to go to Vietnam with his team. He explained the embarrassment that he felt by remaining on Okinawa. Colt soon had his orders to go to Vietnam, but not with his team. Again, he had volunteered to put himself into harm's way.

In September, 1962, Colt was assigned as XO of a B-team in Da Nang, but his tenure was intended to be only a holding position and brief. As second in command, an XO is a kind of "foreman" who does whatever the "Old Man," the CO, wants him to do. Colt did not stay with this B-team long, only about two weeks. The leader of the A-team, A-334, Capt. Terry D. Cordell, was killed when the VC shot down his light aircraft (L-28) while he was marking targets for an air force fighter. The CIA asked the NCOs at A-334 if they knew of someone to replace Cordell, and they said they knew Colt was at Da Nang and that he was their choice. The CIA sent a message to the 1st Special Forces Group Command in Okinawa requesting Colt's assignment. Within a few days, he was transferred to Buon Enao as team leader of Detachment A-334. This unit was the command-and-control team for five other Special Forces A-teams in the High Plateau. Buon Enao was a small Montagnard village near Ban Me Thuot that the CIA turned into a paramilitary training camp. It eventually grew to be a large training center with its own hospital. Colt and his men would see a lot of action in the surrounding areas.

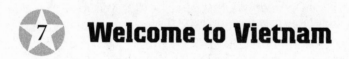
Welcome to Vietnam

COLT WALKED INTO THE MILITARY ADVISORY
Command Vietnam (MACV) Headquarters in Ban Me Thuot in October,
1962.[1] The commander, Colonel "Green," did not care for Special Forces
because they were under the CIA's control rather than under his command.[2]

Colt advised the colonel, "Sir, we've got a wounded Special Forces sergeant, about fifty clicks [kilometers] from here. If we don't get 'im to a hospital quickly, he's gonna die."

Green said, "Well, captain, where is he?"

Colt answered, "Buon Mi Ga."

The commander was surprised. "That can't be. That's VC country."

"Yes, sir," Colt agreed. "That's a VC-controlled area, but it's also where
my men and four hundred of our Montagnard troops live."

That was news to Colonel Green. He thought for a moment and then acquiesced. "We only have one rundown helicopter, one of those banana jobs,
an H-21, but you can use it. They're good on airstrips but not small LZs [land-
ing zones]. See my warrant officer."[3]

Colt raced off to see the warrant officer in charge of the helicopter. To
his surprise and relief, he discovered CWO Alvin "Mississippi" Woods, nicknamed for his home state, who Colt had known in Germany in the 10th Special Forces Group. He told the pilot about the wounded sergeant and showed
him a map of the location, then asked, "Can you fly out there and pick 'im
up?"

Mississippi Woods volunteered. "Yes, sir, if we get an LZ lit up out there."
An illuminated LZ would help him find the camp from the air in the dark and
was necessary for him to land.

Colt asked, "D'ya want me to go along?"

Woods responded: "No, sir. Stay here, get on the radio, and make sure
they're lit up."

After the chopper took off, Colt returned to the headquarters office and
located a five-band voice radio provided by the CIA. He contacted S.Sgt. Tru-

man Foy, a Texan, at the team's camp and instructed him to light up his LZ with potted lights (tin cans filled with fuel soaked sand) set in an L shape. The chopper would come in over the short leg of the L.

That night Mississippi Woods flew what might have been the first helicopter medevac (medical evacuation) of the Vietnamese "conflict." He airlifted the wounded NCO, S.Sgt. Donald L. Jones, from Detachment A-214 under the command of Captain Abernathy, to a Vietnamese hospital in Ban Me Thuot. Colt had not slept for more than twenty hours when he met the helicopter at the hospital. A few minutes later he helped put Jones on the operating table. The sergeant's wounded arm hung only by a few strands of muscle, ligaments, and veins. He watched as a Vietnamese doctor worked on the arm.

As soon as Jones was stable, Woods had him airlifted on a fixed-wing aircraft to Saigon; from there he was flown to Clark Air Force Base in the Philippines. Colt continued his work under the CIA.

WHILE COLT WAS LIVING IN BUON ENAO WITH ONE OF the Montagnard tribes, he worked for the CIA under a case officer known as Jack Bennefield (possibly not his real name).[4] Colt thought that Jack was a good man—for a civilian. Working for the CIA was different from working for the regular army—no mail, no nice mess halls, no chaplain, no nothing. The CIA was unorthodox in many ways. For being so loosely run, it was oddly formal about some things. For example, whenever agency people spent the government's money—and they spent plenty of it—they had to get receipts, tape each one to an $8\frac{1}{2} \times 11$ inch piece of bond paper, and submit the receipts to the accounting department.

Colt was a team leader under Bennefield, who operated from Saigon and only occasionally traveled the three hundred miles north to visit Colt's camp. His trips were usually to issue money, deliver orders, or to make sure that his Special Forces units were carrying out their mission of training the Montagnards and forming them into combat troops. The Montagnards could fight, but they were not organized; Colt and his A-team were training them to be soldiers. And Bennefield let everyone know that the CIA was running the show. He was an "in-charge" case officer.

Colt had two radio operators on his team—Sgt. Harold R. Haney and Sgt. Phillip D. Wilson. All radio contacts with Special Forces headquarters were encrypted messages in Morse code. Each A-team carried secret "DIANA

One-time Pads" of compressed tissues with key codes on each tissue.[5] The pages of each pad were glued together and were separated with a knife when used. One pad was used to encipher, the other to decipher. They were issued to the team leader, who delegated their use to his radio operator. The radio operator kept track of the papers both before and after they were used, then the team leader burned them. No one else was allowed to touch the pads. The team leader was ultimately accountable for these secret documents, and no messages went out without his approval. Nobody, not even the team sergeant, could send a message without authorization. If a security violation occurred, only the team leader would answer to a court-martial.

One night Bennefield went into the radio shack—a real shack, thatched roof, dirt floor, and all—loaded with radios of all types. He told Sergeant Haney that he wanted to send a message. All transmissions were encrypted, so his had to be too. Haney tried to tell Bennefield that he could not send a message without Captain Terry's permission. Bennefield, in his "take charge" way, told Haney to just send it. At the moment the sergeant started to send it, Colt walked in.

In this primitive environment, Colt was reverting to the crude behavior that he had developed on Nan-do. His shack in the steaming hot jungle did not compare with Bennefield's modern headquarters in Saigon. Also, it was Colt's radio room. He verbally blasted both of them and demanded to know what they were doing. Haney stood up, looking embarrassed: he knew he was in trouble, and he knew the captain's temper. Usually Colt got along well with his men and was easy to talk to, but he quickly turned mean if someone crossed him. He viewed this violation of army regulations as a threat to his career, and nothing was more important to him personally. His whole life was centered on, and nothing meant more to him than, being in Special Forces. But his mission was foremost in his mind now, and what Bennefield and Haney were trying to do could endanger it as well.

Haney tried to explain. "We're sending a message to Saigon for Mr. Bennefield."

Colt snapped back, "I didn't see any message!" Bennefield said nothing. Colt continued: "I'll tell you, sergeant. No messages go out over that radio, using that one-time pad, without my signature. It's my neck on the line if something goes wrong and security is breached."

Bennefield then aggravated the situation, saying, "Oh, don't worry about it."

Colt whipped out his 9-mm Browning automatic pistol, grabbed Bennefield by his shirt, and pressed the gun to his temple. He was a trigger pull away from killing him. Colt was not living amid civilization. Life in the jungle was coarse, and his behavior had sunk to that level. This scared Bennefield, and it even scared Colt. He had lost control worse than he had when he beat up that drunken soldier in Germany.

Colt said, "You ever come in this radio shack again, or if you ever talk to my radio operator again, I'll blow your fucking brains out." For emphasis he added, "Have I made myself clear?"

Speaking slowly, Bennefield urged the captain to calm down. Colt lowered his pistol and said that he just wanted to make sure that both Bennefield and Haney understood him. He also told Bennefield that, if he wanted to send a message, he must clear it through him first. Bennefield slowly turned and walked out.

Colt turned to Sergeant Haney. "You should have known better. You know the value of those one-time pads. You know the security procedures."

Haney knew that he had been wrong, and he apologized. Later Colt realized how much he had overreacted and figured that Bennefield would turn him in to the 1st Special Forces Group (Airborne) commander and that the incident would probably go in his record, at a minimum, and could result in discipline as well as possibly go into the CIA record. He could envision some warning in its records on him such as, "Don't hire this hothead. He'll shoot one of our own in a heartbeat." As it turned out, he and Bennefield later ironed out their situation, and to Colt's knowledge the incident was never reported.[6] But Colt's explosive reaction was caused by more than just his anger about the security breach. He had become totally ruthless at this point—the result of being too long in the jungle. For months he had been traveling from village to village, under constant peril of attack from VC; training Montagnards in the use of weapons; and teaching them how to throw hand grenades without hurting themselves, their men, or their families.

COLT'S TEAM HAD BEEN SPLIT IN HALF BY THE CIA, AND his men were heavily burdened with running a supply depot, distributing weapons, and other administrative duties. On one patrol Colt had gone with one NCO and a group of CIDG (Civilian Irregular Defense Group) troops to a small village where they knew a schoolteacher from Saigon had been teaching the local children. Along the way five men from another team joined them and they proceeded together to the village. The teacher had brought his wife and their two small children with him without fear of danger because he did

Colt's house in Buon Enao in the High Plateau. Notice the boy with a toy made from a sardine can.

Transporting Montagnard mercenaries (and friends) in a CIA truck in Buon Enao, with interpreter "Jiminy Cricket" (lower left).

not consider himself part of the war. When Colt arrived, he found the villagers extremely upset. The VC had already been there and had beheaded the teacher, his wife, and their two children, ages three and five. After Colt and his men dug up the bodies, they found that the guerrillas had also castrated one of the Montagnard male babies as a lesson to put the villagers in their place and force them to support the VC.

This savage act infuriated Colt beyond rationality—innocent people massacred for no reason but cold-blooded murder. The villagers knew the direction in which the VC had gone, and one of the men who had joined the American team was known as a superb tracker. The raiders had left only a few hours before Colt and the others arrived. Even though his patrol had been in the jungle for about three days, where they had lived almost like animals, he decided to go after the perpetrators of this brutal act.

It took Colt and his team several days to catch up with what turned out to be a VC propaganda squad. In his determination to overtake these men, he had driven his team to move, without sleep, for three days and nights. They found the seven VC asleep in a hamlet with no security posted. Rather than kill them on the spot, Colt took them alive. It was easy to capture "the bastards," as Colt referred to them; not a shot was fired. His men tied the VCs' elbows behind their backs in the same manner as they had their victims.

He decided to return the prisoners to the teacher's village so the residents could positively identify them; they confirmed that the men were indeed the murderers. Colt held a short meeting with his men (without the CIDG) and explained that they could march the VC back to base camp and turn them in as POWs or they could be executed there. They all agreed that they should be executed immediately so the villagers would witness that justice was done and that the Americans would help them protect themselves against the VC. His men felt that maintaining the villagers' trust and loyalty was essential for their continuing operations in that area.

The next question was how to do it. After some discussion, they agreed that their heads should be cut off with the same weapon used by the VC on the murdered victims, a Montagnard ax used for killing oxen. After consultation with the CIDG battalion commander, they decided which men would carry out the executions. The selected soldiers would then take turns killing the VC, one by one, as the remaining prisoners watched.

The next morning the CIDGs staked the VC to the ground on their backs, with their necks placed on a log. The Montagnard ax had a heavy, wide blade with a small hook on the top end. The hardwood handle was much shorter than that of a normal ax, so the first executioner was very close to the VC when he struck the first blow. Blood splattered all over his face and uniform; a piece of bone struck him in the face, just missing his eye. It took three blows to sever that VC's spine and separate the head from the body. This first executioner warned the others to put on their sunglasses to protect their eyes.

One by one, the killers were executed. The CIDGs hung the severed heads on the village entry as a warning to any other VC who came that way. Colt paid some village men to dig graves and bury the seven bodies. After cleaning up, the team moved out toward its home camp. The villagers no doubt took down the heads as soon as Colt's team left to avoid any retribution. The patrol had a long, quiet march back to their camp. The men all agreed to say nothing about what had been done and to remember the two small children.

As brutal as the retaliation was, Colt felt that this type of justice was needed to show the natives that Special Forces cared about them, were their friends and allies, and would not hesitate to give the VC what they deserved.[7] The captain had become hardened at this point, with all of his training and in his third tour of duty, including Korea. He was mentally tough in every way. He had to be, for he could not let himself become complacent and make a mistake. And the risk of making a mistake was higher because of what the CIA was doing to the A-teams.

In 1962 AND 1963 ONE OF THE CIA'S SHORTSIGHTED decisions, in Colt's opinion, was to split up each of the twelve-man A-teams, both officers and enlisted men, into two teams—probably doing so without telling the 1st Special Forces Group (Airborne) on Okinawa. Of course, the army had two men with certain skills in each team for a reason. The CIA's theory, however, ignored certain facts: a lieutenant cannot always do a captain's job; a backup medic is not as effective as the primary medic; one radio operator cannot stay awake for twenty-four hours a day. Even though team members are cross-trained, a partial team is much weaker than a full one. Col. Robert W. Garrett disagreed with splitting the teams but, for unknown reasons, went along with it. CIA planners must have thought that this was an ideal solution because the teams could then cover twice as much territory. Of course, the men in each half-team were exposed to greater risk. Colt was concerned about the increased danger, but he kept doing his job. As of October, 1962, twenty-four Special Forces detachments were in Vietnam.[8]

The CIA issued funds to Colt from an account they called (for reasons unknown to him) the Parasol Fund. Colt would travel to Saigon and pick up a large cardboard box full of Vietnamese piasters. He would take it back to his camp and use the money to pay mercenaries, buy and repair trucks, buy gas, and pay for other operating costs.

HIS TEAM CONTINUED TO WORK WITH AND DEVELOP A close relationship with the Montagnards. The name "Montagnard" loosely applied to more than a hundred tribes of primitive mountain people, numbering from 600,000 to 1,000,000 at the time and spread all over Indochina. In South Vietnam there were some twenty-nine tribes numbering more than 200,000 people. The Rhade was considered the most influential and strategically located of these tribes in the highlands of Vietnam. Its people were mainly centered around the village of Ban Me Thuot in Darlac Province. The village of Buon Enao had a population of approximately 400 Rhade.[9]

Colt began to learn their language but needed an interpreter's services in many instances. He and his men had learned some Vietnamese when they were on Okinawa, but it was ineffective with the Montagnards, whose village chiefs in the highlands did not like the South Vietnamese and preferred to speak French or their own native language, Rhade. The Montagnards wanted autonomy from the Saigon government.

As a mistreated minority, the Montagnards disliked the North Vietnamese too, but their anger was directed mostly against the South Vietnamese, with whom they came into contact more often. Colt later realized that the North had missed an opportunity to befriend the Montagnards and have them do their fighting for them against the South. Instead, the CIA won their friendship, one of its better achievements in Vietnam.

While the CIA exploited this opportunity, it was the men of Special Forces who cemented the alliance. By treating the Montagnards as equals, sleeping in the same quarters, sitting around the same fires, and eating the same food, Special Forces befriended these indigenous mountain people. They also trained them in modern warfare, provided them with weapons, and became their closest friends, defenders, and confidants.

Special Forces trained thousands of Montagnard tribesmen and armed them with old but working firearms, plenty of ammunition, and hand grenades. The CIA provided Colt and his team with old World War I and World War II weapons, including American M1 carbines, Springfield and Mauser bolt-action rifles, 12-gauge shotguns, 60-mm mortars, Thompson submachine guns, German Schmeisser submachine guns, Swedish K submachine guns, French MAT-49 machine pistols, and British Sten submachine guns. Distributing so many weapons and training the men in their use was a lot of work. Colt traveled across the countryside supervising and assisting his men in this effort.

In one village the chief had allowed Colt and his men to spend the night in a little thatched hut. They had trekked twenty miles that day to reach the settlement, and Colt was exhausted. He built a platform from old ammunition boxes so that he would not have to sleep on the dirt and rolled up his jacket to make a pillow. As he always did, he put his 9-mm Browning automatic pistol under his jacket and kept his hand on it as he slept. He did not put up his mosquito net because he was too tired.

Lying on his right side, he was about ready to fall asleep when he felt something run up and down his leg. He was so tired that he ignored it and started to drift off again. Then, he felt it run up his body and stop on the side of his cheek. He could feel its weight on his face. When he opened his eyes, he saw a large rat sitting there, its tail lying across his nose. He slowly pulled out his gun and, in a flash, swatted at the rat with the barrel as he yelled, "Get off me, you son of a bitch!"

His swat missed the rat. Then he made a mistake. He could see the rat silhouetted in the moonlight as it hopped across the floor toward the door of the hut. He aimed and fired at the rat, "Wham! Wham!" Everyone in the village woke up. Thinking they were under attack, they started shooting into the dark. Gingerly, Colt ran through the tiny hamlet to reach the chief and tell him to order his men to quit firing. It took a good half hour to calm down everyone. He then had to explain to the chief why he had fired his pistol. For months afterward, whenever he saw any of those tribesmen going through the jungle, they hollered at him, "Hey, Commandant, any rats sit on your face lately?"

The chief of another village invited the team to dinner once. Colt's interpreter was a Rhade woman, married to a Vietnamese man, and was called by a name that sounded to Colt like "Hltoin Khaddam." The actual spelling of her name was "Htlôñ Nie Kdam." For convenience, we will refer to her as Ka-Dam.

As they left the dinner, Colt asked Ka-Dam, "What did we eat?"

She replied, "You were eating rats, the only meat these people have."

Colt thought he settled the matter when he told her, "They weren't bad, actually. They tasted like frogs legs."

Ka-Dam, shocked, asked, "You eat frogs legs?"

While Colt was building relationships among the local indigenous, the CIA was getting into trouble with the South Vietnamese government.

IN EARLY 1963 THE SOUTH VIETNAMESE GOVERNMENT became upset with the CIA about the weapons it was distributing to the Montagnards. The CIA operations officer in Vietnam, who reported to the U.S. ambassador in Saigon, had made a previous deal with South Vietnamese president Ngo Dinh Diem that the agency would train and arm the Montagnard tribesmen. President Diem's understanding of the agreement, however, was that Special Forces would issue only single-shot, bolt-action rifles and no automatic weapons. He knew that the Montagnards did not like the South Vietnamese, and he considered them dangerous. When South Vietnam won the war, Diem feared that the tribesmen would rise up against his government.

The Special Forces units did not share Diem's understanding of the agreement. Instead of giving the Montagnards only single-shot rifles, they had armed them to the teeth, including many old but usable automatic weapons. When Diem learned what had been done, Bennefield was summoned to a meeting with the U.S. ambassador, Diem, and other high-ranking officials in Vietnam.

Concerned about a Montagnard revolution, President Diem ordered the CIA and the ambassador to go out again and take back all the automatic weapons. He warned that if they failed to recover the automatic weapons, the South Vietnamese would send in armed troops, seize the weapons by force, and then boot the Americans out of the country.

Bennefield arrived back at Colt's camp with his head hanging low. Colt knew that something was wrong even before Bennefield said anything. "You have to contact all of your teams. Have them get in those trucks we provided and go from village to village and retrieve all the automatic weapons, ammo, and hand grenades."

Colt argued. "There's a war going on around those natives. With the weapons, the VC will leave 'em alone. They need those weapons—to protect their homes and their families—mothers, daughters, sisters, and wives."

Bennefield was not moved. "You have no choice. Get the weapons back by whatever means you must. Buy 'em back or take 'em back by force, if necessary."

Colt warned, "I don't think they'll give 'em up without a fight."

Bennefield would not budge. "Try diplomacy. Go to each village, meet with the chief and offer him money. I want you to personally handle each negotiation." Each tribesman who turned in a weapon would be paid five hundred South Vietnamese piasters. But money was not what they wanted or needed.

Colt had developed a close relationship with many of the Montagnards. For example, while on a combat patrol, his Special Forces team shot a wild boar and shared it with the accompanying Montagnards. The Montagnard battalion commander whacked off the beast's head and threw it in the fire, where it lay all night. As soon as it was daylight, Colt and his men were ready to move out. But they noticed the Montagnard leader standing next to his fire with the well-cooked boar's head in one hand and a large knife in the other.

When Colt approached him to say good morning, the commander whacked off the top of the skull. The brains, bulging out of the head, were well cooked. He invited Colt to share his breakfast. Special Forces trained its men to do whatever was necessary to relate to the indigenous. Talking through his interpreter, however, Colt tried to beg off and said that he was not hungry.

The commander teased him and said something about Colt's not liking hog brains. "Taste it. You'll like it," he insisted.

Colt, like many Special Forces men, always carried a pair of short chopsticks in his shirt pocket should he be invited to a meal. He set down his rifle and told his men to go on without him—he would catch up. Standing around that smoky fire, he shared hog brains right out of the skull with the Montagnard chief. To his surprise, Colt found that wild-hog brains were delicious.

He also carried a small bottle of Tabasco sauce in his shirt pocket. To return the Montagnard's dare, Colt invited him to try a little of it.

"What is it?" the commander asked.

"Taste it. You'll like it," Colt said, repeating the earlier taunt.

He did warn the commander that it was a hot sauce, but to his surprise, he loved it, and the joke was on Colt again.

This kind of close relationship was the only reason why the Montagnards did not kill Colt when he went out to collect the automatic rifles. He knew that retrieving them would be a difficult and dangerous mission.

Colt arrived at the first village in a ¾-ton truck and with a full security force as backup in a 2½-ton truck. He talked with the chief and explained that the Americans needed all of their automatic weapons for another area where the VC were more active. The captain asked him to have all of his people walk to the truck and put their automatic weapons in the back. The Montagnards did not like this order one bit. They were so angry that they refused the money. If they previously had not been treated so well by the Americans and had not grown to like them, they probably would have tried to kill everyone present.

As soon as his men recovered the weapons from that village, Colt ordered them to return to the camp at Buon Enao. He was not going to send them to any more villages. It was too dangerous, and Colt felt that it was not right.

A few weeks later Bennefield visited the camp and asked Colt, "How many weapons did you collect?" Rather than tell him the number, Colt showed him the back of the truck. Bennefield saw immediately how few were there and yelled, "That's nothin'!"

Colt retorted, "Well, we didn't get a very good reception. I'm trying to let things cool down. The word has traveled through the jungle about our first meeting."

At first Bennefield was angry with him, but after he cooled down said, "You've got to get back out there, captain, and get those weapons. President Diem wants those weapons out of their hands or he'll throw us out of the country."

Laughing, Colt said, "If he did, Diem's government wouldn't last two seconds."

He continued to drag his feet, even though Bennefield kept up the pressure. Colt was now totally ruthless and was not afraid of Bennefield or the CIA. More importantly, he was becoming closer to the Montagnards. He felt that it was wrong to take the weapons away from these people because they needed them to defend their homes. He did not care what the agency wanted.

Eventually the CIA's interest in recovering additional weapons faded. Colt and his team continued to train the Montagnards. His men always felt safe when they were with the tribesmen. He came to grow close to these people; as fighters, they were a people to emulate. With them, Colt continued to lead his men on operations deep into enemy-controlled areas until the end of his tour.

Rotation and Ishigaki

WHEN COLT ARRIVED BACK ON OKINAWA from his first tour in Vietnam in March, 1963, he was assigned as commander of the 1st Special Forces (Airborne) Parachute School. The 1st Special Forces (Airborne) had arranged with the U.S. Army to teach parachuting to navy underwater demolition teams (UDTs), marine reconnaissance teams, and army and air force volunteers. Enlisted men and officers from all over the Far East and the U.S. West Coast trained at their school.

Colt's superior officer, Colonel Garrett, reported to Gen. "Small" Paul Caraway, so called because he was quite short. Caraway was a West Point graduate, and both of his parents were U.S. senators. Despite his potentially privileged past, both the enlisted men and the officers thought of him as a good general. He had conducted a number of projects to help the people of Okinawa as goodwill gestures, particularly on the outlying islands.

In April, 1963, General Caraway summoned Colonel Garrett to his office. Colt heard later (from Garrett) that during this meeting, the general had declared that Special Forces were overrated and that he was not impressed just because they jumped out of airplanes. Garrett knew that Caraway had been deriding Special Forces for some time and was surprised when the general suddenly seemed to switch gears. He challenged the colonel to demonstrate that his men were as efficient and as disciplined as he claimed. One of Caraway's "People to People" projects was incomplete, and he wanted help from Garrett's men to finish it before the end of his tour.

Ishigaki was a tiny outlying island 270 miles south of Okinawa, with only a small airport and no regular flights. It needed a channel cut through the coral that blocked the harbor—a channel deep enough to allow large ships to enter and pull up to a pier for docking. The ships would bring needed supplies to the island and would transport its local production of sugar cane, pineapples, and other produce to market. The completion of this project would be a great boon to both the small island's economy and its people's welfare.

The army had hired a Japanese company to build the pier and everything

Aerial view of Ishigaki harbor and channel. A floating pipe with drill head (not visible in this picture) sucked up, chewed up, and spit out the coral debris into the white area, creating new land.

else needed for a seaport. The company's work was behind schedule, however, because of the obstructing reef. Ships simply could not navigate in the shallow water.

Since Garrett commanded the only underwater demolition units in the Far East, Caraway directed him to send his very best team to the island to blast a channel deep and wide enough for a thirty-ton ship to pass from the open ocean through the coral reef and into the harbor. He told the colonel that he would have whatever he needed in equipment, personnel, and explosives. Caraway added that he would be leaving for the States in forty-five days, so Garrett and his men should start work the following Monday and finish the job in thirty days. The colonel could do nothing but agree to the assignment. Colt would be the key.

Garrett left Caraway's office and told his adjutant to have Captain Terry report to him immediately. When Colt received the message, his first thought was that he was in trouble: he knew the general was not keen on Special Forces.

A worried Colt arrived at the colonel's office. Garrett, at six feet, one inch tall, loomed over him. The colonel ordered him to stand at ease while he spelled out the situation. He explained how, "with no disrespect to the general, the son of a bitch had called Special Forces blowhards," and then described the general's orders. Colt could hardly believe his ears as the colonel laid out the mission. Garrett instructed Colt, "Take a complete underwater demolition A-team. Don't just take your team. Handpick the best men from all the teams." He added: "Set up radio communications to my office and report your progress daily. Requisition whatever you need. We'll air drop or ship it to you."

Colt recovered enough to ask, "How much time do we have?"

The colonel responded without hesitation. "Pick your men this afternoon, call them together and brief 'em, tell them to say good-bye to their families, and get them ready to move in the morning. You have thirty days to accomplish the mission."

Colt left the colonel's office with his head swirling with preparation details. Thirty days to cut a ship-sized channel through a coral reef would be extraordinarily difficult. Coral is a soft material, but the volume would be vast, and moving around that much material underwater would be particularly challenging.

He called together all of the NCOs who had completed the UDT school with him. His first choice was M.Sgt. Robert J. "Whisperin'" Smith, six feet, two inches tall, with a deep, gravelly, whisperlike voice from which he got his nickname. Colt also selected Sgt. 1/C Richard D. Fehlner, medic; 2d Lt. Hartmuth D. Guenther; Sgt. Brony Majauckas; Sgt. Ray J. Sakowski; Sgt. 1/C Gilbert A. Secor; Sgt. 1/C Bert M. Smith; and Sgt. Frank Strausbaugh, radio operator.[1] Colonel Garrett called this special project Operation Terry, with orders dated April 10, 1963. Sgt. 1/C Roger H. Kluckman and S.Sgt. Ethyl W. Duffield were added on separate orders a few days later.

The adjutant, Maj. Edgar McGowen, cut the orders to qualify the men for extra-hazardous-duty pay. Also, he informed Colt that, per the colonel's orders, the captain would be taking 1st Lt. James R. Monroe with him as XO. Colt already had one officer with him, Guenther, and did not want to take along another officer, especially one he did not know. With his background, battlefield commission, and field experience, Colt felt that he, along with his handpicked team, could handle the assignment without the extra officer. He politely advised the adjutant that Monroe would not be needed.

The adjutant, a big man with eyebrows so thick that the troops referred to him as "Brow," did not take well to Colt's resistance. He asked the captain if he was questioning the commander's decision. Colt quickly backed off— Lieutenant Monroe would go along as his XO. He soon found out that Monroe was an All Southwest Conference football player from the University of Arkansas.

The next morning Colt learned that a navy UDT had just finished parachute training and wanted to be part of the project. These men had convinced Colonel Garrett that they could show Special Forces how to do the job. Colt told Garrett that did not need any additional help, but the colonel told him to take them along anyway. Colt did not resist further because he thought that maybe the navy UDT could give his men some training and help them do the job.

When the team arrived at Ishigaki by C-130 the next afternoon, Colt made a tactical mistake—he let the navy take the lead in organizing the work, even though he was in command, viewing the mission as more of a training exercise for his men. The cooperating UDT reported to a retired admiral, a highly ranked government civil servant, who represented General Caraway on Ishigaki Island. The admiral already knew that Colt had thirty days to complete the mission.

The next morning the navy team took the Special Forces men out for a run and for a session of calisthenics. In the afternoon they did recon swims, creating maps of the coral, and the navy team trained Colt's men on the use of bangalore torpedoes. The following day they did the same thing. For five days they never started the project.

The navy men loved their marathon training and the comfortable accommodations. The admiral had set them up in a nice villa, with servants to wait on them and their choice of food served in a very elegant dining room. Everything was actually too comfortable. On the fifth day, as Colt was walking to their dining room for breakfast, the admiral called him aside. He pointed out the obvious: "Captain, your teams have been here for five days and have not accomplished anything. General Caraway sent you here to build a channel in thirty days, not to get ready for the Olympics. What are you waiting for?"

Colt explained that they had let themselves become distracted by all the training that the navy UDT wanted to do, some of which was completely ineffective for the mission. For example, they had shown his men how to lay underwater bangalore torpedoes that would not even scratch the coral—they were made for cutting wire nets and undermining foundations. The admiral immediately recognized that the navy UDT was getting in Colt's way and promised that they would be gone that afternoon. But the captain surprised the admiral by asking him to wait until after breakfast the next morning. Without asking why, he agreed.

The next morning Colt called his men together and told them that they were about to have their last run with the navy men. He reminded them how, every morning, the sailors had beaten them back to the compound gate at the end of the run and that some of his team had even dropped out along the way.

"This morning," Colt said, "no one is going to drop out, and as many of us as possible will beat the navy back to the compound gate. You got it?"

"We got it," Colt's men replied in unison.

The UDT had an officer, named Lieutenant Fox, on their team. Over six feet tall, he was, as Colt recalls, a Naval Academy graduate and an accomplished runner. Colt felt competitive whenever he came up against taller men because they always seemed to give him a hard time for his being five feet, eight inches tall. The run was five miles through cane fields and down a dirt road. The men ran in columns of two. On this final outing, when they saw the finish line, a gate at the end of the road, Lieutenant Monroe had the lead on the right and Colt was leading on the left. When they were about one hundred yards from the gate, just before the point where Fox usually incited his men to speed up, both Colt and Monroe took off. The rest of Colt's team followed their lead. The entire team outran the other UDT men except for Fox, but Colt and Monroe both outran Fox.

All the way to breakfast, Fox kept repeating how he could understand Monroe outrunning him since he was a fellow runner, but "I can't believe Mr. Terry outran both of us. Why, he's an old man." At the time, Colt was all of thirty-two years old.

Immediately after breakfast, the admiral told the navy team to get their gear together, that transportation was waiting to take them to the airport. When they asked him why, he simply said that the navy had orders for them to go back to California. In an attempt to reverse the orders, the navy team sent a message back to Okinawa. Colonel Garrett sent back a message that Special Forces was not in a position to help them.

The admiral had kept his promise. Now the entire job was up to Colt and his team. That very morning Special Forces got down to business. Colt and Whisperin' Smith made the first reconnaissance swim. The mission looked impossible—they had to break down a solid wall of coral. Colt told his men that they would start on the harbor side and work toward the ocean. A large round coral head protruded from the water at the entrance to the harbor, which is where they would begin. The navy UDT had told them that the explosives would not need tamping because the water provided adequate resistance, but Colt's team quickly learned that this was not so.

The admiral provided them with a landing craft with a ramp to make the job easier. The first charge was one thousand pounds of C-4 (plastic explosive), but it had little effect. Then they tried two thousand pounds without sandbags, and that did not do much more. After that, the team piled sandbags on top of the explosives and, though it doubled their work, the results were worth it. The first boat they used could haul only four thousand pounds of explosives at a time, which still was not enough. In a few days, after the admiral provided a larger boat, the men tried six thousand pounds. Finally, they were making great progress by placing sandbags on top of six thousand pounds of explosives. Colt radioed Okinawa for five thousand sandbags and an additional twenty thousand pounds of explosives. When the supplies arrived the next day, it was a lot of weight for his team to unload and store. More supply orders would follow.

Each morning two divers made a reconnaissance swim. When they returned to shore, they diagramed on an outdoor blackboard where and how the explosives should be placed that day and the amount to be used. While Colt briefed the leaders on the day's operation, the other men cut detonating cord, primed blocks of high explosives, wrapped the cut cord around the blocks, filled sandbags, and loaded the trucks. They used spools of white detonating cord, about the diameter of clothesline, that burned at ten thousand feet per second to set off all the charges except the first.[2] An electrical charge from a generator, connected by wires to a blasting cap, initiated the detonation.

Sergeant Secor had the responsibility for detonating the charges. When the explosives were in place, he ran the detonating cord to a float where the blasting cap and fuse were attached. When all of the men were back in the boat and accounted for, Secor yelled "Fire in the hole" three times and then twisted the handle on the generator. The men waited a split second for the blast, which sent a plume of water 250 feet into the air, and then headed the boat toward shore.

Loading the LCVP (landing craft vehicle personnel) with explosives at Ishigaki.

Colt planned each explosion differently, targeting each one to produce chunks the size of baseballs. Afterward, the dredge scooped up the chunks, pulverized them, and then sucked them through a floating pipe to be discharged along the edge of the harbor, which created new land for the island every day.

It was a big job for twelve men to prepare and move thousands of pounds of explosives daily, but no one complained—they had good food (thanks to the admiral), stood no inspections, and had almost every night off. When the team arrived on shore after each blast, their work was finished for the day; the water was so cloudy after the explosion that no more work would be possible that day. The men drove the trucks to the villa, showered and dressed, and then headed for the local club to flirt with the girls. The next morning they were back in the water.

As they neared the end of the thirty-day deadline, Colt put Lieutenant Monroe in charge of taking out some small coral heads near the harbor's new pier, recently completed by a Japanese contractor. He told Monroe not to use charges larger than a half pound close to the pier so as not to crack its pilings.

While Monroe was setting the charges, Colt and Secor were making the largest charge of them all. The wall of coral was twenty feet tall in one place and would require a shaped charge. Colt and Secor made the shaped charge by taking a fifty-five-gallon drum and placing in the bottom of it a cone fashioned from galvanized steel (base down). They then took 2.5–pound blocks of C-4, kneaded each one to make it soft and pliable, and then, using an ax handle, packed the explosive around the cone and up to the top of the drum. This took them almost a week, working every evening. Once prepared, the drum was lowered onto the coral wall and covered with sandbags to hold it in place. The cone shape concentrated and focused the explosion to a single point for maximum cutting power. They needed all the men that they could round up to lift the explosives-packed drum onto the truck and then onto the boat.

At the coral site the men took off their life vests, tied them around the drum, pulled the carbon dioxide bottles to inflate the vests, and then lowered the drum into the water. Even with this extra buoyancy, they still had trouble jockeying the heavy container into proper position at the center top of the coral head. When the drum was in place, they applied the "earmuffs."

The use of earmuffs was a trick Colt had learned from the CIA. With the drum in place, the men set two number-ten cans filled with C-4 plastic explosive on either side of the coral head. They set them with delayed detonators tied in to the detonator on the main charge in the fifty-five-gallon drum. When the main charge blew, breaking up the coral, the other two would go off a tenth of a second later, pulverizing the broken pieces; Sergeant Secor came up with the idea of draping sandbags over the coral head and bracing them against the sides of the explosives. The next morning everything was set, and the men detonated the fifty-five-gallon charge and its earmuffs. After the explosion, not a piece of the coral head could be found—it was totally demolished.

Two detonations remained to complete the channel into the harbor. That evening Monroe set off the small blocks of charges to knock out the small areas of coral near the pier.

Afterward, as Colt recalled, Monroe came and told him, "Sir, you'd better go out there. I think one of the concrete pilings on the pier cracked from the explosion."

Colt went and saw for himself. He was surprised at the size of the cracks. He asked the lieutenant, "How much did you set off?"

Monroe replied, "Half a pound."

Colt countered, "No, half a pound wouldn't do that. Something had to be wrong with the pier for it to break that easy."

Colt reported the problem to the admiral. He was mad as hell at first. "I told you to be careful around the pier, captain!"

Defending his team's actions, Colt replied, "Yes, and we were. However, sir, with all due respect, the damage is more than what a half pound could do. Something is wrong with the concrete."

The admiral said, "We paid that Japanese firm millions to build that pier. There had better not be something wrong with it."

Navy engineers took concrete samples from the pier and sent them to a laboratory on Okinawa. Sure enough, to save money, the contractor had used too much sand in proportion to the cement. The admiral thanked Colt and his men with commendation letters for discovering the problem and letting him know as soon as they did. Nevertheless, they still had to finish the job on the channel.

On the last night of the mission, Colt's team had to move the final embankment of loose coral. Through ignorance, someone in the supply depot had included in one of their requisitions a number of eighty-pound cans of ammonium nitrate. Known as "crater charges," the cans were normally used for making tank traps by blowing large craters in the ground. Colt had not used them to remove coral because ammonium nitrate quickly deteriorates in water, and the last thing he had needed was a lot of misfires. On the last night, however, all he had left were the crater charges and some miscellaneous other explosives, and the team had been advised not to bring back any explosives to Okinawa.

Colt told his men that they were going to have a party Friday night. He reminded them there would be a full moon, and to celebrate, they were going night diving. They would put down all of the crater charges against the wall of loose coral and blow it out of sight. He saw it as a celebration to end their mission. But their objective was closer to the town than any of the coral that had been blasted. The men cautioned the captain that having an explosion so close to the harbor and at night could be a problem, waking up everyone in the village and possibly causing some damage. Colt ignored them, figuring that the villagers would be glad to have the harbor open. The men continued to try to talk him out of the plan, but Colt wanted to give them some experience in diving and working at night. His team had never used or placed live explosives underwater in the dark—certainly never four thousand pounds of crater charges.

That night, borrowing an old boat from an Okinawa fisherman, the team loaded it with sandbags, more than fifty crater charges, and all of the other remaining explosives. Colt set up the dive as a formal night-training exercise, in which the men would react as though they were in enemy water, and went down with them to supervise the placement of sandbags and the crater charges at a depth of about forty feet. It was a beautiful moonlit night, and he could see everyone working around him.

When the explosives had been sandbagged and inspected, the divers returned to the boat and pulled it close to the town. Sergeant Secor detonated the charges at 0100 hours (1:00 A.M.). The explosion was much greater than they had expected and broke many windows throughout the small town. Colt feared repercussions, but to his surprise, none resulted. The townsfolk were all out watching the event. Immediately after the explosion, all the locals scrambled into the water and scooped up the fish that had been knocked unconscious by the concussion; some even swam far out and brought back fish in their teeth.

Colt and his team had completed the assignment in thirty days, in accordance with General Caraway's orders. The next day Colt radioed Colonel Garrett that the job was ready for inspection. The colonel ordered his team to stick around until the general inspected the site to confirm that it met his expectations.

The following morning Colt happened to fly to Okinawa for personal reasons, not knowing that the general was flying in that day. Caraway shook every man's hand and gave each a commendation letter. In his remarks to the men, the general took back what he had said about Special Forces being a bunch of blowhards. When Colt returned that night, Monroe told him about

Ishigaki natives watch an explosion, ready to wade into the water to gather stunned fish.

the commendations and presented the general's letter to him. Colt regretted not being there to receive them from the general in person.

WHEN THE TEAM RETURNED TO OKINAWA, IT WAS time for Colt to rotate to the States. In June, 1963, on the way home, he learned that he had been promoted to major. His orders directed him to report to Fort Jackson, South Carolina, one of the basic training centers for the U.S. Army.

He wrote a letter to Maj. Gen. W. B. Rosson asking to change the assignment because he wanted to stay in Special Forces. They told him that they needed officers like Colt down at Fort Jackson—officers whom the men could look up to—and that, for his own career, he would need the experience to stay in and move up the ranks.[3]

In September, 1963, Colt was assigned as XO to a lieutenant colonel who was a battalion commander. Colt had been at Fort Jackson for six weeks before his promotion orders finally arrived. He and his brigade commander, Col. Cecil Hunnicutt, were called up to commanding general Charles DiOrsa's office, where the general pinned the oak-leaf insignia on Colt's collar. Although proud of his promotion to major, he felt unchallenged.

Before long, Colt became impatient and frustrated with working under a battalion commander whose own troops did not respect him. He went to Colonel Hunnicutt and bluntly told him, "I'm wasting my time as XO. Either make me battalion commander or ship me out somewhere where I can go to work." Colt sensed that the colonel did not like his attitude at all.

Hunnicutt got up from his desk, walked around to stand directly in front of Colt, and said, "Well, young man, you think you could command that battalion better than the guy who is there now?"

Colt had his answer ready, "If I can't sir, you can fire me."

The colonel reflected for a moment and then said, "I will. Effective tomorrow morning, you are the battalion commander and you'd better be the best damn one I've got." What Colt did not know was that he had been placed in that battalion because its CO was already under orders to ship out. Colt would now be in charge of training trainers.

ON NOVEMBER 2, 1963, SOUTH VIETNAMESE OFFICERS overthrew Pres. Ngo Dinh Diem in a coup. Dissident military leaders, with the reputed support of the U.S. government, seized him near the Catholic church in Saigon, threw him into the back of an armored personnel carrier, and shot him.[4] The coup shifted the war into a higher gear going into 1964 and increased the demand for experienced Special Forces officers.

COLT WAS STATIONED AT FORT JACKSON FROM AUGUST 1, 1963, until September 1, 1964. In August, 1964, Col. Edwin J. Gravell, who had replaced Hunnicutt as brigade commander, summoned Colt to his office.

Gravell told him, "The conflict in Vietnam is getting a bit more involved, and the 5th Special Forces Group needs qualified officers. You are more than qualified and you've been to Vietnam before."

Colt responded, "Yes, sir, and I don't wanna go back again either."

Gravell continued, "Well, we're sorry, but you've got to go. I wish I could keep you here, but I can't. A new commander for your battalion will arrive tomorrow morning. Turn the battalion over to him by the end of the week."

All Colt could say was, "Yes, sir."

He left the colonel's office and went home to tell his wife, who did not receive the news well. By the weekend, Colt was on his way back to Vietnam. For his service at Fort Jackson, Colt received the Army Commendation Medal for meritorious service from September 7, 1963, to September 11, 1964.[5]

9   Back to Vietnam

WHEN COLT ARRIVED IN NHA TRANG ON September 12, 1964, he reported to the 5th Special Forces Group (Airborne), led by Col. John H. "the Lancer" Spears, who had recently become group commander.[1] Colt quickly went into action. His initial assignment was as liaison officer to the South Vietnamese Special Forces (VNSF) to assist them in writing and editing their Special Forces manual. Because the VNSF were not doing their part, the assignment only lasted about four weeks.

Colonel Spears held a staff meeting every Monday morning. At the end of the meetings, he often announced sudden personnel changes. The colonel meant business: he backed up his men when they knew what they were doing and did it right; otherwise, he reassigned them. At the end of the first meeting after Colt returned from his initial assignment, Spears announced his name among the personnel changes. After the meeting, the colonel told Colt that things were not as sharp at Dong Ba Thin as they should be. A large number of CIDG (Civilian Irregular Defense Group) troops had been assigned as security for the VNSF school but were lax in their job. Spears thought that the current commander was too easy on them. He wanted Colt to instill some discipline.[2]

Colt was assigned as team commander of Detachment B-51 (the VNSF Training Center) and liaison officer between the VNSF school and the 5th Special Forces Group (Airborne).[3] Spears wanted the major to get the CIDG into the jungle to increase offensive operations against the VC. In addition, Colt was to assist the VNSF school, which had no curriculum or standards.

When Colt became team commander at Dong Ba Thin, he learned that his reputation had preceded him. He had been in Special Forces for a long time, and many people knew him. His reputation was generally good, but there was a suggestion of his being a "bad ass." People knew not to screw with him—if he told them to do something, they better damn well do it.

The school's American staff advisors were all highly educated men but, at the time, needed better direction. Colt's XO was Capt. Richard B. Johnson. He also had three other officers and four cream-of-the-crop NCOs, but the NCOs and the officers were not getting along. At Colt's first staff meeting, he told the men that he would keep his mouth shut and his eyes open for the first thirty days. His promise did not last twenty-four hours.

The officers and the NCOs slept in separate prefabricated huts, half wood, half screen, with tin roofs. Each one had outdoor wood-burning hot-water heater. The first morning, when Colt went to shave, he found no hot water. Colt asked one of the officers about it: "It seems the NCOs always have hot water but we don't. Why is that?"

The officer responded: "The NCOs tell our South Vietnamese workers to light the fire in their water heater first. Sometimes they don't light ours at all."

"Is that right?" Colt said. He walked right over to the NCOs' water heater and drained out every drop of hot water, then called out the sergeant major, a big, gruff, two-hundred-pound, six-foot, two-inch trooper: "Let me tell you, Sergeant Major. Starting today there is not going to be any difference between NCOs and officers in this B-team. It will be hot water for you and hot water for them. I don't want to hear about any more of these sorority pranks. This is going to be a straight outfit, and I'm the guy who's going to make it that way. So you'd better ask now if you've got questions because, if this problem comes up again, then it won't be because you didn't know."

The sergeant major did not dare ask any questions. He simply said, "Yes, sir."

After this run in, everything smoothed out. Calling together his team of instructors, Colt asked for their biggest complaints. The men's main concerns were being saddled with the school and not getting into any combat operations themselves. They were concerned that if they were rotated back to the States without having been under fire, they would not earn the Combat Infantryman Badge. Colt had already earned that award both in Korea and in Vietnam, so he knew how important it was to servicemen. The only way for a soldier to earn the badge was to tangle with the enemy. So the major sent out reconnaissance patrols and agents to locate hostile forces, and all of his team members began going on combat operations against VC units in their area. Group by group, the men had an opportunity for action against the enemy. When they left the school, every one of them had earned the Combat Infantryman Badge.

Colt ordered his men to get the team's CIDG into the jungle and to run counterguerrilla operations. The CIDG were on the payroll, and his officers were to make sure that they earned their money. On their orders, the CIDG penetrated farther and farther away from their base, killing or capturing large numbers of VC and pushing them back into the jungle. Eventually the school no longer had to worry about VC snipers sneaking up and firing through the fence or ambushing students going to and from class. CIDG casualties totaled only a couple of wounded men during these operations.

The first time the CIDG ran into the VC, Colt was with them. When the firing began, the enemy ran helter-skelter everywhere. Although the CIDG shot at the enemy, they missed every one of them, and all escaped into the jungle. Colt figured out what was wrong on his way back to camp. He told his XO, Captain Johnson, that they needed to train the CIDG on how to shoot moving targets. Colt came up with the idea of making a sled from a pallet, nailing cardboard targets to it, and then pulling it behind a jeep. They would drive the jeep past the trainees at a distance of twenty-five yards as the men shot at the targets. At first, Colt's XO was reluctant to drive the jeep in front of the CIDG, so the major drove it. On the first pass, his students could not hit the targets at even 5 mph. Once they learned how to lead the targets, they

Veteran staff officers of VNSF school at Dong Ba Thin. Colt commanded a B-team there as advisor for the school. Most of the officers had been fighting for eight years.

began hitting them at fifty yards and 15 mph. Eventually they all became good marksmen, and Colt felt more comfortable taking them on patrols.

During one patrol deep in enemy country, Colt contracted an extremely high fever, with vomiting and explosive diarrhea, and became too weak to walk. It took such a toll on him that he could not travel. He asked his men to put him in a thorn tree where tigers could not get him and to go on without him. In a perfect example of the loyalty among members of Special Forces, Colt's men refused to leave him. He told them to get out of the area and send a helicopter to get him, but they would not agree to that either and stayed with him until he was well enough to walk. After two nights, Colt felt that he was ready to move but was still too weak to walk. One of the CIDG carried him on his back for fifteen miles.

A few weeks later Colt rotated to Okinawa for a brief time, which gave him a chance to recover from the hardships of jungle living. But it was not long before he was back in the action.

On FEBRUARY 15, 1965, COLT WAS LEADING HIS TEAM up a hill to surprise some VC who had set up their camp in a village on the hilltop. As they approached the village, Colt signaled his men to fan out in a skirmish line horizontal to their line of attack. While focusing on his men, he took his eye off the ground ahead of him and stepped into a shallow trap of punji stakes, sharpened bamboo stakes covered with dung or poison, one of which went through his right foot. No one saw it happen except one of the CIDGs, who saw the major pull the stake out of the top of his foot. Colt signaled him to be quiet.

The team had been working its way up the hill all morning and was almost at the top. Colt did not want to blow the surprise. When he gave the signal to attack, the men crested the hill but found that the camp had been recently evacuated. The VC had time only to grab their weapons and run. Pots of hot water were still on the fire; they had even left their chickens and pigs behind.

The CIDG soldier told Xuan (pronounced "soon"), a young medic, about Colt's injury. The medic went to the major and asked if he wanted his foot checked, warning him that he should sterilize the wound because otherwise it would become infected. Colt took off his boot and dumped out a surprising amount of blood. Xuan said that the major could not stay out there in his condition. Colt agreed.

Colt, with his team and
sixty mercenaries, cleared a
helicopter-landing site using
only their knives, like the one
he holds here. Viet Cong heard
them, sneaked up, and started
shooting. Colt had so many
men firing back that the enemy
guerrillas fled.

Colt rests after stepping on a
punji stick while attacking up
a hill.

After the village was secure, Colt was medevaced to a hospital. It was crowded with casualties from a big fight some place. Wounded men were everywhere. He felt that he was not hurt badly and was embarrassed to be there. Because of the crowding, he was lying on a stretcher in the hallway when Major Thompson, the big XO from Delta Project, walked in. Colt saw that two of his fingers were nearly shot off. Thompson was holding them in place as he walked past.

When the major saw Colt on the stretcher, he hollered, "Goddamn it, Colt, I see you're still fuckin' off." He was standing there with two fingers hanging loose and making jokes. Colt was thinking, as he watched the doctor examine Thompson's fingers, that he was not even in the same league with this man. Thompson went back to the States for additional surgery, and Colt never saw him again.

A doctor patched up Colt's foot, and he went right back to the war. On February 23 Colt was awarded a Purple Heart for the injury. But this physical wound bothered him less than the mental pain that would soon follow.[4]

SOON AFTER RETURNING FROM THE HOSPITAL, HE WAS on a mountaintop with bullets flying all around him when he received a radio message from 5th Special Forces Group (Airborne) Headquarters at Nha Trang. His team had walked into the midst of the enemy without either side realizing it. Fortunately, the VC, above them on a mountain, were not very good marksmen. The team's casualties could have been much worse. He had already called for a medevac chopper to pick up two wounded and four dead CIDG.

The message ordered Colt to report to headquarters immediately, so he told his sergeant major, Powell, that he was leaving him in charge. At first he pulled Powell's leg and told him that he was called back to Nha Trang for a party. At that moment they were hiding together behind a rock with bullets whizzing past them. The sergeant major, taking the bait, became extremely upset. "How can headquarters possibly care about a party while we're in a firefight? I recommend, sir, that you send back a message telling them that you're needed right where you are."

Colt laughed. "Oh, this firefight's not all that bad," he said as he tried to calm down Powell. "You can handle it." He finally confessed that the message was not an invitation to a party after all but instructions for him to return to headquarters immediately. "It must be something serious. You keep your head down, sergeant; you still have a long way to go in this army," he told him. Colt was awarded a second Combat Infantryman Badge during this tour for operations like these.[5]

The major rode along with the casualties in the medevac helicopter to Nha Trang and reported to Colonel Spears. The colonel was not big, but he was tough, smoking cigars constantly. Spears called Colt into his tent, his makeshift command post. It had a little bar in it, and a few of the colonel's staff were attending a meeting there. Spears introduced him as his "young major who had just come in from a hell of a firefight."

Colt added, "It's probably still going on."

The colonel continued the small talk and told Colt that the inspector general was coming down to examine his camp. He said that he expected Colt to have the place in top shape. Colt told him that he had left a good man in charge. Spears then invited him to make himself a drink and sit down. He dismissed the rest of his staff so that he and Colt would be alone.

As the others left the tent, the colonel turned serious. "Now, I don't want you to go off the deep end with what I'm going to tell you. I want you to know that, when I was a young officer, what's happening to you right now happened to me. If I had gone off the deep end, do you think I would be sitting here talking to you now?"

Colt responded, "I don't know; what is it, sir?"

Spears said, "We got a message down through the chain of command that you may have some problems at home that you need to go back and resolve. General Westmoreland's office has issued a thirty-day leave for you to go back to the States. I know the first thing you're going to want to do and that's the wrong thing."

Confused, Colt asked, "What problems?"

Knowing how Colt probably would react, the colonel tried to moderate his comments. "Well, it looks like there are people living in your house. Also, your wife was in an accident with your car, and there were some other people with her. You are a good officer with a long career ahead of you. You might even make general. But you could ruin your career if you lose your head."

Colt almost did. He now understood why Spears was dancing around the issue. Colt listened to the colonel, but he did not really hear what he said. He had left his second wife behind at Columbia, South Carolina, by her choice, where she worked for the Internal Revenue Service. Like him, she was athletic, and she was a good match with Colt but wanted no part of the army lifestyle. After a while, she apparently got tired of being alone. Their elderly neighbors, Colt heard later, had taken exception to his wife living with two men while Colt was fighting for his country.

The neighbors, who considered the major a war hero, called their senator in Washington, who called the secretary of defense. The latter's office sent a message to the secretary of the army, who forwarded it to DCSOPS (deputy chief of staff for special operations). From there, it went to the theater commander, General Westmoreland, and then to Colonel Spears. This was the actual chain of events, according to Colt's recollections.

"You've been out in the jungle shooting people, and it would be easy for you to go back there and shoot somebody. Don't do something stupid, for your own sake," Spears advised.

Colt acknowledged the colonel's instructions, saluted, and left the tent. He went back to camp and packed his Israeli Uzi and three ammunition magazines in its CIA-issued briefcase. If he were caught transporting this weapon, he would go to Leavenworth Prison for "the long course" (that is, for a long time, breaking rocks). But he did not care.

Colt was still in a combat frame of mind when he left Vietnam. At home he spent his entire leave trying to find his wife and the two men, but they had left before he arrived. He discovered that the men were officers from a nearby air force base and learned their names from some NCOs stationed there. One of the men had paired up with his wife, while the other one paired up with one of her coworkers at the IRS. The fact that one soldier would be with another officer's wife, while the husband was in combat no less, was an insult to Colt and his principles of justice. Their living in his house compounded the insult.

Having learned their names and ranks, Colt went to their group commander, who refused to do anything. He told the major to find his "old lady" himself and throw her out in the street—adding insult to insult, Colt felt.

Colt located his car, which was not seriously damaged. He put the car and his furniture in storage, closed his house, turned it over to a realtor, filed for divorce, and headed back to Vietnam. Being left by his wife put Colt in a reckless frame of mind, again.

⭐ 10 **Pleiku and Martha Raye**

IN JUNE, 1965, COLT WAS ASSIGNED TO
Detachment C-2 at Pleiku, Vietnam, as XO under Col. William A. Patch.[1]

At that time, in the mid-1960s, a number of field-grade officers were transferring into Special Forces in Vietnam so that their records would show combat in a Special Forces unit—a card punched on the way up their career ladder. Patch, the son of a general, had no prior experience with Special Forces; as Colt recalls, he had just come from the John F. Kennedy Special Warfare Center and was assigned to the C-team.

When Colt was first introduced to the colonel, Patch commented that he thought they might have met before. He did not remember Colt from their previous meetings, and the XO did not remind him. Indeed, he had met Patch when Colt was a young major stationed at Fort Jackson. Assigned to participate in a war game as part of planning for an invasion of Cuba, Colt had been the airborne advisor to a Marine Corps general and a navy commander in charge of the preparations. Patch was then in the 82d Airborne Division, directing the main element to be parachuted into "Cuba" on the simulated invasion. The commander's staff, which included Colt, was assigned to play the role of the enemy.

Colt had read an obscure top-secret intelligence report indicating that Cuban prime minister Fidel Castro had his tanks driven onto lowboys (trucks that haul cranes), chained down, and parked in underground bunkers in Havana; that way, he could quickly dispatch them at high speed to the location of an invasion. Castro believed that he could have those tanks rolling off the trucks so quickly that invading troops would be wiped out.

Because the intelligence was classified top secret, Colt figured that it was probably true. Based on this information, he did what Castro would have done, deploying his tanks rapidly on trucks. His tactics resulted in Patch's men being wiped out during the simulated invasion of Cuba. The colonel did not like that at all. Colt gave all the credit to the intelligence report.

In Vietnam Colt grew to really respect Patch's leadership style and felt that he definitely turned things around for the better. In his opinion, Patch became an outstanding Special Forces commander, partly because he was an inclusive leader. As his XO, Colt had a vital part in helping the colonel plan the C-team's operations. Patch also utilized Colt's ten years of experience with Special Forces, realizing that he could lean on the major and count on him for straight answers.[2]

Even so, while Colt was XO of Detachment C-2 at Pleiku, he sometimes wondered if Colonel Patch just liked him a lot or possibly subconsciously disliked him a lot. The colonel kept assigning Colt to the most dangerous missions. Each time, Patch joked, or so it seemed, "What's it gonna take to get you killed, major?" Of course, Colt always told his CO that each assignment was a "piece of cake." Colt really did not need help from Patch to endanger his own life.

CAPT. JAMES CONWAY, A YOUNG, TALL, FRECKLE-FACED, redheaded pilot, visited Colt at Pleiku. Conway had been with Special Forces back in the States and had been a member of the Armed Forces Day rappelling demonstration team with Colt in Washington, D.C. He had transferred out of Special Forces to attend army flight school. Conway and another pilot, Charlie Thompson, arrived at Pleiku in two Mohawks—twin-engine, two-seater ground-support bombers.

In his Tennessee drawl Conway said to him (as Colt recalls), "Sir, I heard you're up here kickin' the VC's ass."

Colt responded, "Ya got that right."

Conway, speaking for himself and Thompson, added, "We wanna come up here and fight along with y'all."

Colt was flattered but warned, "You don't wanna do that. You'll get yourself killed."

Conway countered, tauntingly, "We can't live forever."

Colt asked, "What d'ya got out there?'

Conway answered, "Two Mohawks."

The major looked them up and down and, with a gleam in his eye, acquiesced. "Okay, how 'bout flyin' a mission for me?"

Conway said, "You got it, sir." Thompson agreed too.

Colt outlined the mission. Some of his men were operating on the Cambodian border near Duc Co. The Special Forces Detachment A-253 camp at Duc Co, also known as Chu Dron, was opened in May, 1963, and continued to operate until it was turned over to the control of the South Vietnamese Army on October 31, 1970.[3] The North Vietnamese Army (NVA) was reported to be sneaking down inside or along the border. Colt had also received an intelligence report that NVA units were going into Cambodia to lick their wounds, regroup, and come back into Vietnam to fight again. He wanted to find evidence in Cambodia to substantiate this information. Conway and Thompson thought nothing of the danger and agreed to fly the mission. Colt advised Patch, who just smiled and said, "Go get 'em, major."

Colt climbed into one of the Mohawks with Conway, who gave him a quick orientation on the ejection seat just in case they had to bail out, and they took off. With Thompson trailing slightly on their wing, they flew low to the Cambodian border and looked for signs of NVA.[4] Having not seen anything, Colt suggested that they drop down just above the treetops to reduce exposure time in case they drew enemy fire. As they came around the bend of a river, NVA soldiers suddenly opened up on them. They barely saw anything before a .50-caliber bullet crashed through the canopy, missing Conway's head by inches. The planes returned to Pleiku without further incident. Both Colt and the pilots, however, were unsure whether the NVA who shot at them were in Cambodia or in Vietnam. As the war progressed, this question would grow in importance. After his close call with Conway, Colt got a break from the action.

IN MID-1965, MOVIE ACTRESS AND COMEDIENNE MARTHA Raye visited Colt's camp twice.[5] The first time she was at Colonel Patch's C-team headquarters at Pleiku for about two weeks, and Colt came to know her fairly well. Raye always marveled at Special Forces men, particularly the contrast between their ability to kill people and their ability to be total gentlemen in the presence of ladies.

At the end of her first day in camp, Raye came into the mess hall and asked Colt who had put the guards on her shower.

"I did," he said.

"I can understand why you would put one guard on my shower, but why would you put two guards on it?" Raye wondered.

"The first one is to watch that no one comes near when you're showering, and the other one is there to watch the first one," he said. Colt's response made her let out one of her famous belly laughs. Martha Raye, as an entertainer, made others laugh, but she appreciated a good joke as well.

On the final day of her second stay at Pleiku, Colt had come in from an exhausting mission and was lying down. But at that time, Raye was about to give her last show at the camp, during which Special Forces was going to make her an honorary colonel. One of the C-team officers came to Colt's room to get him out of his bunk and over to the club.

The officer, Capt. Jerry Dodd as Colt recalls, reminded him that it was "Maggie's" last night there, and they wanted him to present a plaque to her. Needing sleep just then, he tried to beg off. Dodd insisted that Colt had to be the one to present it. Finally, the major gave in, dressed in a clean uniform, and walked over to where the farewell party was taking place. Raye, dressed in a slinky black dress, was on a stage built of empty ammunition boxes. Above and behind her was a banner that read "Maggie, we love you."

Everyone became quiet as Colt walked onstage. He told Raye that the plaque was a small token of their appreciation for all she had done for Special Forces, not only in the C-team compound but also in the more remote A-team camps in the VC's backyard. After entertaining the men at an outlying camp, she had returned to Pleiku to entertain the men there each evening, and then the next day she went to another outlying camp.

While Colt was expressing their appreciation, he became a bit choked up. He really liked Maggie. He bowed his head so no one would see that he was getting teary eyed. While looking at the floor, he also tried to think of what to say next. Raye, realizing what Colt was feeling and that the moment might become awkward for him, looked out at the crowd and said loudly, "I don't know if he is at a loss for words or is looking down the front of my dress."

The whole place erupted. Colt did not need to say anything more. All the men were delighted with Martha Raye's visits, especially considering the dangers surrounding the camps.

COLT HAD AN ACTIVE SOCIAL LIFE, SANDWICHED BRIEFLY between and in sharp contrast with his experiences in combat. At one point he was seriously dating a Chinese girl. While he was back in combat, two of Colt's "friends" tricked the girl into believing that he had been killed so that she would go out with them. They took advantage of her in a weak moment. The main culprit was a lieutenant colonel, "Crusty." Colt found out what happened on his next leave and was furious. He vowed to get even.

A year passed after that leave, and Crusty happened to stop at Pleiku on his way back to his own camp. Colt, acting as if nothing had happened, invited Crusty to have a few drinks with him and one of his company's surgeons, Dr. Cramer. Colt got Crusty drinking in their camp's team house while subtly staying sober himself, drinking rum and cokes without the rum. The conversation happened to drift to the subject of circumcision, during the course of which Crusty revealed that he had never been circumcised. Colt saw an opening to get even.

Colt started playing up the benefits of circumcision. Looking to Dr. Cramer, he said, "Tell him, doc, until you've been circumcised, you really don't know how good sex can be."

Crusty turned to Cramer and asked, "Is that true, doc?"

Cramer went along with Colt's game. "Yeah, that's right. It's a simple operation. We give you a local, do the surgery, and the next day you're back in action."

By this time Crusty was drunk, so Colt went for the close. "Hell, doc, we got our own operating room right over there. Why don't you do Crusty a favor and circumcise him here tonight." Crusty, in a stupor, agreed.

With a martini in his hand, Crusty walked over to the operating room, assisted by the others. The doctor asked, "You sure ya wanna do this?"

Crusty answered, "Hell, yes. If Colt says I haven't had real sex yet, then I'm gonna get circumcised, tonight."

Colt stayed long enough to see Crusty drop his trousers and shorts and get up on the table. When the doctor brought out a needle to stick into the head of Crusty's penis to deaden it, Colt left.

The next morning Crusty woke up sober and in severe pain, with a big bandage on his penis. To say he was furious would be an extreme understatement—he was beyond livid. He managed to get his uniform on but could barely walk. Colt was leaving the mess hall with a cup of coffee in his hand when Crusty saw him. He yelled, "You little son of a bitch. When I catch you, I'll kill ya."

Colt, staying about twenty yards away from him, replied: "Looks like it might be some time before I need to worry about that. Besides, I owed ya. Next time, don't fool with my Chinese girl friend."

Crusty, suddenly wising up, screamed back: "Why you fucker! That's why you did this. I'll kill you for sure." But he never did catch Colt. Obviously, Colt could hold a grudge when he felt someone had wronged him. But he also had a passionate affinity for people who did things right.

These brief recreational respites gave the men a reprieve from war at the moment, though not from what was ahead. The time had come for Colt to do what no one else would do—that for which fate must have saved him throughout years of combat.

11 ⭐ Colt's Finest Hour

IN AUGUST, 1965, COLONEL PATCH AND COLT
tried to explain to the commander of an army medevac helicopter unit, Colonel "Trembley," that Special Forces had American and CIDG casualties numbering forty dead and one hundred wounded at Duc Co and needed his help. The camp also was running out of ammunition and needed medical supplies. Patch asked Trembley to take in supplies and pick up the wounded.

Colonel Trembley told him that there was no way he was sending his men in there—it would be suicide. He reminded Patch that the NVA had nearly wiped out a South Vietnamese paratrooper company Patch had sent in.

Patch and Colt were furious when they left Trembley's quarters, but they knew he was right; they could not blame him. The NVA had Duc Co surrounded with three regiments that were pouring fire in as fast as they could load their weapons. Trembley believed that he would lose at least 60 percent of any helicopters sent in there, and he had flatly refused—with sound reasoning.

They next contacted a combat-operations helicopter unit. But its commanding officer also refused to pick up anyone at Duc Co. He said that his gunships would continue to conduct periodic combat sorties against the NVA in that vicinity, but that it was impossible for his choppers to land there—the NVA would "shoot the shit out of them." The American operations combined had already lost five choppers before they even attempted to land in that area.[1] Patch and Colt requested help from every known unit in the region, and none of them would risk the potential losses.

Duc Co was under constant pressure. NVA soldiers crawled up close to the camp at night and lobbed grenades into the compound. The men inside the perimeter were strained to the breaking point from the nightly attacks and constant shelling. Knowing they were surrounded and nearly out of ammunition and medical supplies intensified their stress.

The next morning the C-team radio operator told Colt that the XO from Duc Co, Lt. Sario J. Caravalho, was on the radio and wanted to talk with him.[2]

Colt went down to the radio shack, picked up the mike, and said, "Go ahead." He heard a tough man in serious straits.

Caravalho's voice, as Colt recalls, was tremulous. "Sir, I don't know who to turn to but you. You're the only one that I know who'll listen."

Trying to calm the lieutenant, Colt responded, "Wait a minute, Tiger, the colonel knows you guys need help."

Caravalho said, "It's worse than that, sir. If you can't get us some ammunition today, we won't be here in another day. It will be knives and hand-to-hand and then that's it."

Colt was angered to think that it might come to that. He said, "Caravalho. I give you my word: I'll find a way to get out there. Tell the men to hang on and I'll be there. And when I get there, I want some support."

The lieutenant replied, "Okay, sir. I knew you'd help us."

Without a word to Colonel Patch, Colt drove a jeep to II Corps Headquarters. Nearly despondent because of the rejections he had already experienced, he asked the air force liaison officer, a stocky lieutenant colonel named "Phillips," for assistance. At first Phillips was cordial, even polite, until Colt told him what he wanted.

"Do I understand you correctly, major? You're asking for an aircraft to fly out to Duc Co with supplies and ammunition?" Phillips asked in an agitated voice.

"That's right, colonel," Colt replied.

Colonel Phillips seemed to come unglued and nearly jumped across his big desk—in his big, comfortable office. "There's no way in hell you're going to get a goddamned airplane from us! I know what's going on out there. I know how Special Forces are getting their asses kicked out there!" he shouted.

Colt responded: "That's true, sir, but there are three NVA regiments surrounding us. That camp wasn't designed or staffed to hold off three infantry regiments. If we don't get some ammunition and medical supplies to our men, they're gonna be killed or taken prisoner. I just talked to the XO a half hour ago. He said they might last one more day."

Phillips just shook his head.

What happened next, Colt thought later, was miraculous. At that moment two air commandos walked through the door. They were reporting to the liaison officer that they had finished their mission and were going to get haircuts and something to eat. Air force captain Earl Van Inwegen, the pilot, was a six-foot-one-inch blond fellow who looked like Charles Atlas, the famous 1950s bodybuilder. Air force captain Gerry Fritz, the copilot, was a small Scots-Irishman with flaming red hair.

With a new audience, Colt tried again to convince Phillips: "I've been to everybody, and no one will help."

"I don't blame 'em—that's a suicide mission," Phillips said.

"What's a suicide mission?" Van Inwegen, as Colt recalls, asked.

"You don't want to know about it," Phillips said, trying to exclude the pilots. But they insisted on knowing about it.

A large map lay on the big conference table in the middle of the office. Colt grabbed the map and turned it around to show the air commandos where the camp was located, right along the Cambodian border. He described how the NVA had surrounded them. He continued: "Forty men are dead, and a hundred wounded. Americans, Montagnards, and ARVN [Army of the Republic of Vietnam] paratroopers need evacuation, and there's a decent runway out there. I'm tryin' to get someone to fly out there with ammunition and medical supplies."

When the pilots asked how much weight he was talking about, Colt simply said, "As much as you could haul."

The pilots looked like they were thinking about it when Phillips jumped up and yelled, "There's no way in hell you're gonna fly anything or anyone out there."

The two must have known the colonel well because they just let him rant and rave and waited patiently until he was done. Then they told him that they could do it, no problem.

Colt went for the close. "I'll get the plane loaded. Just tell me where it's parked and the tail number."

Van Inwegen put on the brakes. "Slow down," he said. "We'll fly your mission, major, on one condition."

Colt did not hesitate. "Name it!"

"We'll go, if you go with us," Van Inwegen said.

Colt knew it was dangerous, but he did not hesitate to agree. "You've got it. I'll be there." Van Inwegen gave him the tail number, and the major was out the door and down the stairs in seconds. Breaking a land-speed record, at least for a jeep, Colt returned to camp. He found the supply sergeant and told him what he needed. "Get that aircraft loaded, right to the ceiling, with ammo and supplies," he ordered.

Colt had no time to get back to headquarters and tell Colonel Patch about the flight. While he was talking to the sergeant, Capt. Alan T. "Tom" Cramer, one of the two C-team surgeons, was standing nearby and overheard him.

"You're gonna need a doctor out there," Cramer said.

"You could get killed on this trip, Doc." Colt warned.

"Well, just to remind you, I joined Special Forces to do this job," the doctor argued.

"Okay, Doc, go help pick out the medical supplies," Colt replied.

Captain Cramer had been in country for only about a month. While the sergeant and his men got everything to the aircraft, Colt retrieved his pistol belt and canteen, loaded up on ammunition for his Uzi, grabbed a sandwich, and headed for the airfield. When the supplies arrived, the plane's loadmaster, Airman 1st Class Ray Satterfield, and the crew chief, M.Sgt. Robert Taylor, did a speedy job of getting everything onboard.[3]

As the plane taxied down the runway, the pilots quizzed Colt on how to find Duc Co. He stood between Van Inwegen and Fritz in the cockpit and gave them directions. Taylor sat on a rack of electronic gear in the pilots' compartment. In the rear of the C-123, Cramer sat in the only seat, by the right door across from Satterfield, who sat on the floor.

Colt had been to Duc Co so many times that he could have found it blindfolded. He told the pilots to follow the dirt road due west out of Pleiku as though they were driving to Cambodia. A dirt runway ran right past the front of the camp. Van Inwegen mentioned that he assumed Special Forces had control of the runway.

"Of course, they do," Colt snapped back, even though he did not know for sure.

He radioed the camp to tell the men that he was coming in with a loaded C-123 and to lay down supporting fire. Also, they should have ammunition bearers ready because the aircraft had to be unloaded quickly. He emphasized that the wounded had to be ready to be loaded as soon as the ammo and supplies were off the plane. The dead would have to be retrieved later.

As the plane came in low over the camp, Van Inwegen started to circle. Colt grabbed his shoulder and told him not to circle—the enemy would know that they were going to land and have more time to shoot at them. NVA gunners had shot down other aircraft that had approached the camp. A wrecked helicopter sat next to the runway. "Just fly straight in," Colt advised.

Van Inwegen dropped the wheels, and the plane drifted onto the runway. The NVA had a two-man .50-caliber antiaircraft gun on a tripod hidden in the high grass at the end of the landing strip. It immediately opened up on the C-123. The incoming fire sounded like someone throwing rocks against the side of a tin building. A bullet screamed through the cockpit, right past Colt's nose, and missed Van Inwegen's head by inches. It slammed into the radio equipment on the wall behind Fritz, just a few inches from the crew chief's head. Colt was still standing up next to Fritz.

The plane rocked and rolled as a rain of bullets scored many hits. In the rear, sitting amid the ammunition, Cramer and Satterfield each had their head between their knees to avoid being struck. After the C-123 landed, Van Inwegen taxied to where the camp gate was and turned the aircraft into position to take off immediately after exchanging cargoes. As the plane pulled up to the gate, the ammunition bearers, with their security laying down protective fire, swarmed from the camp. Van Inwegen left Fritz at the controls to keep the props turning and helped Colt, the crew chief, and the loadmaster pass the ammunition and supplies to the bearers.

Colt handed a case of ammunition to a little South Vietnamese paratrooper, who walked no more than twenty feet from the plane before a mortar round hit him squarely in the back, splattering him all over the runway. Machine gunners at the end of the strip were still hosing down the plane with a wash of bullets. The C-123, as tall as a two-story building, looked like the Empire State Building sitting on that runway. Fritz kept the engines running while trying to duck bullets. The doctor, meanwhile, had taken cover in a ditch alongside the runway to keep out of the way while he waited for the wounded to be brought down.

As soon as all of the ammunition was unloaded, Colt yelled, "Load the wounded. Don't worry about strapping 'em down—just drag 'em in and leave 'em on the floor any way they fit. That machine gun will shoot this plane to pieces if we don't get it off the ground soon."

If a mortar round hit the plane, they all knew that it would be gone and them with it. Cramer had abandoned the relative safety of his drainage ditch and was back aboard helping the wounded. When the forty most critically injured had been loaded, Colt left the cargo hold, ran to the front of the plane, and yelled up to the side window, which was open.

"Fritz," he yelled, "rev it up and get the fuck outta here!"

"I'm waiting for Captain Van," he yelled back.

"He's on. Go! Now! In another minute, ya won't be able to. You've got a flat front tire already."

"What about that gun at the end of the runway?" Fritz asked.

Colt looked down the runway. "Don't worry about it—I'll take care of it right now!"

He pulled back the slide on his Uzi and started running down the runway toward the enemy machine gun. Cramer, Satterfield, Taylor, and Van Inwegen had all the critically wounded loaded. The plane was already rolling as Colt came within range of the enemy gunners. As he sprinted toward the antiaircraft gun, two NVA soldiers, who were security for the .50-caliber, jumped out of the grass at the side of the runway. A burst from Colt's Uzi dropped them both, and he kept running, not stopping to check if they were dead.

At the end of the dirt strip, Colt opened up on the NVA soldiers behind the antiaircraft gun as he ran toward them screaming, just like he learned to do in Ranger school. The gunners were so focused on shooting at the huge aircraft that they never saw him until he was right on top of them, hurling profanities at them. They pushed the machine gun over and ran into the jungle. He heard one of them yelling in Vietnamese, "That man is crazy." Colt probably was crazy at this point; all he wanted was for the brave air commando crew to get home safely and for the wounded to have their best chance at recovery.

Kicking up a cloud of dust, the plane lifted off right over Colt's head. At this moment Colt realized that he was out of ammunition, saying to himself, "You stupid son of a bitch. You'd better get your ass out of here." He waved at the aircraft and crew as he ran back toward the camp gate. The antiaircraft gun had hit the plane in some vital places. He could see hydraulic fluid pouring out as it passed overhead, but it could have been worse. The huge C-123 had sat on the runway for an eternity—about fifteen minutes—while the enemy lobbed mortar rounds and gunfire at it.

Cramer began operating on the wounded while they were still in flight. The plane was diverted to Saigon. When the pilots tried to put the wheels down, they would not drop into position. The runway was foamed, and the plane made an emergency wheels-up belly landing. No one was hurt, and all forty wounded men were saved thanks to Cramer and the brave air commandos who flew them out of Duc Co.[4]

WHILE THE C-123 WAS ON THE GROUND AT DUC CO, the men inside the camp had fired a 4.2 mortar, with a four-thousand-yard range, so often as suppression fire that it turned red hot and they ran out of ammunition. When Colt got inside the gates, he found the mortar pointed into the camp. He figured that the men had probably done this to use the last rounds to blow the camp apart had they been overrun. Colt ordered Lieutenant Caravalho, "Turn the damned four-duce around and start dropping everything you have on the surrounding enemy, day and night, until you run those bastards out of the jungle."

He did just that. After two days of fighting against the resupplied Americans, the NVA units had had a bellyful. With the combined effort of the men at Duc Co, U.S. Air Force bombers, and the South Vietnamese II Corps task force fighting its way into the village, the NVA withdrew.

A couple of days later, a chopper was able to land and pick up Colt. When he returned to Pleiku, Colonel Patch asked the major where he had been, knowing full well where he had been. Colt joked, "Trying to get myself killed, sir." Patch was astounded when he heard the details of the trip to Duc Co. Colt gave credit for the rescue to the air commandos.

Within a few days, Dr. Cramer recommended Colt for the Silver Star, but for unknown reasons it was never processed, and the only reward he ever received for this action was the thanks of the men who were at Duc Co. Without question, because of Colt's determination and the bravery of those who joined him, more than five hundred men were saved. Cramer was awarded a Bronze Star, and Van Inwegen, Fritz, Satterfield, and Taylor all received the Distinguished Flying Cross. This group of just five men (including Colt) disregarded their own safety and risked their lives to save forty wounded plus the lives of the camp's defenders, denying the enemy the capture of a key Special Forces position and a victory that they badly needed at that point in the war.

Such valor on the part of all five men was of a level that probably deserved the highest recognition of our country, the Medal of Honor, had witnesses been able to see all that happened that day. Even Gen. H. Norman Schwarzkopf, in his autobiography, calls this flight "the most heroic act I'd ever seen." Yet for these men and others like them, they were simply doing their duty and what they were trained to do.[5] Afterward, Colt went on leave to Saigon. It was September, 1965.

 **12** **Plei Me**

WHEN COLT RETURNED FROM SAIGON, Colonel Patch told him that an attack had occurred while he was away. The colonel had received an intelligence report that the NVA had moved into and taken over the district town of Le Thanh. Not believing that the enemy could have advanced that far, Patch wanted to know whether the report was true. He ordered Colt to fly out to the town for confirmation. The major flew out with a pilot nicknamed "Red Baron" who was as "loose" as Colt when it came to dangerous missions.

Le Thanh, as they found it, was just a wide spot in the road with a few dozen razed buildings. As the report had stated, NVA soldiers were all over the town. Bivouacked in straight lines on both sides of the main street, they were squatting around small fires and cooking their morning rice. Their rifles were stacked.

Colt and Red Baron flew down the main drag to take a close look. The Vietnamese were caught so off guard that not one shot was fired at them. Red Baron suggested making another pass. Colt agreed, and the pilot pulled the plane right down on the deck, swerving from side to side to avoid hitting poles and buildings. They were so close to the ground that they could see the soldiers' pith helmets, epaulets, camouflage, uniform insignias, and even the kinds of weapons they carried. On this pass the bullets whizzed by. In a plane full of bullet holes, they landed safely at Pleiku. Colt never saw Red Baron again.

He reported to Colonel Patch that NVA units were in Le Thanh and that they had taken a few shots at the plane. Patch asked once again, "What's it going to take to get you killed, major?" and then laughed, though in a strange way, Colt thought.

The colonel called for an air strike. Within minutes a sortie of jet fighters ran the NVA out of that town with bombs and guns and pretty much wiped out what was left of the town in the process. Colt's attention then turned again to Duc Co, the Special Forces position that was under constant attack.

SOME CAMPS WERE MORE DANGEROUS THAN OTHERS, and Duc Co was still one of the most hazardous. The VC and the NVA were putting a lot of pressure on the A-team camps along the Cambodian border. Colonel Patch had transferred Capt. Richard B. Johnson, Colt's former XO at Dong Ba Thin, to Duc Co because it was a major hot spot. Johnson had already served a lot of time in dangerous action, even though he was only about twenty-five years old, and Colt felt that he deserved a safer location. But the colonel insisted.

After three months at Duc Co, Johnson returned to the C-team compound by chopper specifically to see Colt. When he asked Johnson how it was going out there, the captain confided that it was "rougher than a cob" and asked to speak with Colt in private. They went over to the little mess hall for a cup of coffee. The establishment was not much, but it was better than the mess halls in most other camps. When they were alone, as Colt recalls, Johnson told him, "Sir, you've known me a long time."

Colt confirmed this, "Yep. You were a good XO for me. As far as I'm concerned, you've been doing a damn fine job out at Duc Co as well."

Johnson confided, "That may be true sir, but I wanna transfer out."

Colt was shocked. "What?"

Johnson, who had to be worn down and tired, said, "I want to get the hell out of Special Forces and out of that camp."

Colt replied: "Why? You're gonna make it. You're gonna break out of there."

Johnson felt differently. "No, no way. The jungle is right up to our front door. The VC and NVA are sneaking right up to our barbed wire and shooting my men right through the wire."

Colt asked, "What are ya doing about it?"

The captain explained, "I'm sending out patrols, trying to drive the enemy away, but the jungle is so thick around there that they're right on top of us and we can't see 'em."

Colt sat there and thought out loud, "We can't spray herbicides out there, it would be too close to the camp." Then he had an idea: "We can do the next best thing. I'll start recruiting people for you, not soldiers, just people who can operate a machete, a scythe, or other cutting tools. We're going to clear that jungle back for five hundred meters, all the way around that camp."

Johnson asked, "Sir, could we do it?"

Colt countered, "We can, Johnson, if I get you the manpower. I'll put them on the payroll and fly them out there, but there is one thing you've got to be careful about. I won't be able to security check these guys. Some of them might be enemy agents. At night, you'll have to pen them up some place where they can't do any harm and keep a guard on them. I'll send you as many as I can recruit, and I can recruit a hell of a lot of 'em. There are all kinds of people looking for work. We're going to feed 'em too, that will draw even more." Food was scarce for civilians. He continued: "So, tell ya what. Give me thirty days, no, give me sixty days. If it isn't better in sixty days, I'll help you get a transfer."

Johnson thought for a moment and said, "Okay, sir."

Colt knew how bad the place was, and he had only the highest respect for Johnson, who was only being honest. He had already proven his courage to Colt, so that was not the issue. The camp was just a giant nightmare.

The major started recruiting immediately. In response, civilian applicants piled into his camp looking for work. Through his interpreter, Colt asked each man if he could cut grass and chop down trees, explained the conditions of his employment, and assured him that he would be paid in cash and furnished free room and board. He made sure that the men understood the job, but he could do nothing to verify that they were not VC. Johnson would just have to provide the best security he could and, beyond that, take his chances.

Colt flew so many civilians to Duc Co that Johnson and his men were astounded. Within thirty days the workers had cleared one thousand meters around the camp.

A few months later Johnson's tour was up and he stopped by and thanked Colt before he returned to the States. Colonel Patch recommended the captain for the Bronze Star, which was awarded. Colt felt that any officer or NCO who spent more than six months at Duc Co deserved at least that much recognition.

Colt felt good about being able to help such an outstanding officer. But Duc Co was still one of the most dangerous camps in Vietnam. Another hot spot was Plei Me.[1]

IN OCTOBER, 1965, THE S-2 (INTELLIGENCE OFFICER) was reporting a buildup of NVA troops in the area around the Special Forces camp atop a hill called Plei Me. The Americans expected the enemy to attack, but no one knew that the NVA was already entrenched on the surrounding three hills, all higher than Plei Me and perfectly positioned for the enemy to fire down into the camp, awaiting orders to open fire.

Colonel Patch arranged for Colt to fly out in an L-19 to get a firsthand report of what problems the men were having and to let them know that everyone was behind them. Colt made his own decision to take the mail and a case of beer along as morale boosters.[2]

Plei Me's dirt airstrip was adjacent to the camp.[3] The L-19 landed, on an upslope, rolled over the top of the hill and then downhill, and finally turned around to taxi back up the runway to the camp gate. It was late afternoon when Colt arrived, and he could not stay long; the plane had to take off before dark.

The pilot carried the mail and Colt carried the case of beer as the two walked about one hundred yards to the gate. At the time, no one suspected that NVA soldiers were already dug in along the runway. They must have watched Colt the entire time and had to have been under strict orders and strong discipline to allow a Special Forces major to walk unmolested into the camp and not kill or capture him for valuable political propaganda.

The Special Forces team sergeant, a tall, lanky trooper from North Carolina, and the team XO, both of whom Colt had known back in the States, met him at the entrance. They may not have realized that he would do anything for them, but they should have realized that he did not have to be there. His visit was a demonstration to them that they were not alone. Once inside the perimeter, they took Colt to their team house, which was more underground than above, a dark bunker of a place. He sat down to talk and have a beer with the men. One of the other men came in and took the mail—letters from home—to hand out to the rest of the garrison. Colt also had brought cigarettes for the Montagnards—he always took care of those who took care of him.

The team commander reported that they had had several probes in recent weeks—NVA patrols coming down off their hills and taking potshots at them through the wire. Usually, before the NVA launched a major attack, they probed the enemy position to learn the layout and test the defenses. The Plei Me camp had barbed and concertina wire all around and Claymore antipersonnel mines spaced along the perimeter.[4]

It was getting late, and the major had to fly out. He gathered up the outgoing mail and walked to the gate, accompanied by (according to Colt's recollection) the team commander, Capt. Harold Moore; his XO, Lt. Robert

Berry Jr.; and the team sergeant, M.Sgt. Everett Hamby.[5] The men told him to be careful and reminded him that NVA personnel looked to kill Special Forces officers especially—his head would make a fine trophy on their wall. Colt could not believe the men were worried about him. He saluted them and turned to walk with the pilot toward their plane.

He and his pilot safely reached the plane, cranked it up, and took off. Of course, Colt did not learn until the next day that he had walked back past very disciplined, dug-in, and well-hidden NVA soldiers.

That night the enemy started shooting at the camp from their foxholes, but they did not immediately mount their full assault. They increased their probes during the night until all hell broke loose at 2300 hours (11:00 P.M.) on October 19, 1965. The C-team at Pleiku sent in air strikes and gunships and dropped napalm all around the camp. Two U.S. jet bombers were shot down. One pilot bailed out and hid in the woods until a chopper was able to get in and rescue him. Another helicopter pilot was shot through the heart and flew his chopper into the side of the hill.

When it was apparent that reinforcements would be needed, Delta Project, based at Nha Trang, was alerted with orders to move to the C-team compound in Pleiku.[6] Two companies of the 91st Airborne Rangers Battalion of the Army of the Republic of Vietnam (ARVN) were also sent in, under the overall command of Gen. Vinh Loc, the II Corps tactical-zone commander. Lt. Col. John C. Bennett, deputy group commander of 5th Special Forces Group (Airborne), was dispatched by Col. William A. "Bulldog" McKean to assist Colonel Patch. With no specific order other than Patch's general consent, Bennett became the OIC (officer in charge) of the operation. Patch assigned Colt to provide Bennett and Delta Project with whatever support they needed.

Commanded by Maj. Charles "Charlie" Beckwith, Delta Project was a uniquely organized group of Special Forces assigned to do special operations and provide reinforcements in only the toughest situations. Plei Me was under attack by three NVA battalions. Its defenders needed Delta Project and the ARVN Airborne Ranger companies to reinforce them and possibly break out into the surrounding hills to drive off the NVA units. Colonel Bennett wanted Delta Project on their way to Plei Me within twenty-four hours. He ordered Colt to reconnoiter the area around the camp and locate a landing zone for the Delta Project team as close as possible to the camp but far enough away not to be detected, so the NVA would not know that Plei Me was about

to be reinforced. Bennett cautioned Colt not to telegraph his position by cir-
cling the area or showing special interest in a particular piece of terrain.

Near dusk, Colt went out in a chopper. He picked a landing site far
enough from the camp to reduce the odds of Delta Project being ambushed.
That evening, before the briefing, he showed the site on the map to Bennett,
who agreed that the location was a good choice.

C-team and Delta Project officers met to review their readiness for the
next day's operation. Colonel Bennett stood by as the officers went over their
plans. When they started talking about logistics, such as batteries, rations,
and medical supplies, a strange thing happened. Every time they mentioned
an item, Beckwith said that he was a little short on it because he had left in a
hurry and asked the C-team to help him out. As the C-team's XO, Colt had
a good supply of everything and told Beckwith in each instance, "We've got
you covered."

Again, when they got to radios and Beckwith again asked for help, Colonel Bennett, normally a quiet and reserved officer, began getting quite exas-
perated. He had taught Russian and English at West Point—a smart man and
highly decorated. When the subject turned to ammunition, Beckwith once
again announced that he was a little short on M16, M79, and M60 machine-
gun rounds.

Before Colt could say anything, Bennett shocked everyone with language
that he seldom used: "Damn it, Charlie. What the hell did you come up here
to do—fight or fuck?"

After a pregnant pause, Colt stepped in. "That's no problem, sir. We have
ammo out the kazoo."

"I hope so!" the colonel said. "I'm glad someone came prepared for this
war." He then ended the meeting.

Delta Project and the 91st Airborne Rangers took off early the next morning. The Special Forces teams dropped into Colt's targeted landing zone
without resistance but ended up having to cut their way through several kilometers of jungle. Fortunately they arrived without detection. When they were
near the A-team's camp, they called by radio to have the gate opened. As Colt
recalls, the first two to emerge from their cover within the tall elephant grass
were a big American major (Delta Project's XO, Charles P. Thompson), six
feet, two inches tall and 240 pounds, and, beside him, a South Vietnamese
lieutenant (whose name Colt does not recall) who was only five feet tall. As
the strange probabilities of war would have it, the first casualty that day was

the little South Vietnamese lieutenant, struck between the eyes by an NVA bullet, killing him instantly. Thompson did not get a scratch. The Americans got inside safely, but several other South Vietnamese were killed.

The Delta Project troopers and ARVN Rangers fought side by side with the A-team and the camp's Civilian Irregular Defense Groups (CIDG) for three days but were unable to drive the NVA forces from the surrounding area. They called the air force for heavy air strikes, but even these did not drive off the enemy. On the third day Beckwith contacted Colt by radio. After blasting him for picking a landing zone that required his men to hack through kilometers of jungle, Beckwith asked Colt to send more American troopers.

When Colt asked him why, he said that it was going just terrible—the "little yellow bastards," referring to the ARVN Rangers, would not move outside the camp's defensive perimeter. Colt knew that Beckwith should not have said that on an open mike from which the Rangers could hear his transmission. But the major always told it like it was, and the Rangers could not accuse him of saying anything behind their backs.

Colt heard later that, when Beckwith had finally had enough, he announced to the South Vietnamese, "If you bastards won't attack, then I'll do it myself." Even the Americans thought it was too dangerous and decided not to follow him.

But Beckwith did what he said. With his M16 and some hand grenades, he charged up the hill in front of the camp alone, with the NVA throwing everything they had at him. He was hoping that the Rangers and his NCOs would follow him, but they did not. Naturally, Beckwith could not take the hill by himself, but he did kill a number of NVA soldiers before he had to retreat. He returned to camp without a scratch. The carnage that he left behind was extensive enough that the NVA had difficulty in evacuating all of their wounded for several nights. Likewise, some of Beckwith's men, seriously wounded days before, had not yet been medevaced. Colt decided to do something to get those wounded men out.

BECKWITH HAD THREE HELICOPTERS AT THE C-TEAM'S base in Pleiku. He was not using them because their American pilots were on R&R (rest and recreation). These Sikorski H-34s were so large that the pilots sat about two stories above their cargo and passengers. Each helicopter had a single large rotor on top, a small rotor on the tail, and a large opening on the right side where a sliding door had been removed. Also in Pleiku were the three famous South Vietnamese pilots, nicknamed "Cowboy," "Khoi," and "Loc," assigned to Delta Project to fly those helicopters, who were waiting either for the operation to be completed or to be called on to participate. These men normally flew only special operations for the Delta Project and to "put out fires," that is, to assist camps with reinforcements in an emergency or when a camp was under attack. In Colt's opinion Plei Me was a camp under attack.

With the recent intensity of the battle at Plei Me, its airstrip was unusable. Only helicopters could go in, and they had to land in the middle of the camp. Because the camp was on a hilltop, the choppers would stand up so high that they would be sitting ducks for NVA mortars and gunfire. Despite the danger, Colt needed them to bring in supplies and pick up the wounded. He had tried but could find no regular U.S. Army or U.S. Air Force teams willing to land there.

Colt found Beckwith's three South Vietnamese pilots sitting in the C-team's makeshift club. They were dressed in black jumpsuits and lavender scarves, just like South Vietnam's prime minister, Nguyen Cao Ky, wore when he flew. These men did not drink alcohol; they were sipping 7-Ups. They had known Colt for several years, and they liked and trusted him.

Colt asked, as he walked up to them, "How you guys doin'?"

They could sense that something was up right off the bat. In Vietnamese Colt's rank of major was called *thieu tá* (pronounced roughly "Que-tah.") They answered, "We're doing all right, *thieu tá*. How are you doin'?"

Colt confessed, "I came over to ask you guys for a favor."

"Yeah, we heard you got some problems," came the response. "How's our old buddy Beckwith doing out there?"

Colt said, "Well, he's hanging on. I need you to fly out to Plei Me and get some wounded out for me. I don't want this cleared with Beckwith because he'll say no." The choppers and pilots were Beckwith's, and he would have a hard job replacing them if they were lost. He probably would not risk them, but Colt would. "I'll pay you whatever you want—whatever amount of money you need," he told them, then added, "I know you guys are off duty, but how about doing this for me?"

They talked in Vietnamese for a few minutes. Even though Colt spoke some Vietnamese, he could not get the gist of what they were saying. Finally they said in English, "Okay, we'll do it, but we want three cartons of Salems and 150,000 piasters." This was not a lot of money in dollars, about $1,500, but it was a lot of Vietnamese money in terms of quantities of bills.

Colt told them, "Don't worry about the cigarettes; I already got 'em." He did not smoke, so he had accumulated cigarettes from his service allotment. He never sold them, as some soldiers did, but gave them to the natives in exchange for favors. Colt continued, "Let me talk to Colonel Patch about the money." Special Forces had local funds in Vietnamese currency for certain operations, but Colt needed his commander's approval to pay the pilots with CIA money.

When he told the colonel that he had three pilots willing to fly to Plei Me, Patch asked, "What are you waiting for?" Colt explained that he needed 150,000 piasters to pay them. The colonel was not fazed and dispatched him to the adjutant's office with authorization to get it from the safe. When Colt finally had the cash in hand, the bills filled three large canvas bags.

The pilots invited him to go on the first trip and show them the way. Colt did not think that he was needed for the operation, but since they invited him, he went. An hour later he was sitting on the side seat in the back of Cowboy's H-34 facing the opening where the sliding door used to be. Cowboy, at the controls, sat above and to Colt's left, and his copilot sat to his right.

They flew to a point directly above the camp at four thousand feet. NVA soldiers blazed away at them, but their fire was ineffective at that altitude. Suddenly Cowboy turned the helicopter on its side and dropped more than thirty-six hundred feet toward the camp. It dropped so fast that Colt thought that it had been hit and was about to crash—that his time must have finally come. He was looking straight down at the ground below through the wide-open doorway, only his safety harness and the helicopter's inertia kept him from falling out. The chopper dropped straight down until, at the last moment when it was about four hundred feet off the ground, Cowboy flared it out and set it down in the middle of the camp. By dropping out of the sky like that, the aircraft was not hit by a single bullet.

Cowboy kept the engine running while medical supplies and a couple of cases of beer and cans of water were offloaded and wounded men were placed onboard. The chopper was on the ground for no more than three minutes, but bullets were flying all over the place, some snapping into its aluminum sides. Normally a helicopter rises up a few hundred feet before moving out laterally, but not this time. Cowboy barely got his machine off the ground before he put the nose down and they were gone, flying low between valleys of jungle forest until they were out of range—true contour flying, right on the deck.

As soon as they arrived at the base in Pleiku, two Special Forces medics,

Jimmy L. McBynum and another named "Johansson," walked over to Colt and asked permission to go out to Plei Me on the next flight. He gave them a point-blank no: "Plei Me was bad news—bullets flying everywhere." The medics countered that they would wear flak jackets. As Colt looked at McBynum's face, he could have sworn that he saw a ghost. The sergeant suddenly appeared to go pale, and Colt knew in the deep recesses of his subconscious that the man would die.

Colt tried again to dissuade the two men—they did not need to go out there, but he appreciated their offer. He even argued that the space on the chopper was needed for the wounded, but the sergeants persisted until he finally agreed to one trip. McBynum would go on one chopper and Johansson another as long as they wore their flak jackets.

Three helicopters flew on the next mercy mission as Colt remained in the operations area at the C-team base. The first one sat down on top of the hill as bullets snapped through its sides. McBynum was helping load a wounded man when a bullet hit him just below the bottom edge of his flak jacket, where he had no protection; it went clear through his abdomen. Another bullet smashed his right leg so badly that the bone was sticking out of his upper thigh. Johansson landed in the next chopper and did not get a scratch. War was being arbitrary again.

A couple of hours later, Colt was still in the operations office in Pleiku when word came over the radio that McBynum was in the Special Forces hospital. The hospital had two good surgeons, and both were operating on him at the same time. As soon as Colt heard the radio report, he ran to the hospital, but he was too late—McBynum had died. The bullet that went through his abdomen had hit his spleen and liver as well as his lungs.

Cowboy, Khoi, and Loc airlifted every wounded man out of Plei Me. They each made six roundtrips, but by the end of the day, two of the choppers were so damaged that they could not have made another trip. Colt met the last one coming in. The engine was shot up so badly that the pilot, Cowboy, had great difficulty in controlling the chopper as it slipped from side to side. According to Colt, if the South Vietnamese pilots had not been so good, they never would have made it back to Pleiku, especially on the final run. They did not even land where they normally did but just plopped their machines down in the camp's yard. All three aircraft needed to be completely rebuilt, and topnotch mechanics were needed to overhaul and repair them extensively. Cowboy, Khoi, Loc, and their copilots all survived that day without a scratch. Colt could not help but love these South Vietnamese Air Force (VNAF) helicopter pilots—they were true heroes. But neither Colt nor any of these VNAF officers received any decoration or recognition for their bravery this day.

Beckwith was mad as hell at Colt when he discovered how badly his helicopters had been damaged. Also, Colt figured that Beckwith probably was still upset with him for picking the landing zone. But he got over his anger and did not hold it against Colt for taking the initiative.

MEANWHILE, THE BATTLE AT PLEI ME RAGED ON. Finally, the ARVN formed an armored column, went in by road, ran off the NVA, and relieved the camp on October 28, 1965, after "one hell of a fight." The South Vietnamese needed armored personnel carriers, tanks, and troops to do the job—and they fought all the way to the camp. Patch sent Colt out to Plei Me one more time to survey its condition after the battle and report back.

Colt described his feelings in a letter, dated November 5, 1965, written to his wife at the time, reflecting back on his visit to the camp before the attack:

> It was hard to realize that just 10 days ago, the bullets were flying in all directions and so thick you couldn't walk across this dirt airstrip. As I stood there just quietly trying to understand how it all happened, I could still smell the dead bodies and see NVA positions that they had dug at night along the airfield. It was very quiet and death seemed to hang over the camp like a heavy fog that refuses to leave.
>
> As I talked to some of the SF [Special Forces] men, I could see or at least felt like they were still in a state of trance or numbness, like they didn't believe the nightmare they had just lived through. I kept joking with them and finally they began to smile and laugh a little. I had to pull every problem out of them and finally found out what they needed to rebuild their camp and get it back in good shape.
>
> They brought in a new NVA prisoner while I was there and he was just about dead from going without food and water. He was wounded too. The first thing these "tough gangsters" did to him was to give him first aid and water. After he recovered some, only then did they question him. I had to leave to get back to Pleiku for another mission.
>
> I would have given a million dollars to capture the picture I saw, looking back—the three of them standing there in front of the shattered gate and cratered camp, the young 23-year-old captain on one

side, the old 6'4" team sergeant in the middle, and a 21-year old lieu-
tenant on the other side. All of them wearing their pistols slung low
like a group of Texans and I thought if only our grandfathers could
see them now. They looked like Davy Crockett, Jim Bowie, and Colo-
nel Travis at the battle of the Alamo. I got a big lump in my throat just
seeing it and knowing how much of themselves they had already given
to hold that camp.

When Colt inspected Plei Me, he found a scene so grotesque that he could never have imagined it.[7] The NVA had placed antiaircraft guns all around the camp and had trained conscripted VC to man them, shackling the VC to the guns so that they could not run away. The ARVN troops found the VC hanging dead, still shackled to their guns. Beckwith took photographs of the scene and sent them to C-2 headquarters for developing and then on to the 5th Special Forces Group Headquarters in Nha Trang. Group headquarters then forwarded them to General Westmoreland's headquarters, where, according to Colt's recollections, they were distributed as examples of how the NVA treated the local VC. The NVA reportedly later defended their action as being done at the request of the gunners as a "guarantee" of their heroism.[8]

Plei Me was saved because of Major Beckwith and his Delta Project, even though the South Vietnamese general Vinh Loc saw the rescue differently, giving all the credit to his forces and not even mentioning U.S. Special Forces in his account of the seige.[9]

AROUND CHRISTMAS IN 1965, COLT HAD A CHANCE FOR some R&R and a trip to Saigon to see his new girlfriend, Jane Maeda. He hitched a ride on an air force C-130 late in the evening and flew in the cockpit with the pilots and loadmaster. To Colt's shock, amazement, and pleasure, while in flight, the pilots were able to provide him with an improvised hot Spam sandwich and an ice-cold beer—but only for him, the crewmen were all business.[10] What a way to start his R&R—a hot sandwich and a cold beer at twenty thousand feet over Vietnam! For Colt, it didn't get much better than that in a combat zone.

As the plane approached Saigon, the pilot swung his aircraft out over Cambodia, a bit, and then back over the Mekong Delta. The sky lit up with enemy tracers, and the pilot commented about how pretty they were. Colt just hoped that they would land safely. He had a date with this beautiful American lady who worked as a civilian for the U.S. Agency for International Development in Saigon. He did get down safely and did go out with her that evening.

After their date, Colt returned Jane to her apartment building in Saigon, a modern French structure where female U.S. Embassy employees lived. The building had no elevator, so they were walking up the stairs when they heard a familiar voice drifting down the circular stairway from above. Neither of them could quite place it. Suddenly John Wayne appeared in front of them with a female embassy employee on each arm. Everyone stopped, and one of Wayne's escorts introduced him to Colt and Jane. Wayne told them to call him "Duke" and went on his way.[11]

In early 1966, when Colt returned from his R&R, he found John Wayne at his camp.[12] Every morning for about five or six days, Duke had breakfast with Colt and the other officers. They talked and joked, and the actor got along well with all the men. After breakfast each day, Wayne and his film crew would fly by helicopter to a different A-team camp and shoot footage of the camp and team as research for a movie about the Green Berets.

Each evening Wayne returned to the C-team compound, where Colonel Patch had set up accommodations for him. He ate with the men and then headed to the camp's team house, or club, for a few drinks. The club was more like a thatched hut, but it served all kinds of beer and booze. Wayne would not let anyone pay for anything the whole time he was there.

Colt went to the club about 2200 hours (11:00 P.M.) when his XO duties allowed him time to socialize, and he sometimes had a drink with Duke. One night he had just completed checking the perimeter and headed for the club to have a beer before hitting the sack. On the way in, he had to stop to let Duke out, who was on his way to the urinal, which was located just outside the club. As he opened the door, Wayne stepped to one side. Because Duke was their guest, Colt stepped aside to make room for him to exit. As he did, Wayne stepped to the same side. They shuffled back and forth a couple of times.

Finally Wayne stopped, puts his hands on his hips, and said, "Major, either you get the hell out of my way or I'm gonna pinch your head off."

Still wearing his 9-mm Browning automatic pistol, Colt unsnapped the flap as though he were going to draw on Wayne and said, "You do, Duke, and I'll shoot your balls off."

Duke turned to the men sitting in the bar, all within easy earshot, and said, "You know, I believe the little son of a bitch would do it."

They all laughed, and one of the men at the bar yelled, "And he would too."

After having a beer and discussing jungle natives with the actor, Colt offered to introduce him to the Montagnards. He alerted the tribesmen at one of the A camps that a famous American was coming to meet them. They arranged a big sacrifice in his honor to make Wayne a member of their tribe.

The ritual called for them to kill a big buffalo and to cut out its heart and put it in a bowl. When Wayne arrived, they asked him to take off his right boot and sock. A witch doctor did a chant while the other Montagnards dipped cotton in the blood of the buffalo heart and wiped it across his toes.

While the witch doctor chanted, Wayne was required by the natives to suck homemade rice wine through a bamboo straw stuck in a large earthen vat of a homemade alcoholic drink while sitting on a log stool. When the blood ceremony was completed, the Montagnards put a brass bracelet, made specially to fit, on Wayne's large wrist, making him a brother of the tribe.[13]

The Montagnard tribesmen greatly impressed Wayne, as Duke impressed Colt. Colt also had a great affinity for the actor and the characters he played in his movies. Like Wayne's movie characters, Colt felt that it was his sworn duty to right every wrong.

Being assigned to a C-team kept Colt close to danger. His next assignment would move him into Saigon, but his new mission would be just as dangerous.

⍟ 13   **Project Flying Horse**

IN EARLY 1966 LIEUTENANT COLONEL
Bennett, who had recently left his position as XO of the 5th Special Forces
Group to set up a new team, C-5, requested that Colt leave his current C-
team assignment in Pleiku and move to Saigon to join him. Colt joined Bennett as his XO in establishing the top-secret project. Bennett's assignment, as
Colt understood it, was to obtain intelligence about enemy operations inside
Cambodia. Colt's mission, code named Flying Horse, was to form, organize,
and train secretly a detachment of indigenous Montagnards and Cambodians
living in Vietnam that would be sent into Cambodia to collect intelligence on
the placement and movement of NVA or VC units within its borders. Enemy
forces were already known to move into and out of Cambodia along the border, but the mission of Flying Horse was to search for operations stationed
inside Cambodia.[1]

When Colt was first assigned to Project Flying Horse, it had no detachment designation other than C-5; it would later become Detachment B-57.[2]
Under C-5, there were other special projects, such as B-50 (Omega), B-51 (the
South Vietnamese War College at Don Ba Thin), and B-52 (Delta Project).
Some of the special projects and special operations were brought into Saigon
and hidden within elements of the Command Liaison Detachment, which
had maintained a presence in the capital since 1962. They were all extremely
sensitive politically and highly classified at the time. Colt would need to be
very careful in how he went about establishing operations.

Indigenous Khmer controlled the southern end of the Cambodian Seven
Mountains region that Colt would search, more so than did the Cambodian
government.[3] They were the most violent and unpredictable group of fighters
in Cambodia and Vietnam—ruthless radicals with their own agenda and not
under anyone's control. To operate in the assigned areas, Colt would need
the cooperation of the Khmer and other ethnic groups, which would not be
easy to obtain.

SOON AFTER COLT ARRIVED IN SAIGON, HE CONTACTED a Special Forces NCO, M.Sgt. Charles E. "Snake" Hosking Jr., whom he had known for years. Snake had connections that could introduce him to the leaders of the indigenous Khmer tribes living along the Cambodian border. He took Colt to a temple in Saigon to meet its chief monk who knew the leaders. Although Colt had trained some of these indigenous at one time, he did not have such personal connections through the monks, with whom Snake had developed an unexplainable rapport that even money could not buy.

Hosking was about to rotate to the United States, and he wanted Colt to carry on the relationship that he had developed with the monks. He would introduce Colt to them as his "number-one man." If the introduction "took," Colt would be able to succeed at his assignment. If not, he would have a very difficult time placing his men into the area of operation—it was that simple.

After Colt met the monks, some of them traveled with him into Cambodia and introduced him to the indigenous Khmer leaders, who agreed to assist Colt's men. Thanks to Snake and the monks, Colt was accepted by the indigenous and able to start operating in the Seven Mountains area at will. He returned to Saigon and continued to run his operation from there.

WITH CIA FUNDING, COLONEL BENNETT LEASED A VILLA in Saigon for the Flying Horse unit's headquarters and staffed the mission entirely with Americans. Keeping an operation secret from the South Vietnamese government was unprecedented. Until then, American and South Vietnamese forces had jointly conducted all operations. In addition, U.S. State Department officials had made it clear that they did not want Special Forces going into Cambodia. Diplomats had assured Prince Sihanouk of Cambodia that Americans would not cross his border. Because of the rocky history between the Khmer tribes and the Vietnamese government, the U.S. government did not want the Vietnamese to know it was working with them.[4]

Colt started reconnaissance operations with two teams and a single individual. At first he believed that the mission could operate all of its teams out of a city in the High Plateau region of Darlac Province in South Vietnam, but operating from there was too visible. Since people were asking too many questions, he stationed the teams in different areas of South Vietnam. One team, consisting of a major, a captain, and an NCO, went to work in the Mekong Delta. The second team, consisting of two NCOs, went to the Seven Mountains area. Colt also assigned a single individual, Sgt. Howard A. Stevens, to an area where a Special Forces A-team would be able to provide security and support, the vicinity of Duc Co in the High Plateau along the Cambodian border.

The mission of Flying Horse had nothing to do with what the Cambodians were doing. The teams were directed to recruit indigenous personnel and secretly infiltrate them into Cambodia from South Vietnam, up and down the border, to gather intelligence on any established operations of the NVA, VC, or the Chinese military (if any). They were to determine unit identification, size, makeup, and transportation (for example, truck, bus, ox wagon, or other means) and the extent of any military activity in Cambodia. They were also to develop a network of agents among the indigenous living near the border.

Location was not the mission's only problem. Initially, when indigenous agents were dispatched into Cambodia by American helicopters that landed close to or just inside the border, enemy groups almost immediately captured them, never to be seen again. The teams did everything possible to prevent detection during insertion—even requisitioning new, specially built helicopters that were painted black, had all markings removed, and had special rotors that traded altitude capability for lateral speed.[5] The pilots were typically young second lieutenants straight from their initial training in the States, looking a lot like high school kids.[6]

When Colt briefed the new pilots on Flying Horse, he informed them how and where they would be flying. He also told them that they have to leave behind everything that could possibly identify them as American military personnel. They had to wear civilian clothes, black pajamas, or whatever garb they could find, but no uniforms, no labels, no markings, and no IDs. Even though these steps were taken, it was hard to disguise young American men. If they were captured in Cambodia, they were on their own. Colt gave each pilot ample opportunity to withdraw—there would be no hard feelings, and they could transfer to a regular army unit without prejudice. Not one pilot backed out.

The helicopters could not attain high altitude quickly, but they could fly fast on the level. Unfortunately, they were noisy, and this attracted attention when they landed to drop off the agents and their bicycles. Too often the indigenous agents disappeared, even though Colt never lost a pilot. He would later give up his black helicopters to other projects.[7]

COLT CONTINUED TO PUT AGENTS INTO CAMBODIA, using them to infiltrate the Seven Mountains area, and worked for six months to insert a three-man American NCO team along with an indigenous team to look for NVA soldiers. Unfortunately, they were not finding the evidence his mission sought.[8]

He felt that the time had come for a bolder plan. He pulled Sgt. 1/C Bruce Baxter from other duties and placed him on "special assignment," a technique commonly used by intelligence units to hide a human resource from the formal army organization.

One day in early 1966, Colt asked Baxter to do something so dangerous that he had to make it clear to him that accepting the assignment was his choice alone. Baxter did not hesitate for a moment. Colt told him that Flying Horse was getting nowhere. Agents, both South Vietnamese and indigenous, were returning with nothing to report, when they returned at all. Special Forces needed to break out in a new direction to learn what was going on in Cambodia. Baxter told Colt to name it, and he would do it.

The major was careful to explain that what he was about to ask the sergeant to do could get him into fatal trouble—and not just with the enemy. He wanted Baxter to secretly play the role of a deserter in Cambodia. Colt again told him that he could say no, with no hard feelings on Colt's part and with no effect on his career. Baxter's resolve remained steady. Colt explained that he would furnish money, a fictitious passport, transportation, and anything else Baxter needed to get underway. He would provide him as much support as he could, directly and only from him, but it would be limited.

The plan included Baxter finding a way to make friends with someone in the Australian Embassy and asking that person to send information to Colt in the embassy's diplomatic pouch. Communicating this way was a risky venture, but Colt knew that the Australians had a pouch that went from Phnom Penh to their embassy in Saigon. He had arranged with the Australians to recognize a code name and to forward the pouch to the American Embassy in Saigon, where Colt would pick it up.

He took Sergeant Baxter, dressed in civilian clothes and carrying a false passport and money, to the airport. As he said goodbye, Colt never felt so bad about anything in his life. He had put this NCO's life as well as his career on the line. The only people who knew about Baxter's mission, to Colt's knowledge, were Colt and Maj. Harry Ching, S-2 with the 5th Special Forces Group (Airborne); Colonel Bennett may also have known, assuming that Ching kept him informed.[9] If anything happened to the few who knew, Baxter could have been headed to Leavenworth charged with desertion or even worse.

After Baxter arrived in Phnom Penh, he soon made friends with a good-looking Australian woman who worked at her country's embassy. The sergeant was diligent about his job. One day he even rode on top of a bus with pigs and chickens, just as the natives often did, all the way to the Vietnam border, and surreptitiously took photographs along the way. Colt thought it was a miracle that Baxter was not discovered and killed. He sent his pictures to Saigon in the embassy pouch and also sent at least a postcard almost every day. This stream of postcards helped inform Colt that Baxter was still operating effectively. Colt recalled providing photos to Colonel Ching on at least three occasions. The range and quality of Baxter's pictures were excellent.

During a period of six months, however, not one picture, or any other evidence collected by Baxter or any of the agents whom Colt had spread over a distance of more than 350 miles, revealed the presence of organized operations by the NVA or the Chinese in Cambodia. Along the border, they did run into VC patrols, but no large-scale operations.[10]

Baxter did a superb job, but Colt recalled him to Saigon in late 1966. When he did, the sergeant was angry about it because he had become romantically involved with his Australian contact. Colt had him rotated back to the States for his own good, but he soon found his way back to Vietnam and joined up with a cross-border operation into Laos, operating out of Da Nang. For his work in Cambodia, Colt recommended Sergeant Baxter for the Silver Star. (Colt recalls that Baxter received instead the Bronze Star.) Baxter's departure was not the end of Flying Horse. Colt continued to run his operation in the face of inexplicable obstacles. One example was his attempt to acquire a small aircraft. It all began with a message from the CIA.

AS XO FOR COLONEL BENNETT, COLT HAD TO RECEIVE and read all messages transmitted to Flying Horse.[11] One morning in March, 1966, Maj. "Joe Ferrington" took a message from one of C-5's radio operators and, after reading it, started to run, literally, out the door toward the colonel's office. Colt stopped the major and ordered him to explain why all the excitement about a routine message. When he did not respond immediately, Colt took the message from his hand and read it. What he read was a memo from the CIA saying that Flying Horse had an additional $3.2 million for its top-secret project, along with instructions that the money had to be spent by June 30, the end of the fiscal year. To spend $3.2 million in three months would not be easy.[12]

After reading it, he had Ferrington take the message over to Colonel Bennett's office. Colt could not help but notice the major's unusual behavior, for messages were seldom delivered with such urgency, particularly one concerning budgetary matters. There was little specific need for that much money, and Bennett would have a challenge in determining how the team (C-5) should best use it in gathering additional intelligence. Soon after receiving the message, Ferrington, along with Capt. "Tom Cooper" and an NCO, moved—without notifying Colt, which they normally would have done. They apparently had dealt directly with Bennett.

It soon became clear to Colt that Ferrington and Cooper were spending a lot of money while not producing any intelligence at all. Colt became suspicious about their operation, particularly since they appeared to have a direct line to Colonel Bennett. He had his own idea for spending some of the $3.2 million—he could help the mission by buying two French-made civilian light aircraft. The planes were quieter than the helicopters and would work well for dropping off agents in Cambodia, as they could land on any dirt road.

Colt was astonished when the Bennett turned down his request for the aircraft. He had asked for only $80,000, and the planes would have definitely assisted the mission. His commander's exact words, as Colt recalls them, in turning down his request, were, "No, you've got to find some other way to do it." Because the rejection made no sense to him, he became even more suspicious, asking himself, "What was this money being used for?"

Taking Colonel Bennett up on his suggestion to "find another way," Colt and one of his officers, Capt. Jerry "Tiger" Walters, reconnoitered a local aviation unit with several small aircraft that were not being used. Walters had obtained a pilot's license when he was sixteen years old, but he kept it secret because he did not want to fly all the time for the military. When the commander of the aviation unit refused to lend a plane to them, the officers hatched a plan to "borrow" it, which they did a few days later.[13] Walters flew it to a small airfield outside of Saigon, covered it with camouflage nets, and left it there while they searched for a pilot.[14] Colt knew that it would take a very experienced pilot to fly a light aircraft below radar and land on dirt roads at night. Finding one to fly it regularly into Cambodia would prove difficult. Colt continued to focus on his secret mission, but changes in leadership made his job more difficult.

14 Operating along the Cambodian Border

IN MAY, 1966, COL. WILLIAM A. "BULLDOG" McKean left C-5, and a month later Col. Francis J. "Blackjack" Kelly arrived to replace him as 5th Special Forces Group (Airborne) commander at Pleiku. In June, 1966, Lieutenant Colonel Bennett rotated back to the States, promoted to (full) colonel, and assigned, as Colt recalls, as deputy commander of the 82d Division. After Bennett left, while a replacement was being assigned, for about six months as Colt recalls, Colt served as the CO of C-5, Project Flying Horse.[1]

Kelly was a big man—six feet, two inches tall—a former New York City cop, and tough. While the troops feared him, Colt has always felt that he was a good man. He believes that Colonel Kelly saw his officers in only two ways— those who were with him, and those who were against him. If he perceived that a man was not with his program, he was soon gone. When he first arrived, Kelly insisted that every officer in the field come to headquarters and meet with him. When it was Colt's turn to appear before him, an old friend, Col. John S. "Jack" Warren, whom Kelly had recently brought in as his deputy commander, gave the major a big buildup.[2]

When Colt arrived for his scheduled visit, Colonel Warren told him that all he had to do was to salute; mind his military manners; and, if he had the opportunity, tell Colonel Kelly that he was behind him 100 percent—this last suggestion being the key.

Warren had done a good job. After Colt saluted and greeted Kelly, the colonel returned the salute, rose from his desk, and walked around it. He came straight up to Colt, gave him a hug, and addressed him by his nick-name, "Skosh" (Japanese for "small"), telling the major that he had heard a lot of good things about him. When Colt politely thanked him, Kelly slapped him on the back and told him that he was glad to have him as one of his officers. Any time that he needed help, all he had to do was ask, and he would get all the assistance he needed. Colonel Warren, standing to the side, just stood there smiling like a possum and winked at his friend as he left. Colt left feeling assured that he would have Colonel Kelly's support.

COLT'S FLYING HORSE OPERATIVE AT DUC CO, SGT. Howard Stevens, was still recruiting Montagnards and sending them into Cambodia. According to Colt, Stevens was a smart, independent trooper. He was stationed so far away that the major did not see him often. On one visit to Duc Co, Colt arrived just as Stevens was leaving the camp with a large reconnaissance patrol of about sixty-five men, mostly indigenous; the major decided to tag along with them.[3]

On a trail a good distance from Duc Co, they stopped at a small stream to get water. The air was steamy, with a temperature over one hundred degrees and humidity close to 100 percent. When the 1st Air Cavalry arrived in country, in September, 1965, it started sending its NCOs to Special Forces camps for on-the-job training, continuing to do so into 1966.[4] Stevens, a veteran NCO with three years of service in Vietnam, had two Air Cavalry NCOs, both of them new to Vietnam, on this patrol. The two "Green Peas" were loaded down with all the paraphernalia that the 1st Air Cavalry forced them to carry on patrol. Special Forces, in contrast, traveled very light. For example, steel helmets were too heavy and hot for one-hundred-degree weather, but the 1st Air Cavalry required its men to wear them. Fortunately most of them were smart enough to ignore that rule.

At the stream, Stevens put out security in all directions. He told one of the Air Cavalry NCOs, Sgt. "Ray Curtis," to take two of the indigenous up the trail about one hundred yards and set up security there. If Curtis saw anyone coming down the trail, he was to send one of the indigenous back to let him know. The three men went up the trail, and Stevens sent another small security team to their rear and down the trail. On one flank, away from the stream, there was a small hill about the size of a house. He set sentries there too as well as on the other flank across the stream. The rest of the men began to fill their canteens.

The patrol had not been there ten minutes when Curtis came running back down the trail. Stevens heard his equipment clanging before he was even in sight. The man's eyes were the size of half dollars, and he had lost his steel helmet. Between huffs and puffs, he kept blurting out over and over, "The mother-fuckin' North Vietnamese are coming down the trail. The mother-fuckin' North Vietnamese are coming down the trail." Curtis was so excited that every other word out of his city mouth was "mother-fuckin'" this and "mother-fuckin'" that.

Stevens, as Colt recalls, told him, "Calm down and tell us exactly what you saw."

Curtis repeated, "North Vietnamese are comin' down the trail—a whole bunch of 'em."

Stevens asked, "How many?"

Beginning to calm down but glancing back over his shoulder, Curtis said, "Twenty or thirty, I'm not sure … with stuff sticking out of their pith helmets."

Stevens then turned to Colt and asked, "What should we do?"

Making an obscure reference to an old Lone Ranger joke, he answered, "What do you mean 'we,' paleface? You're the one in charge of this operation."[5] Colt liked Stevens and joked with him regularly.

"There's no time for bullshit, sir—we need to decide quickly!" Stevens retorted.

Colt finally laughed and told him: "We have two choices. Our patrol can make a run for it back to camp, or you can set up a 'hasty' ambush." "Hasty" refers to a specific way of setting up an ambush. Colt was an expert on the subject and loved it.

Stevens asked, "Where are we gonna set the ambush?"

Pointing up the hill behind them, Colt explained, "When the enemy comes into the killing zone, shoot from up there. Put some security back down the trail with a Claymore mine and hide a team up the trail with another one." The Claymores would stop any enemy who got away. Each mine weighs 3.5 pounds and is powered by C-4 explosive. It propels fragments that resemble $7/32$-inch steel ball bearings as fast as bullets in a sixty-degree fan pattern as high as eight feet for a distance of sixty yards.[6]

Stevens followed Colt's suggestions and set up the hasty ambush in less than five minutes. He ordered men to set off the Claymores as soon as the shooting began. Stevens told the men who were going up the trail to hide and not to move. They needed to be well concealed because the enemy would have to pass right by them on the way down; when the ambush began, they were to kill any enemy soldiers who came back up the trail. The men readied the Claymore down the trail, but Stevens changed his mind about putting one up the trail. He did not say why, but Colt figured that he probably was not sure that the Green Peas knew how to handle the weapon.

The NVA party walked into the ambush exactly as Colt and Stevens had planned. Forty soldiers came to the exact spot where Stevens's patrol had stood minutes before. They noticed no footprints, smelled no unusual odors, and sensed no danger. Without establishing any security, the Vietnamese took off their packs and set down their rifles. If they had taken the time to set out sentries, they might have found the Claymore or seen something to warn them that enemy troops were nearby. Barely glancing around, they waded into the water and started splashing each other in horseplay. Stevens looked at Colt.

"Now," said the major.

The Americans and the indigenous killed thirty-nine NVA soldiers in less than three minutes. The Claymore went off as planned, and none of the Vietnamese was able to get back up the trail. Only one NVA soldier escaped—across the stream.

Immediately Stevens and his men searched the bodies and collected the rifles. They looked for information about the unit and how long the soldiers had been on the trail. Letters found on the men indicated that they recently had been in Hanoi. Later Stevens would turn in the documents to the S-2 at Pleiku. About a week later, the lone, sick, and starving ambush survivor surrendered at the nearby A-team camp at Duc Co. He had thrown away his rifle and everything else except the clothes that he was wearing—a blue turtleneck sweater, khaki pants, and Bata boots.[7]

Stevens was doing such a good job at Duc Co as the intelligence sergeant, General Westmoreland wanted to hear directly the top-secret intelligence that Stevens was collecting. From time to time, the general would fly in to meet with Stevens.[8] It was a long trip for Westmoreland, even though he had his own airplane, but it was his way of staying in touch with the men on the front lines and the intelligence they gathered. Although this attention might have been good for Stevens's career, it was tough on the team leader, who had to provide security, keep the camp tidy, prepare for the general's visits, and keep everyone in clean uniforms whenever he was there. It also caused problems for Stevens's group commander, Colonel Kelly.

Kelly was bothered by the fact that Westmoreland, the commanding general of all U.S. forces in Vietnam, was visiting one of his master sergeants without the colonel being involved. Colt was not bothered by the visits at all because they were not interfering with his team's mission. Kelly, of course, knew that Stevens was also working for Colt on the secret Flying Horse project. After a number of Westmoreland visits, Kelly transferred Stevens into

5th Special Forces Group Headquarters, as 1st sergeant, for no other apparent reason than to keep track of Westmoreland's visits.

Colt was livid. He called everyone he thought he could without revealing his mission. His direct contact with 5th Special Forces Group Headquarters was Major Ching. But his complaints to Ching went unanswered. Neither Stevens nor Colt was happy about the reassignment, but there was nothing they could do. This transfer shut down Colt's operation in Cambodia west of Duc Co. While Stevens's reassignment damaged the operation, worse news would soon follow.

A WEST POINT LIEUTENANT COLONEL, "CLYDE Humphreys," who wanted to get his ticket punched for serving with Special Forces in combat was terrified of Colonel Kelly. The colonel assigned him as commander of Ho Ngoc Tau, the base camp of Operation Omega, and commanding officer of Flying Horse. Colt was expecting a new commander to be assigned to C-5 (Flying Horse) soon and the project possibly to be given to Humphreys. But before that occurred, Colt was acting CO, primarily reporting directly to the S-2 for the 5th Special Forces Group (Airborne), Major Ching, who was in charge of the intelligence-gathering aspect of Flying Horse. Colonel Humphreys had been briefed on Flying Horse but should have known more than he did about it. This unfamiliarity would present problems for Colt.

The camp at Ho Ngoc Tau was close to Saigon. The VC plagued it occasionally, but it was relatively safe. It should have been a good assignment for a new commander. The all-black helicopters with short blades, formerly used by Colt to drop agents into Cambodia, were kept there, under Humphreys's command, for other special operations.[9]

One day Colt told the operations officer that he wanted to use one of the helicopters the following night. When the officer asked him how long it would be out, Colt said probably all night because he had to drop off some weapons near Seven Mountains. Of course, he planned to fly into Cambodia, but he could not tell that to the operations officer, saying only that it was part of a top-secret project. Furthermore, the operations officer was not to mention anything about the project to anyone. Colt promised to be back before sunup, and the officer signed out the helicopter to him.

To Colt, that was the way such operations should work—everybody helping each other when they could—though, in reality, it often was very difficult to get cooperation when he could not tell people about his mission. The three NCOs in Cambodia had requested his aid in arming indigenous reconnaissance teams with BARs, M1 carbines, Thompson submachine guns, and hand grenades. Far out in the jungle, the NCOs were exposed to the enemy and doing dangerous work. They had not found any established NVA troop operations in the Seven Mountains area, but they regularly ran in to VC traveling to and from the area.[10]

Colt loaded the helicopter with as many arms and as much ammunition as it could carry, plus some mail and beer for the NCOs. The pilots, young army officers in civilian clothes, followed the terrain's contour from Saigon to Cambodia. When they arrived at the rendezvous point, the landing zone was lit up. As soon as they touched down, Colt and the pilots offloaded the weapons and supplies and talked to the NCOs for a few minutes before leaving. The NCOs' morale was high, and they appeared to be doing great.

Arriving back at camp well before daylight, Colt and the pilots tied down the chopper, refueled it, filled out the maintenance log, and went home to bed, thinking that everything was fine. The next morning Colt checked in with 5th Special Forces Group (Airborne) Headquarters, as he did every day, in case the S-2 or Colonel Kelly wanted something. The adjutant had sent him a message stating that Colonel Humphreys wanted to see him as soon as possible at Ho Ngoc Tau.

As part of his low-profile mission, Colt dressed in civilian clothes and lived with his girlfriend in Saigon. He was not supposed to visit the camp during daylight hours in civilian clothes because NVA spies and the VC were always watching. A single civilian going in and out of a Special Forces camp would raise their suspicions, and they might follow him when he left and attempt to capture or assassinate him. Despite the risks, Colt immediately left for headquarters in his jeep.

He greeted Colonel Humphreys with a salute, even though he was dressed in civilian clothes, and wished him a good morning. Without returning the greeting, the commander went directly to the reason for ordering Colt to come in.

"I understand that you used one of the group's classified choppers last night," he said.

Colt responded, "Yes, sir." Then, hesitatingly, he asked, "Do you know about Flying Horse?"

Humphreys, straining his memory, answered, "Yes, they briefed me on it. Top secret. You're in charge of the project down here."

Colt said, "Yes, sir. What I'm about to tell you is top secret and you can't repeat it to anyone." He really did not need to tell him that—it was SOP (standard operating procedure).

Blasting the major, Humphreys yelled, "I'll be the judge of what I tell others."

Technically, Colt was not required to tell the colonel anything about Flying Horse. Only out of courtesy to his rank and to solve whatever problem he had, Colt briefed him on the NCOs in Cambodia. Before he could finish, though, Humphreys rose from his chair and started screaming at him. "Are you telling me, major, that you have three American NCOs living in Cambodia with indigenous?"

Colt was proud of that accomplishment and explained: "Yes, Sir. It took us three months to set it up and three months to get them in there. We took weapons to them last night."

Humphreys yelled, "Don't you realize that you could get those NCOs killed, major?"

Colt thought the colonel had gone off the deep end. With a slight smile, he responded, "Yes, Sir. This is war. You and I could get killed too, at any time. They know the risk. They volunteered for Special Forces."

Humphreys asked, "Does Colonel Kelly know these NCOs are over there?"

Colt answered, "I'm sure he does because I report everything to his S-2, Maj. Harry Ching. He has a staff meeting every Monday morning. I'm sure Major Ching tells Colonel Kelly everything we're doing in Flying Horse."

Humphreys said, "I don't think so. If Colonel Kelly knew those people were in there, he'd hang me." He snapped, "You get them out, immediately. That's an order." Colt could not challenge Humphreys's order without going over his head, and at the time, he did not feel that was appropriate.

After working for many months to get the men in there, Colt had to move them out in a matter of days. Every one of the indigenous Khmer quit. The entire operation was lost. Colt reported what had happened to Ching, who reported it to Kelly.

Later Colt heard that Colonel Kelly called Humphreys on the carpet, crucified him, and then shipped him to another unit. They never saw him again. Colt felt that Humphreys was not as concerned about the NCOs as he was about his own skin. Unfortunately, this team already was pulled back, lost to the mission. Soon afterward, a new CO arrived.

In LATE 1966 A NEW CO, LT. COL. DONALD WOOD, arrived from the United States to replace Colonel Bennett. Colt knew Wood as a "by the book" officer—so straight, Colt thought, that he was almost a Special Forces misfit.[11] A few days after Wood arrived, the major was summoned to his office in Saigon. When Colt arrived, Wood first asked him for a briefing on their mission. He told Wood about the project and the problem of getting people into Cambodia without their being picked up and killed.

He then surprised Colt by stating, "I understand you stole an airplane."

Realizing that he was about to be in big trouble, Colt did what he had to do to protect his mission—he lied. "No sir. We asked one of the aviation units if we could use a light aircraft, but when they turned us down, we forgot about it." Persisting, Wood asked if the major was saying that he did not have a stolen army aircraft stashed away on some airfield. Colt simply responded that the colonel's information was wrong.

Wood apparently had no reliable evidence because he never brought up the subject again. Colt felt that he and Captain Walters had better get rid of the plane, however, and asked Jerry to call his Vietnamese girlfriend, who also happened to be the daughter of Saigon's police chief. Colt wanted her to convey a message to her father. Jerry had taken some men into Cambodia recently to spring the chief's daughter from the local jail and was, at the time, on especially good terms with him. Besides, everyone knew that the police chief was trafficking in all kinds of goods.

Colt and Jerry asked the police chief to hide the airplane until such time as they could use it. He agreed for a price and on one condition—they had to deliver the aircraft to a warehouse in Cao Lanh. They agreed to his terms. Colt and Jerry disassembled the plane so it would fit on a lowboy truck and drove it to the warehouse at night, along with the twenty-five bags of rice requested as payment for keeping the aircraft under wraps. Colt believes that it was still in the chief's warehouse when the Americans pulled out of Saigon in 1975.

Jerry was upset because Wood had put the skids on the use of the army's airplane. To get even, without Colt's knowledge, he moved the colonel's fancy new black jeep, which Wood had only had for about a week, across town and parked it in plain sight on a well-traveled street.[12] Even though it was reported stolen numerous times during the days that followed, the vehicle was never located. A couple of months later, after Wood had been reassigned as XO of a C-team up north, Jerry insisted that Colt meet him in

front of U.S. Military Police Headquarters in Cao Lanh, the big ethnic Chinese area in Saigon.

Colt drove over to Cao Lanh and found Jerry standing in front of a dirty abandoned jeep parked at the curb directly in front of the Military Police building. When Jerry, with a sly smile, rubbed away the dirt over the jeep's markings and ID number, Colt immediately recognized it as the one stolen from the colonel. He looked at his friend in amazement and directed him to clean it up and take it back to their headquarters in Saigon; Jerry was to leave it there and not say anything to anybody. No one else ever knew what had happened to Wood's jeep. It was subsequently found and would later be used by the colonel who would replace Wood. Although stealing the jeep was mischief, stealing the airplane was only one of many attempts on the part of Jerry and Colt to complete their assigned mission. But as much as they tried to hold the secret project together, it continued to unravel.

15 $3.2 Million Missing and Elephant Missions

BY LATE 1966, THE TWO SPECIAL FORCES
officers, Major Ferrington and Captain Cooper, who Colonel Bennett previously had dispatched to the Mekong Delta to collect intelligence and who had received a large portion of the mission's $3.2 million had still not submitted any good intelligence.[1] Colt had been conducting his own investigation and met with Colonel Kelly at least once while filling the command gap between Bennett's and Wood's tenures. When Wood arrived, Colt briefed him on the matter.

The officers had recruited a South Vietnamese man as an agent. This man turned out to be a double agent, working for both the Americans and the North Vietnamese. The officers had no idea about his duplicity, but being in intelligence, they should have known. Colt did not know that he was a double agent either until the Counterintelligence Corps (CIC) uncovered his dual status. A CIC officer, "Tim Hammond," told Colt of the agent's duplicity and was present when the major told Ferrington and Cooper to "kill the agent—ace him, ax him, shoot him—whatever it takes, but get rid of him." The two officers argued for ten minutes that the man was okay. But Colt was convinced that the CIC information was accurate and stood by his order.[2] After the two officers left, he told Hammond to let him know when the agent's body showed up. The CIC had their own man watching the officers.

A few weeks later Colt learned that the double agent was still alive. He heard this news when learning that the situation had taken a turn for the worse.

At a bar in the delta, the agent had had a fight over a girl with a Vietnamese schoolteacher who he then shot. The South Vietnamese police arrested the man and began interrogating him. The double agent began to compromise Flying Horse, exposing it to the South Vietnamese government. The police, of course, knew nothing about C-5's secret operation. Colt told Ferrington and Cooper that before the South Vietnamese finished their interrogation, the agent would "sing like a mockingbird" and tell the police everything he knew. Ferrington tried to convince him that the man knew nothing of value, but Colt believed that he knew better.

Colt had planted two Special Forces NCOs in the South Vietnamese police station, posing as civilian public-safety officers for the U.S. Agency for International Development (USAID), employees working for the State Department.[3] They were there, purportedly, to teach the police about security measures. Colt knew that the murderer had already informed the police that he was an agent. Initially they did not believe him because they thought that he was just trying to get off the shooting charge. When the interrogators asked him for whom he worked, the agent named Ferrington. One of the two USAID officers, realizing that the whole operation was now "blown wide open," excused himself from the questioning and immediately radioed Colt.

Colt sent his XO, Captain Walters, down to the delta to find out what was going on. If Jerry confirmed that the operation was blown, he was to get both Ferrington and Cooper out of the country, hopefully before the South Vietnamese government found out what they had been doing.

Walters learned from the two USAID officers that the agent had revealed the name of one of the officers. He told the police that he also knew a captain was involved, but he did not know his name. Walters quickly put Major Ferrington on a flight to Okinawa. Captain Cooper was already on orders to rotate back to the States, so Colt expedited his departure in case the police identified him.

Before Ferrington was put on the plane, he asked Walters if he could go to his villa to get some personal things. The captain sent an NCO with him to be sure the officer came back. The NCO called an hour later to report that Major Ferrington was burning every document in the villa. Walters sped to the house, but by the time he got there, Ferrington had all the records burning. When asked why he had done this, the major claimed that he wanted to keep the network from being revealed. Walters did not believe him.[4]

The South Vietnamese police tried to "roll up" (investigate up the line) the operation based on what the agent had told them, but they were unable to find a major by the name Ferrington. Apparently the national government never found out what the police had learned. If they had, the consequences could have rippled all the way up to the U.S. president.

Colt began to dig into what these officers had done with all the money allocated them. Oddly, given the CIA's normal practice of documenting every expense, records for the money were conspicuously absent. Ferrington, Cooper, and Ferrington's team sergeant, "Jackson," were placed under charges and their movements restricted. Jackson told Walters at the time (as Colt recalls) that Ferrington and Cooper were laundering the money through a Chinese bank, but that was all he knew about it. This was possible, but Colt could not prove it and had trouble believing that the major and, possibly, the captain had been stealing intelligence funds.

A CIC officer arrived in Okinawa with charge sheets accusing Ferrington of embezzling the portion of the $3.2 million for which he could not account. Yet he failed at one of the most basic duties of every CIC officer. This man, with many years of experience in the CIC and commissioned by the president of the United States, forgot to read Ferrington his rights under Article 31 of the Uniform Code of Military Justice and, even more absurd, failed to ask him to sign a copy of the article. This breakdown in standard procedure was more than unprecedented, it was unfathomable to Colt, who became even more suspicious.[5]

Colt would never know for sure, but he suspected that the CIC officer deliberately failed to read Major Ferrington his Article 31 rights. Whether due to poor judgment or intentional action, the U.S. Army afterward had no case against the major. After the judge threw out the case, Ferrington was transferred to Washington, D.C.

Under normal circumstances, both Major Ferrington and Captain Cooper would have been drummed out of Special Forces. But the next thing that Colt heard was that the major had been sent to DCSOPS, deputy chief of staff for special operations, in Washington and then soon afterward was back in the same Vietnamese town where he had been operating, though now working for the CIA as a civilian. In Washington the captain was also working for the CIA. Colt wondered if they both had been working directly for the agency all along.

Colt's own investigation led to the Vietnamese widows of two civilians who had been killed while working for CIA-backed operations. The agency was still supporting the two women. Colt believed, but could not substantiate, that they were the funnels through which the money flowed to a Chinese bank.[6] He had been unable to confirm his suspicions, but the more he looked into the matter, the more he came to believe that the major and the captain probably did not take any of the money for their own benefit. It did appear to Colt, however, that the two men were laundering money through the two widows for some unknown reason. Was it a form of payback, or was the money going elsewhere? Was the CIA using the money for other purposes?[7]

Obviously the range of Colt's investigation was limited to his area of authority, but he became convinced that the entire operation was set up to launder money. He was not angry about the fact that the two officers were not court-martialed because he believed that they were only following orders. What did anger him was his growing suspicion that all of his team's efforts—sending Baxter into Cambodia, assigning the NCOs to the delta, and using Stevens at Duc Co—might have been a phony cover for the real purpose of diverting the money. It infuriated Colt to think that hardworking soldiers might have been risking their lives in the jungle for a mission that might have been a sham. Of course, he had no proof, just many coincidences that did not add up. In any event, Colt's ability to investigate was drawing to a close.

LT. COL. PATRICK MURRAY ARRIVED TO REPLACE Colonel Wood in late 1966. The following January Colt was transferred to Ban Don. Murray had been drafted into Special Forces from military intelligence (MI), and Colt felt that he wanted an XO who was also from MI. Colonel Murray was very straight with him and asked the major where he wanted to be based. Colt suggested Ban Don because he wished to see the mission through and knew that area well. He also knew the Duc Co area, but Stevens was already there, so Ban Don made the most sense to him. Colt asked for Capt. Jerry Walters as his XO and that his interpreter, Ka-Dam, and a couple of favorite NCOs accompany him. Murray asked him to write up an operations plan. After a few modifications, the colonel approved it and arranged for Colt's team to be based with an existing A-team in the region.

Some time after he arrived in the Ban Don area, Colt and his team had been staying in a small Montagnard hamlet in Vietnam near the Cambodian border for more than a week. The few houses, open to the outside, had dirt floors and no running water. Colt and his team were there to help dig a well for the villagers.

One night one of the Montagnards reported to him that their commander's wife had gone to the stream around sundown to get water and had not come back. Native commanders often traveled with their whole families, moving from village to village as the military camps moved. Colt told the man to round up flashlights and about twenty-five of his fighters in case they ran into any VC. In addition to the danger from the enemy, tigers roamed the area at night.

Colt and the group walked cautiously down the trail toward the stream. The men called the woman's name but heard no response. They feared that

Some Viet Cong had occupied this house under jungle canopy just a day or two before Colt's team found it.

Colt drinks with a female agent, who spoke six languages and recruited insurgents for him, in her store in the jungle near Ban Don.

A Saturday night bath for Colt and his friend, Chaum, a young elephant that he loved like a dog. Earlier when he had taken her to be tamed, her mother, chained to a tree, tore it down to remain with her baby.

either the VC had captured her or a tiger had killed her. Suddenly Colt stopped. His jungle-tempered nose had picked up a scent of burnt wood. He told the men to move farther down the trail so he could determine if the odor became stronger. About twenty yards down the path, he stopped again and called to the Montagnard battalion commander, Yi Yhu. He told Yhu about smelling burnt wood back up the trail, though there were no fires out there and he did not now smell it where they stood—it was not being carried on the breeze.

Yhu asked Colt to show him where he had noticed the odor. Arriving back at the spot, Colt told the commander to start calling his wife's name. Sure enough, she was high up in a thorn tree and spoke in a small voice that she was okay. Colt had smelled the smoke on her clothes from her having cooked over an open fire all day. The Montagnards had not smelled it because they lived with the fires day in and day out. The commander's wife explained that she had seen a tiger at the water hole and had climbed the tree so it would not see her, then she had fallen asleep.

For months, whenever the Montagnards saw Colt, they yelled to him,

A leopard killed by accident when Colt's team, while coming back from Cambodia, shot at an antelope at the instant the cat attacked it. It provided breakfast, lunch, and dinner for the whole village.

Colt shares homemade alcoholic hooch with Montagnard tribesmen who operated with elephants at Ban Don. The Sar, or village chief (out of picture, to right), who ruled over a group of villages in Darloc Province switched over to supporting the Americans after Colt had his medic treat the man's eighteen-month-old baby for malaria.

Colt's elephant patrol without baskets atop the animals. They used baskets only when taking supplies into Cambodia.

"Hey, Commandant, you smell any women up in trees?" It was about as annoying as being asked if any rats had sat on his face lately. Of course, the tribesmen would not joke with him if they did not like him.

Colt's time in the Ban Don area was full of uncommon experiences. When he had visited Ban Don in 1962, he had met some of the elephant owners of the region. After his reassignment to the area in January, 1967, Colt re-established his relationship with the tribe's elephant men. After some lengthy negotiations, he hired them to take his teams on cross-border trips at night.

Colt personally led many of the elephant missions up to twenty miles into Cambodia, where agents and their equipment were quietly dropped off. A roundtrip took all night, and riding an elephant was a tough job. Sitting in a swaying basket made some of the men sore and seasick, yet they had to stay constantly alert for patrols of VC and NVA soldiers.

To get into camp on elephants was also potentially dangerous. The animals had to cross a river, shuffling their way down steep, slippery banks so that they could ford it. They never slipped going down the slippery banks. Although the elephants were about ten feet tall, the river was deep enough to cover their backs, and some water even flowed into the passengers' baskets.[8] Only by standing up in the basket could Colt stay dry. On the other side of the river, the banks were just as steep, and the elephants had to crawl on their knees to get up the slope. But these huge animals were so agile that, even when stumbling on rocks in the river during pitch-black darkness or climbing banks on their knees, they never dropped any of the men. Colt fell from an elephant only once, breaking his hand in the process, yet it was his fault, not the elephant's. He ran this operation from Ban Don for nine months.

During these months of reconnaissance operations into Cambodia, Colt and his teams found no evidence of large-scale organized enemy operations, only small groups of VC and NVA soldiers moving along the border and in and out of the country. Other U.S. intelligence sources reported NVA and VC activity in Cambodia, but at a time when the intelligence community wanted hard evidence to throw back at world opinion, as hard as they tried, Colt's teams located no objective verification.

After his time in the Ban Don area, which ended in March, 1967, Colt went to Nha Trang for processing back to the States.[9] For him, the war was coming to an end.

16   **Reflection**

UPON HIS DEPARTURE FROM VIETNAM, COLT was given permission to visit Bangkok, Hong Kong, Okinawa, Taipei, Hawaii, and Japan, and he visited them all. On his way home Colt learned that he had been promoted to lieutenant colonel.[1] He was ready to return stateside for good when he was rotated back. With eighteen years in Special Forces, nearly half of that time in combat zones, and five years in the line of fire, he felt that he knew as much about its operations as anyone. After three tours in Vietnam, Colt's time was up too; he had had enough of the CIA and war. He had survived when literally hundreds of his friends and fellow troopers had not. He was ready to go home even though the fighting was still going on and he was leaving behind many friends who would remain in danger. His fiancée had already gone to her parent's home in Hawaii, and Colt was on his way to join her.

Public support for the war was waning in 1967, and the United States was beginning to give up on it. On the way home a navy pilot asked Colt how he felt about fighting a losing war. He explained that the North had no navy and no air force. The United States had its navy's huge guns and aircraft operating at will up and down the coastline and its air force doing the same along the Cambodian border. In fact, the navy was so powerful that it scared the Americans, as well as the Vietnamese, onshore when its guns opened up on the coast. The air force's B-52 bombers also scared the Americans, including Colt, when they operated along the Cambodian border. Because Colt's mission was top secret, the air force had no idea where he and his men were operating.[2]

Colt believed that the United States and South Vietnam could still win if we truly wanted to do so. He also felt that the Americans should never have picked that fight in the first place if we did not have the will to win it.

But he no longer needed to worry about such dangers; someone else would. As Colt flew from Vietnam to Hawaii, he had other things on his mind. His military career was nearing its end, and he was about to be married for the third time, to Jane Maeda. Even though their plans were already made, when Colt arrived in Hawaii, he asked Jane's parents for their permission to marry her, which they gave. Once they married, Jane's father, Shigeto Maeda, became one of Colt's closest friends.

ALONG WITH COLT'S PROMOTION TO LIEUTENANT colonel came his appointment as the director of instruction, U.S. Army Special Forces School, at Fort Bragg. Later he was assigned to be the training-group commander.[3] His job was to pass along his knowledge and skills to new Special Forces trainees. He did not pass on only what he had learned about procedures and techniques but also told them about the deeds and actions of those who had gone before them. He wanted the men to understand the standards that had been set and what would be expected of them. Under Colt's influence they learned that each one of them mattered—to the mission, to their teammates, and to their country.

Besides reliving his experiences for his men, he also had occasion to have someone else relive one for him. One evening soon after he arrived at Fort Bragg, Colt and his sergeant major, McRae, walked into the Special Forces Parachute Club, a unique and exclusive establishment for the officers, team

Colt promoted to lieutenant colonel at Fort Bragg Special Forces school.

leaders, and NCOs of Special Forces, where the men all drank together. Unlike other military clubs, there was no separation of officers and NCOs. Just inside the entrance, the floor stepped down to a lower level.

Traditionally when a senior officer walked in, someone would yell "At ease!" Everyone would then stop talking and sit at attention until the officer yelled "Carry on!"

Colt felt embarrassed by this ritual when it was done for him, but it was tradition. That evening, as expected, when Colt and Master Sergeant McRae stepped down to the club level, someone yelled "At ease!"

"Carry on!" Colt quickly replied.

A half-smashed NCO sitting at the bar turned around and saw Colt. He stood up and yelled another "At ease!" He walked over to Colt and said loudly to everyone in the room, "I want you all to know that this is the sweetest son of a bitch that ever walked this fuckin' planet."

McRae was about to accost the man, but Colt stopped him. He recognized the man as one of the Green Berets from Duc Co.

"You see, this colonel here was the only son of a bitch who would come to our aid at Duc Co," the NCO continued. Everyone started clapping and yelling. The trooper gave Colt a big bear hug, and they reminisced for a few minutes about the close calls of that day. The NCO then gave Colt what he considered to be the highest compliment that a soldier can offer to a senior officer.

"If it hadn't been for you, sir," the NCO said, "our asses would still be out there. You saved our lives." This tribute from an NCO meant more to Colt than any award the army ever had or ever could give him. Only those who had been at Duc Co could fully appreciate how much it meant to him.[4]

AS HE TRAINED THE NEW TROOPERS, COLT OFTEN SPOKE of the men who had helped him in his career and of his courageous friends who had died in combat. Despite the many acts of bravery that Colt displayed throughout his career, in the author's opinion, his view was that many other men were superior to him in their performance and courage. Several of them frequently came to mind.

Capt. Joseph Ulatoski, his commanding officer on Nan-do in North Korea, was subsequently assigned to a top-secret project for which he learned to read, write, and speak Russian fluently. He was then assigned in the Soviet

Union as a military attaché. Ulatoski was smart and someone who "punched his tickets" with real and dangerous experience. Over the course of thirty-two years, he served four tours in Southeast Asia. He moved right up the ladder and retired with a permanent rank of colonel and a temporary rank of brigadier general. Colt has always felt that Joe Ulatoski was an extraordinary and exceptional officer.

Sgt. Norman L. Bell, the Canadian who was shot by the sniper next to Colt in the graveyard in Korea was, in fact, not killed as Colt had thought.[5]

Capt. Jones Epps, the brave officer who survived so many battles in Korea that killed many other officers, survived his war experiences, was awarded the Silver Star five times (according to Colt's recollection), eventually retired as a full colonel, and passed away due to natural causes in 1992.

Colt lost track of Kim, his young interpreter on Nan-do, but believes that he was smart enough to have attended South Korea's equivalent of West Point and would have graduated at the top of his class.

Col. Aaron Bank, the first commander of Special Forces, Colt believes was a dedicated and exceptional officer. On his reassignment from that duty, Bank received, in the opinion of many of his men, less than fair treatment, considering all that he had accomplished. When he formed the original 10th Special Forces Group (Airborne) in 1952, he commanded young men, mostly bachelors bursting with energy who were rebellious and prone to getting into trouble. If too many disciplinary incidents occurred in one group, the commander was held responsible and could be reassigned or relieved. Bank was exposed to that risk with such rebellious young men under his command.

As an example, one morning the inspector general was due to examine Bank's 10th Special Forces Group (Airborne). The previous evening after their cleaning detail, some of the men had overimbibed and were still drunk that morning at inspection time. They were so hung over that one hid under his bed behind his shoes, and another hid in a wall locker. When the inspection was called, the team sergeant, Master Sergeant Mancuso, got out as many men for the lineup as were able. Each one wore a short jacket in the style of the one worn by Gen. Dwight D. Eisenhower. Eventually the sleeve cuff of the "Ike" jacket rubbed against a man's watch and became frayed, and it was supposed to be repaired whenever this happened.

The inspector general, upon seeing a sergeant's damaged cuffs, told him that he looked good except that his cuff was "a bit frayed." Rather than simply agreeing to have it fixed, the sergeant, who was still drunk, remarked, "My fuckin' jacket isn't '*fraid* of nobody, sir!" This was the type of discipline problem that would reflect poorly on the commanding officer.

Eventually Bank was transferred to the Southern Area Command Headquarters. His officers and NCOs, however, have never forgotten him. Each year until he died in 2004 at the age of 101, the colonel and his wife were honored guests at the annual Special Forces reunion. And if one asks any Special Forces man to name the father of their organization, the reply invariably will be "Col. Aaron Bank."

Colt remembered other men.

Capt. Thomas Wantling earned five Silver Stars in Korea for bravery, according to Colt's recollection. After his time in Vietnam, he retired from the army as a captain and died a few years later. Colt feels that he was a real warrior and a lively character.

Sgt. Fred Funk, the medic, became a Cobra helicopter pilot and chief warrant officer, stayed in aviation and Special Forces for thirty years, and then retired but continued to work on aviation side of Special Forces as a civilian.

Maj. Charlie Beckwith, leader of Delta Project at Plei Me and other major battles, survived the Vietnam War. Afterward, he formed and led Delta Force, a private group of mercenaries, which he trained in the United States, led on clandestine raids in other countries, and deployed to provide security for presidential candidate H. Ross Perot in 1992. He died quietly in his sleep at his home in Texas on June 12, 1994. To Colt's knowledge, Beckwith never received any type of military medal or recognition during his years of brave service.

Khoi, the South Vietnamese helicopter pilot who flew into Plei Me to rescue wounded under heavy fire and who Colt so highly respected, was killed sometime later in Military Region One when his chopper crashed into a mountain during bad weather.[6]

Lt. William J. Eisenbraun, another brave Special Forces soldier whom Colt particularly liked, tried unsuccessfully to get assigned to the 5th Special Forces Group (Airborne) in Vietnam. He volunteered as a MAAG (Military Assistance Advisory Group) adviser and later was captured in Vietnam. After several years as a prisoner of war (as Colt recalls), members of the NVA beat him to death.

M.Sgt. "Snake" Hosking rotated to the States and became a Special Forces instructor at Fort Bragg. He hated stateside duty, though, and volunteered for another tour in Vietnam. After his return, while a member of the 5th Special Forces Group (Airborne), he served as company advisor in the III Corps

CIDG Reaction Battalion. During a combat operation in Don Luan District, according to Colt's recollection from reports he received at the time, Hosking was preparing to feed a captured VC sniper, who had been shackled to a post, and had released his shackles to hand him a bowl of rice. Suddenly the prisoner grabbed a hand grenade from the sergeant's suspenders. Snake immediately realized that the prisoner would use the weapon against the company command group, two American and two Vietnamese officers who were sitting a few feet away. With utter disregard for his personal safety, Hosking forced the grenade against the guerrilla's chest, wrestled him up against the post, and covered the grenade with his own body until it exploded. The blast instantly killed both men. By absorbing the full force of the exploding grenade with his body and that of the enemy, Hosking saved the other members of his command group from death or serious injury. He was posthumously awarded the Medal of Honor for his bravery.[7]

Three years after S.Sgt. Donald Jones had his arm almost shot off, while Colt was on his third tour of duty in Vietnam as a major and XO of a C-team,

Interpreters Ka-Dam and Jiminy Cricket with Harry Elkims and Jerry Walters (second from right). The interpreters were not evacuated when the United States pulled out of Vietnam. The North Vietnamese killed both of them after the war.

Jones, then a sergeant first class, came walking into his camp. It was like a re-union with a long-lost son. Because he had already been shot seriously once, Colt offered to assign him to a quiet area. Jones would hear of nothing but the toughest area, and so received assignment to Duc Co. He survived, rotated back to the States, and became an instructor at the Green Beret school. Colt's recollection is that he retired as a sergeant major.

Sgt. Bruce Baxter, the young faux-deserter while in Detachment B-57 with Colt, was killed in a helicopter crash while leading Spike Team Idaho on a cross-border operation into Laos along the infamous Ho Chi Minh Trail on November 9, 1967.[8] He was awarded a posthumous Distinguished Service Cross.[9] Bruce and Snake were very much alike, in Colt's thinking—true rebels who were willing to die for their country.

Ka-Dam and Jiminy Cricket, Colt's interpreters, went to work for other U.S. military officers after he left Vietnam. Colt heard later that they were captured, tortured, and killed by the North Vietnamese after the United States left them behind during the evacuation. Colt has reflected that losing the Vietnam War did not bother him as much as losing friends like them and so many others.

None of these brave people risked their lives for glory or riches. They did what they did for their country, their allies, and their friends. Colt would carry his memories of them for the rest of his life.

EVENTUALLY COLT'S MILITARY CAREER CAME TO AN END. Under pressure from Jane to retire, he decided in December, 1969, to leave Special Forces forever in August, 1970.

When an officer retires from Special Forces, he is usually honored with a ceremonial parade. Many of Colt's friends—NCOs and officers alike—had died in Korea or Vietnam. Some were still in Vietnam and other places around the world. Too few were left or in the vicinity of Fort Bragg for a proper gathering upon his retirement, and Colt felt no connection with the people at Fort Bragg at that time. Also, he did not want the NCOs, like so many of those who had taken care of him all those years, to have to march on a parade field in the hot sun, which he knew they hated to do, especially for someone whom they did not even know. For these reasons he declined the honor of a ceremonial parade and quietly faded away.

His permanent grade was lieutenant colonel, though later, after spending many years in the army reserves, Colt was promoted to colonel. But because of an incident that had happened before he left Vietnam, Colt subsequently was reduced one grade. Just as he was rotating home, Colt got into a fracas with a big, arrogant colonel who refused to send in an extraction team to save two Special Forces men who were wounded and hiding along a trail behind enemy lines in North Vietnam. Colt threatened the blow the man's head off if he did not make an effort to save the troopers, unfortunately a threat made in front of witnesses. The arrogant colonel attempted to get Colonel Kelly to court-martial Colt, but he would not do it. After Colt rotated home, the arrogant colonel took the matter to another ranking officer. They tried to bring him back, but he was traveling to various places (as mentioned earlier) and was not located. Actually a message did arrive from Colonel Kelly directing Colt to return as soon as possible, but the NCO who received it asked Colt if he wanted the message or if he could just "ash can" it. Colt never took receipt of the message.

The arrogant colonel later hired a civil lawyer and tracked Colt down and threatened him with a court-martial. Colt was required to appear in federal court, where the arrogant colonel's lawyer had brought a witness, an NCO; Colonel Murray had been asked to be a witness, but he declined. A CIA man was also present but did not say anything during the proceeding, probably to protect against the disclosure of classified information. Colt agreed to a one-grade reduction to settle the matter on the condition that no record was made of the charges.

After the proceeding, the CIA man said to Colt, "Maybe next time you lose your temper, you'll learn to keep your mouth shut." Colt said nothing. Later, when their bodies were recovered, he learned that the two Special Forces men were killed the same day that the arrogant colonel refused to send a rescue team.

Colt recognizes that he overreacted and was wrong to threaten to blow the brains out of an obstinate senior officer. He was hot tempered, no doubt, and was also rebellious in his behavior, especially when men's lives were in danger. But Colt also learned to be calm in battle.

MANY SOLDIERS IN COMBAT NEVER KILL AN ENEMY directly. Colt personally killed more than forty enemy combatants during his military career. Nearly all were trying to kill him at the same moment. He was no born killer; he did not like killing people. His southern Christian mother taught him to believe that one does not kill, and this lesson always reverberated in Colt's mind.

Colt standing in front of his quarters at Fort Bragg with his lieutenant colonel's nameplate on it.

The execution of the VC propaganda team gave Colt bad dreams for ten years. Waking up in a cold sweat, he thought that he could see their heads hanging from the plumeria tree in the front yard of his house in Hawaii. Despite the nightmares, Colt still feels that what they did to those murderers was the right thing to do.

When asked how he feels about his killing experiences, Colt said, "Many times you don't see people being killed—you don't see them go down—on either side. When the enemy charges, to take the territory you are defending, they come out like ants and you see many of them die. You may see a dozen killed at one time, but you're rarely sure it was your bullets." He tries not to think about the enemy that he knows he killed. Instead, he remembers how lucky he was to survive.

COLT LIVED THROUGH THE BETTER PART OF FIVE YEARS of his life in combat, under fire, during two wars, not counting his years of dangerous training. He survived and emerged from these experiences more intact, both mentally and physically, than many people who spent a single tour in combat. His deeds demonstrated that he was tough as well as brave, but Colt's view is that he was amazingly lucky.[10]

He might have been the one shot running up that hill in the Korean graveyard. The explosives in his pockets might have been ignited when he was up the river in North Korea. He should have been with Lieutenant Naylor-Foote when he was captured in Korea. He could have been captured at Plei Me or blown up by mortars or shot with .50-caliber bullets at Duc Co. In Korea and Vietnam he might have been killed or captured numerous other times. Even though he was often in danger, Colt's focus was always on his mission and his men.

When asked for a single word to describe Special Forces, he said, "Dedication." Colt defines "dedication" as "commitment to mission, to country, to fellow soldiers, and to family—even under bad commanders, conflicting orders, and horrendous conditions. It is all about continuing on, no matter what, to complete your mission."

But as much as Colt epitomized dedication to Special Forces through all the years and all the combat, he also remained in close contact with his mother. Before Colt retired, his mother was able to see him promoted to lieutenant colonel at Fort Bragg and tell him how proud she was of him. She was also able to see the house he was assigned, with a lamppost in front of it with a plaque showing his name and rank. Colt always felt that he survived so many combat experiences because his mother prayed for him so much. She passed away at age sixty-seven in 1972.

Colt's next mission would be to adapt to civilian life. After so many years in the service, it would not be easy.

 **Retirement**

AFTER LEAVING SPECIAL FORCES, COLT
lived for a time in Las Vegas, Nevada, but he continued to be bothered about
the $3.2 million that was missing from the Flying Horse mission.[1] He sent a
registered letter in a double envelope marked confidential to General, formerly Colonel, Bennett, Colt's former commander, around March, 1970, containing all of the information he knew about the operation. The letter listed
the unanswered questions still haunting him. Bennett was now commander
at Fort Carson, Colorado, and Colt felt that he was certainly in a position to
know, or to discover, if there had been a hidden purpose to the Flying Horse
mission.

Colt locked a copy of his lengthy letter in a briefcase and stored it in a
closet in his apartment. A few weeks later, while still waiting for a response
from the general, Colt discovered that someone had surreptitiously entered
his apartment. His belongings were not obviously disrupted, but Colt sensed
that something was wrong. When he checked his briefcase, the lock had been
picked, and his copy of the letter to General Bennett was gone.[2] Colt did not
hear back from the general but would not give up.

When Bennett retired from the army, he was recruited by the White
House to serve as a deputy assistant to Pres. Richard Nixon. Among his duties while at the White House was to supervise the editing and printing of the
transcripts of the Nixon tapes before they were released to the media. Bennett
was apparently a very close confidant to the president.[3]

Colt wrote twice more to the general (once was merely a Christmas card
and the other regarded a Honolulu newspaper article about Bennett). He
did not remind him about his earlier letter but hoped the general might be
prompted to bring up the subject. He even spoke briefly with him once by
phone, but since it was not a secure line, Colt did not ask about the letter.
The general never acknowledged the registered letter even though Colt did
receive the registered-mail receipt.[4]

General Bennett stepped down from his government post before Nixon resigned the presidency and retired to operate his own small airline in Alaska. Colt would not speak with Bennett again, but he would later hear some disturbing news about him.

A few years later, when Colt was in Hawaii, he met and got into a conversation in a used-car lot with a retired army colonel whom he had not met before. Colt recalled that the man was a West Point graduate and had been in Bennett's class, stating that the general was a close friend. He told Colt about Major Ferrington working for the CIA after his return to Vietnam. He also mentioned that General Bennett had resigned his political appointment in disgust after transcribing the Nixon Tapes and had retired to Alaska. When Colt asked about the general living in Alaska, the colonel responded that Bennett was dead and that he believed that "they killed him"—referring, Colt presumed, to the CIA. This colonel told Colt that, while flying one of his small airline's aircraft in Alaska, Bennett had mysteriously disappeared without a trace.[5]

Colt did not believe that the disappearance was in any way related to the money, but it ended any chance for him to learn more about it. He was never able to uncover the truth and finally gave up on the subject and tried to settle into retired life. Unfortunately his life would continue to be unsettled. In 1982 Colt's marriage to Jane ended after twelve years. He married again soon after, to Vera.

COLT WOULD HAVE TWO SERIOUS BRUSHES WITH DEATH in civilian life. Once, much of his body was set on fire from an aerosol can exploding while cleaning a stove. The other time was when he came within minutes of killing himself during the long and painful recovery from his burns and his mounting medical bills.

When he finally began to improve from his burns, his relationship with Vera came to an end. For a short time he worked as an undercover detective for a security firm in Tampa and then moved back to Hawaii to be closer to his son. But living in Hawaii proved much too expensive for him. Colt returned to Florida and settled in Winter Haven, where he met and married his fifth wife, Pat, whom he has described as his "last wife."

Colt remains unusually active. Although he gave up parachuting and hang-gliding in 1989, when he turned sixty, he continues to lift weights, run, and play racquetball. Now in his seventies, he still lifts weights daily. In 2005 Colt is happily retired in sunny Florida.

HOW DID COLT SURVIVE ALL OF HIS WAR EXPERIENCES? He says that it was God's higher purpose, his mother's prayers, and extraordinarily good luck. Of course, it was also due to excellent training, hard work, and good instincts. Any bravery that Colt displayed was only because of how much he cared for his fellow soldiers, especially his NCOs, and how well he was trained.

When asked to sum up his life, Colt said: "I wouldn't want to do it again, but I'm glad I did it. Now that I think back . . . was I really able to carry six hundred pounds of rock and sand onto a railroad bridge in Germany and simulate blowing it up? Was I really able to convince a stationmaster in Ogden, Utah, to slow a freight train to 15 mph so we could load six hundred pounds of sandbags off it and jump off while it was rolling? How did all the training get done, and no one get hurt seriously? How did I survive so many battles?" When asked what he wants to be remembered for, Colt responds, "For always looking after my men."

Col. Sherwood J. "Nick" Carter describes Colt as "a good combat leader," saying, "I'm glad he's my friend and was on my side in the two wars I fought with him. . . . He's a man among men and has always been."[6] Sergeant Funk describes Colt as "a Superman in Vietnam! He worked hard and he worked us hard." M.Sgt. Walters, after a long career in Special Forces, has told Colt, "Sir, I don't report to you any more; so I don't have to butter up to you. You were one of the best fuckin' officers we ever had." To Colt, this was the highest praise that he could receive—the admiration of a fellow Special Forces NCO, especially one who had been in special forces for many years.

A Special Forces NCO stationed at Fort Bragg during the 1960s offers the most interesting view of Colt's character. When asked if he knew Colt, he said that he had heard of him. When asked what impression he had of him, he thought for a second before slowly and deliberately responding, "a quiet hero." In a way he was. Curtis "Colt" Terry had a hot temper that got him in trouble often, but his motive was almost always in standing up for one of his men or for others who could not stand up for themselves.

Notes

PREFACE

1. Some U.S. Army Special Forces soldiers object to being referred to as Green Berets, claiming that a green beret is a hat, not a soldier. While the author respects this point of view, most people know the Special Forces as the Green Berets, and that name is held in the highest respect around the world. Colt Terry refers to himself as a Green Beret, so I have used that term at times in this book in referring to this great fighting force.

2. This book primarily reflects Colt Terry's recorded recollections during more than twenty hours of interviews conducted in 1999 and 2003 and many follow-up discussions. Colt provides the dialogue in most cases, based on his recollection of events. Steve Sherman and Edward J. Rasen Jr., recognized military historians, reviewed this book, and some edits were made according to their recommendations.

INTRODUCTION

1. "The History of the 10th Special Forces Group (Airborne)," http://www.soc.mil/SF/history.pdf. Colt joined the 10th Special Forces Group (Airborne) on July 24, 1952.

CHAPTER 1

1. Military records, in Colt's possession.
2. Ibid. See also note 6 below.
3. Physical-test scorecard, military records, in Colt's possession.
4. Military records, in Colt's possession.
5. Ibid.
6. The date of departure of 187th Airborne Regimental Combat Team from Camp Stoneman, California, was September 6, 1950. They arrived in Japan on September 20 and were, four days later, sent to Kimpo Airfield near Seoul. "187th Infantry Regiment," Army Historical Foundation, http://www.armyhistoryfnd.org/armyhist/research/detail2.cfm?webpage_id=390&page_type_id=3.
7. Ibid. For Colt's MOS as radio and radar repairman, see his application for Special Forces Duty, July 8, 1952, military records, in Colt's possession.
8. For lists of additional books on the Korean and Vietnam wars, see Korea Web

Weekly, www.kimsoft.com/2000/book0520.htm; and The Army Historical Foundation, http://www.armyhistoryfnd.org/armyhist/research/detail2.cfm?webpage_id=380.

9. Paratrooper Combat Jumps in Korea by 187th ARCT, http://home.hiwaay.net/~magro/parakorea.html. The total number of troops who jumped was 2,860 men, including all of the support companies. Also dropped were over three hundred tons of equipment and supplies. See "Jack Cicolello," Paratrooper Combat Jumps in Korea by 187th ARCT, http://home.hiwaay.net/~magro/cicolello.html. At roughly sixty-two loaded and armed troops per aircraft and about fifteen tons of supplies per aircraft, the author estimates that seventy-one C-119s and forty C-47s were needed for the entire operation.

10. "Fairchild C-119J 'Flying Boxcar'," http://www.wpafb.af.mil/museum/outdoor/od26.htm; Nick Dramis, "Munsan-ni Combat Jump," Paratrooper Combat Jumps in Korea by 187th ARCT, http://home.hiwaay.net/~magro/dramis.html.

11. Sergeant "Hiller" is the first of the pseudonyms used in the book.

12. On the wounding of 1st Lt. Herbert J. Hedrick on March 25, 1951, see "187th Abn Regimental Combat Team, Letter 'H'," Korean War Casualties, http://www.2id.org/187-h.htm.

13. The Silver Star is awarded for "gallantry in action against an opposing armed force." The Bronze Star is for "heroic or meritorious achievement of service, not involving aerial flight, in connection with operations against an opposing armed force." The award order for gallantry or heroic service against opposing armed forces is: the Medal of Honor, the Distinguished Service Cross, the Silver Star, the Distinguished Flying Cross, the Bronze Star, the Army Commendation Medal with V device, and the Air Medal with V device. These are the medals awarded for gallantry and heroic service—that is, bravery. U.S. Army Decorations Page, http://www.inxpress.net/~rokats/decora.html. The statement that Jakaitis received a Bronze Star is based on Colt's recollection.

14. Colt thinks that the doctor's name may have been Major Carver. He was treated for pneumonia and for infections of both heels from blisters.

15. Colt's recollection is that the hospital was in Uijongbu.

16. For information on Captain Miley being wounded, see "187th Abn Regimental Combat Team, Letter 'M'," Korean War Casualties, http://www.theriver.com/Public/gcompany/187-m.htm.

17. For confirmation of Operation Killer and its official date range, see "Operation Killer, 20 February–6 March 1951," map 25, http://www.army.mil/cmh-pg/books/korea/maps/map25_full.jpg. For Operations Killer, Ripper, and Courageous, see "The Korean War: Operation Killer," http://www.multied.com/korea/op_killer.html; and "The Korean War: Restoring the Balance," U.S. Army Center of Military History, http://www.army.mil/cmh-pg/brochures/kw-balance/balance.htm.

CHAPTER 2

1. The name of the hill is confirmed by the documentation of Cpl. Rodolfo P. Hernandez's Medal of Honor. See "Medal of Honor Recipients: Korean War," U.S. Army Center of Military History, http://www.army.mil/cmh-pg/mohkor2.htm.

2. For date, see ibid.

3. During an interview, while telling this story, Colt suddenly realized that some of the men whom he shot while protecting his lieutenant that day were unarmed support troops carrying packs of food and supplies. Colt felt bad when he realized this. But to him, it was simply self-preservation that day, shooting at anyone who was not in an American uniform.

4. "Medal of Honor Recipients: Korean War," http://www.army.mil/cmh-pg/mohkor2.htm.

5. According to Colt's recollections, the number killed was even greater, but according to the 187th RCT Veteran Association, in a telephone conversation with Colt, this is the correct figure.

6. Colt's recollection is that the number of commanding officers who were killed, wounded, or transferred was between twenty and twenty-five.

7. The order to shoot every fallen enemy soldier, as Colt recalls, was an informal oral command given as a precaution against losing any more men to enemy who might be "playing possum."

8. 24th Replacement Co. to Misc. Group 8086th, Special Orders Oct. 19, 1951, military records, in Colt's possession. This document confirms that Colt was transferred in grade as master sergeant from the 24th Replacement Company.

9. Verbal Order of the Commanding General (VOCG) Eighth U.S. Army Korea (EUSAK) Lt. Col. Westmoreland (authorized), Special Orders, Oct. 14, 1951, copy, military records, in Colt's possession..

CHAPTER 3

1. Military records, in Colt's possession.

2. Westmoreland commanded the 187th Airborne Regimental Combat Team in operations in Korea in 1952–53. In November, 1952, he was promoted to brevet brigadier general and in July, 1953, to permanent lieutenant colonel. In July he moved to deputy assistant chief of staff (G-1) of manpower control and served in that capacity until 1955. "William C. Westmoreland," U.S. Army Center of Military History, http://www.army.mil/cmh-pg/books/cg&csa/Westmoreland-WC.htm. Westmoreland also was an instructor at the Army War College in 1951–52. Craig M. Keeney and Carolina Columns, "A Chronicle of Extraordinary Service: The Military Career of Gen. William Childs Westmoreland," 1–6, and William C. Westmoreland Papers, c.a. 1900–2000, gifts to the Manuscripts Division, South Caroliniana Library, Univ. of South Carolina, Columbia. But whether consistent with the foregoing or not, Colt's assignment to the 8086th Army Unit was authorized by "VOCG EUSAK Lt. Col. Westmoreland." Special Orders, Oct. 14, 1951, copy, military records, in Colt's possession.

3. Westmoreland was chief of staff of the 82d Airborne Division at that time, remaining so until 1950. He was promoted major in July, 1948. Keeney and Columns, "Chronicle of Extraordinary Service," and Westmoreland Papers.

4. Attempts to confirm that Westmoreland dispatched a C-47 to pick up Colt and

fly him to Taegu were unsuccessful. Brian J. Cuthrell, Manuscripts Division, South Caro-liniana Library, after searching Westmoreland's papers, commented: "There are few doc-uments from the Korean War period and no mention of Task Force Kirkland. The papers are more extensive beginning in the 1960s. In the Military Papers series (1936–1972): en-tire run of correspondence dated 1926–1959 fits in Box 1 [i.e., one linear foot in legal-size folders], while Box 2 contains letters ca. 1960 Jan.–1962 June. I discussed with colleagues if such information on special ops would be unclassified even at this point in time?" Cuth-rell, e-mail to author, Mar. 23, 2004.

5. Task Force Kirkland is mentioned in several references. For example, see "United Nations Special Operations in Korea," http://www.korean-war.com/specops.html; and "Korea—Guerrilla War," http://www.kimsoft.com/korea/ccrak.htm. No rec-ords of the CIA operation out of the large villa were located. First mention found of Task Force Kirkland was on April 30, 1951; the first elements arrived at Nan-do on May 19. On September 27, 1952, Task Force Kirkland was changed to a regiment designation. "The Children's War in Korea," http://www.kimsoft.com/korea/a-chrono.htm.

6. There also are two different spellings for the name of the island, "Nam-do" and "Nan-do." The most common use appears to be "Nan-do." See military history, U.S. Army, and U.S. Navy official Web sites such as "Raiding the North Korean Coast," Mili-tary History, www.military.com/Content/MoreContent?file=PRwhaleboat; and James A. Fields Jr., "Two More Years," chap. 12 of *History of United States Naval Operations: Korea,* www.history.navy.mil/books/field/ch12a.htm. Efforts to determine the accurate name of the island through North Korea went unanswered. Colt recalls that the Koreans had another name for the island as well but could not remember it.

7. According to Colt, Nan-do had a low rocky area where boats could barely pull up in calm weather and would have to be very careful in offloading men and supplies, one person or item at a time. Sometimes heavy items, like fifty-five-gallon drums of oil, would be floated in and pulled up on the rocks by hand. Some supplies were airdropped by para-chute.

8. The fifteen-mile distance between Nan-do and the North Korean mainland is approximate, based on "United Nations Special Operations in Korea," www.korean-war.com/specops.html. Yet according to the map at this site and the author's own measure-ment against the map's scale, the distance appears to be less than eight miles. Colt does not know the distance himself but recalls that he could see people along the coast with a pair of high-powered binoculars.

9. Colt also reports that, at times, he used a crossbow with steel arrows to shoot sentries along the coast. For evidence that C-3 explosives were used in Korea, see "Korea Pics," http://www.tjbooks.com/koreapics.htm.

10. The training at Sokchori, South Korea, is documented in "United Nations Spe-cial Operations in Korea," http://www.korean-war.com/specops.html. A good source on the 8240th Army Unit–Guerilla Section is "Korea—Guerrilla War," www.kimsoft.com/korea/ccrak.htm.

11. For confirmation that the B-26 bomber was used for agent insertion, see "North Korean Spy Operations," http://www.kimsoft.com/korea/eyewit9d.htm. Colt's recollec-tion is that the aircraft was an A-26, an earlier model. Charlie Harper (USAF, ret.) spent

four years in operation of the A/B-26 and has heard from others that the CIA used the aircraft in Korea. Harper, e-mail message to author, Mar. 24, 2004. Harper also cites a book that identifies three B-26s in use by the CIA during the Korean War. See Dan Hagedorn and Lief Hellstrom, *Foreign Invaders: The Douglas Invader in Foreign Military and U.S. Clandestine Service* (Voyaguer, 1994), 169.

12. One source indicates that 70 percent of agents dropped into North Korea came back. See Carl Bernard, "Re: 50 years ago today—29 Sep 1950," e-mail to Korean-War-L, Oct. 1, 2000, http://www.korean-war.com/Archives/2000/10/msg00043.html. According to Colt, the information on how many teams were lost was considered top secret by the CIA at the time, but he is quite certain in his recollection that he was told that eight teams were lost. He did not know for sure how many teams existed. Colt knew the leaders of two of the teams that were lost, both formed after he had left Korea and after Special Forces was organized: one was lead by a Lieutenant Castro and the other by a Lieutenant Payne, both from the 77th Special Forces Group.

13. Four PT boats were given to the Republic of Korea in early 1945. "The Fate of PT Boats," PT Boats, Inc., www.ptboats.org/20-11-05-fate-001.html; "U.S. PT Boats List: Numerical List of Boats," www.hazegray.org/navhist/pt/list.htm. Colt did not know about the South Koreans having the PT boats: they were not part of the operation; their arrival was unexpected; he did not know where they were based; and he never saw them again. Also, according to Colt, the two sampans were a little larger than typical sampans; each would carry eight to ten men. On some raids he had to make more than one trip to shuttle all the men. For a record of sampans being delivered to Nan-do, see "Korean War: Chronology of U.S. Pacific Fleet Operations, May–August 1952," http://www.history.navy.mil/wars/korea/chron52b.htm#may.

14. USS *Higbee* (DD-806) operated with Fast Carrier Task Force (TF) 77 from March 18, 1949, through February 8, 1951. "DD-806 DANFS," www.hazegray.org/danfs/destroy/dd806txt.htm. It returned to Korea twice more, including screening the light cruiser USS *Manchester* (CL-83) on February 3, 1952. "Korean War: Chronology of U.S. Pacific Fleet Operations, January–April 1952," www.history.navy.mil/wars/korea/chron52a.htm. According to Colt, TF 77 operated all around Nan-do. See also "United Nations Special Operations in Korea," www.korean-war.com/specops.html.

15. The USS *Iowa* (BB-61) operated around Korea from April 8 to October 16, 1952. "Iowa," http://www.hazegray.org/danfs/battlesh/bb61.htm.

16. The USS *Manchester* (CL-83), a light cruiser, operated off the east coast of North Korea from September to October 29, 1950, with TF 77 and on December 3, 1950, rejoined TF 77 until June 1951. She returned December 8 and operated in Korean waters until May 14, 1952. She returned again to Korea on March 4, 1953, rejoining TF 77 until July 23. "Name search," http://www.nwc.navy.mil.usnhdb/ShipLookup.asp?ShipID=USCL00083; "History," http://www.ussmanchester.com/htdocs/History/History.htm.

17. The cruiser USS *St. Paul* (CA-73) joined TF 77.3 in Korea in November 9, 1950, through June, 1951. She rejoined the force November 27, 1951, through June 24, 1952. She returned once again from March through July 27, 1953. "St. Paul," www.hazegray.org/danfs/cruisers/ca73.txt.

18. The cruiser USS *Rochester* (CA-124) joined TF 77 from July 3, 1950, through Au-

gust 25, 1950. She continued serving in Korea from September, 1950, through January 10, 1951; returned on November 21, 1951, and served again through April, 1952, with TF 77. She arrived back with TF 77.1 (support group) on December 7, 1952, and remained through April 6, 1953. She again served from February through August 6, 1955. "Rochester," www .hazegray.org/danfs/cruisers/ca124.txt.

19. All five of the ships listed above were present for between four and seven months of the nine months that Colt was on Nan-do (October 19, 1951–July 7, 1952).

20. The delay for the timer in a U.S. hand grenade ranged from four to five seconds, depending on model. "World War II Medal of Honor Recipients T–Z," see Robert M. Vaile, http://www.medalofhonor.com/WorldWarIIV-Z.htm. For information on the damage caused by hand grenades, see "MJA: Nocera, What Makes a Grenade," http:// www.mja.com.au/public/issues/may19/nocera/nocbox.html. According to "U.S. Hand Grenades" (http://www.rt66.com/~korteng/SmallArms/grenades.htm): "*Fragmentation grenades* ... contain an explosive charge in a metal body, designed to break into fragments upon the charge exploding. They have a killing radius of 5–10 yards, and fragments are dangerous up to 50 yards. Normally thrown less than 35 yards, that means 'duck' until they explode, and the time delay after pulling the safety pin was from 4.0–4.8 seconds."

21. For events involving Naylor-Foote and his role as a CIA officer, see Lee Wha Rang, "U.S. CIA Operations in Korea—1950–1955," http://www.kimsoft.com/korea/ eyewit9.htm; and (more extensively) "From Pak's to Pyoktong," Memoirs of Duane Thorin, http://www.usgennet.org/usa/topic/preservation/journals/pegasus/peg-p.htm. For the attempted rescue, see "January–June, 1952," HU-1, Helicopter Squadron One: The Korean War Years, http://www.geocities.com/seaunit_5/pages/1952Jan.html.

22. For a photograph of the USS *Manchester* showing its fantail landing platforms, see "Photo #NH 97200: USS Manchester in the Mediterranean Sea, March 1948," http:// www.navsource.org/archives/04/0408305.jpg.

23. Colt refers to this boat as a junk but said it was a pitiful craft with a small engine, a "one-lunger," that chugged when it was engaged and ran fairly quietly when the engine idled. It could transport about thirty to thirty-five armed men. At 8 knots per hour (9.3 mph), the vessel could travel about thirty-seven miles in four hours.

24. It was a known navy procedure to locate a boat at night with radar, sneak up on it, and then hit it with their arc-spotlights while yelling "hands up." For destroyer USS *Douglas H. Fox,* see "Raiding the North Korean Coast," Military History, www.military .com/Content/MoreContent?file=PRwhaleboat. When challenged as to his recollection that a ship as large as a cruiser could not have been the type of ship that stopped them, Colt was firm that it was a cruiser. If he happened to be mistaken, it could have been a destroyer accompanying a cruiser.

CHAPTER 4

1. Copy of letter, June 25, 1952, military records, in Colt's possession.

2. In recommending Colt for the promotion, Ulatoski wrote: "Sergeant Terry has performed numerous duties including: First Sergeant, Operations Sergeant, Intelligence

Sergeant, Demolitions NCO, and Small Boat NCO. He [*sic*] been responsible for the instruction and training of the Indigenous personnel at this base and has instructed in the following subjects: Mortar, Machine Gun, Browning Automatic Rifle, Carbine, M-one Rifle, Foreign Weapons, Map Reading, Demolitions, Tactics and the adjustment of Naval Gunfire.... During his time with Task Force Kirkland Sergeant Terry has at all times demonstrated a strict sense of discipline, enthusiasm in his work, initiative, knowledge, ability, and soundness of decision. He has a high type character and is very intelligent. He has a very high sense of duty to his country and is an honorable soldier." Letter by 1st Lt. Joseph R. Ulatoski, CO, Feb. 27, 1952, copy, military records, in Colt's possession.

3. Undated document, military records, in Colt's possession.

4. Colt no longer has this document, and the author was unsuccessful in obtaining a copy of it from the U.S. Navy History unit. Among Colt's military records is a letter dated October 14, 1957, where CWO L. Edelstein, Asst. Adj. is requesting a copy of the commendation from the Adjutant General, US Army, referencing that, "It would have been from Admiral Dyer, US Navy, Task Force 77, pertaining to directing Naval fire behind enemy lines and an attached response stating that the requested Letter of Commendation submitted with efficiency report for 1st Lt. Curtis D. Terry, while serving with FECID (Korea) during 1952 is not of record in this office," signed Herbert M. Jones, Major General. CWO L. Edelstein, Asst. Adj., to Adjutant General, U.S. Army, Oct. 14, 1947, and attached response from Maj. Gen. Herbert M. Jones, n.d., copies, military records, in Colt's possession.

5. For the origins of the 10th Special Forces Group, see "The Early Years: 1961–1965," http://www.army.mil/cmh-pg/books/vietnam/90-23/90-231.htm. See also "The History of the 10th Special Forces Group (Airborne)," http://www.soc.mil/SF/history.pdf.

6. Military records, in Colt's possession. Colt's application is in the form of a letter signed by Capt. W.L. France, assistant adjutant general, to Commanding General Logistical Command, APO 343, July 8, 1952, which reads in part: "Volunteered for Special Forces training with permanent grade of Mstr Sgt and temporary grade of 2nd Lt. Recommending approval. Experience stated to include: Parachutist, radio operator, demolitionist, combat infantryman, directed fire behind enemy lines, directed naval air strikes behind enemy lines, one combat jump with 187th ABN RCT, jumped behind enemy lines with guerilla teams, demolition work behind enemy lines."

7. Colt no longer has a copy of his orders for the Officers Infantry Basic Course, but did provide a copy of a record noting his graduation from the Psychological Warfare Center at Fort Bragg (Feb. 2–Mar. 30, 1953), which was part of his training. The U.S. Army Psychological Warfare Center was renamed the Psychological Warfare School on December 10, 1956. See "A Brief History of Special Operations Forces," http://www.soc.mil/sofinfo/history.shtml.

8. Article 31 of the Uniform Code of Military Justice prohibits "Compulsory Self-Incrimination." See "Uniform Code of Military Justice," http://www.military-network.com/main_ucmj/main_ucmj.htm.

9. Naylor-Foote was a POW for twenty months, which would make his period of captivity from September 7, 1952, to approximately May, 1954. See "Korean War Project," http://www.koreanwar.org/html/units/usaf/335fis.htm.

10. For additional information (unflattering) on Naylor-Foote, see "The Ride to Panmunjon," http://www.usgennet.org/usa/topic/preservation/journals/pegasus/peg-zi .htm.

11. Army officers who were disciplined, depending on the severity of their breach of conduct, could receive a reduction in rank, a transfer, a dishonorable discharge, or, if a criminal offense, a prison sentence, with hard labor for the worst crimes.

12. During his life, Colt would be married five times and divorced four. He would lay the blame for his failed marriages on his youth, his unwillingness to settle down, his extensive involvement in training new Green Berets, and his overseas tours of duty, which took him away from home frequently.

13. "Special Forces 'A' Team Organizational Structure," www.soc.mil/SF/Ateamfs1 .shtml.

14. This explanation of how Special Forces teams are organized was provided by Colt's recollections and personal experiences.

15. This description of the mission of Special Forces is from Colt's recollections and experiences. Others have described the Special Forces mission similarly. See Charles M. Simpson III, *Inside the Green Berets, the First Thirty Years: A History of the U.S. Army Special Forces*, 1. For a current official statement of the mission, see "Special Operations Forces Reference Manual," http://www.fas.org/irp/agency/dod/socom/sof-ref-2-1/ SOFREF_Ch3.htm.

16. Colt's personal experiences working with the CIA were limited but consistent with what others have said about how the agency often gave direction to, recruited from, and at times even infiltrated the ranks of Special Forces. For references in support of how the CIA was involved in controlling Special Forces, especially during the early days of Vietnam, see "The Secret Team," http://www.ratical.org/ratville/JFK/ST/; "Results of the 1973 Church Committee Hearings on CIA Misdeeds ... ," http://pw1.netcom.com/ ~ncoic/cia_info.htm; The Phoenix Program, http://pw1.netcom.com/~ncoic/cia_info .htm; "Appendix I," "Domestic Counterterrorist Trainings: A Dangerous Trend," http://www.brianwillson.com/awolcounter.html; and "Vietnam Studies, U.S. Army Speical Forces, 1961–1971," http://www.army.mil/cmh-pg/books/Vietnam/90-23/ 90-23C.htm.

17. For information on the origin of the Green Berets, see "The Green Beret," http:// www.101st.org/RB6/beret.html.

18. For information on John F. Kennedy's visit to authorize the wearing of the green beret, see "Place of Honor for Green Beret," http://www.jfklibrary.org/gberet.htm.

19. This story is based on Colt's recollections. While unable to find any other instances of a similar experience, we were able to confirm these facts about the C-47: it could fly at a speed as low as 95 knots (KIAS—knots indicated air speed); parachute drops were usually made when flying at about 115 KIAS since it was a safer speed for the aircraft and any faster might tear the parachutes; the pilot normally slowed the engine on the side from which the troopers jumped; and the normal speed of the aircraft was 130 KIAS. See "Flying with the 71st Troop Carrier Squadron, 437th Troop Carrier Group," http://216.239.41.104/ search?q=cache:4dWJC10NCMIJ:www.71stsos.com/FlyingWithThe71st.pdf+%22air+sp eed%22+combat+jumps+Korea&hl=en&ie=UTF-8. Also, Colt said that by his recollec-

tion, Sergeant Wolf pulled in all the used static lines before Colt slid down the remaining jumper's line. He said that the airflow along the fuselage from the engines pushed them up against the aircraft, which they were hitting. Colt first wrapped his legs around the man and was thinking about how difficult it was going to be to try and cut the static line, so he yelled at the young trooper, and as soon as he did, the man let go.

20. See "77th Special Forces Group (Airborne) 1953–1960, Fort Bragg, North Carolina," http://www.groups.sfahq.com/77th_special_forces_group.htm.

21. See "1st Special Forces Group (Airborne)," http://www.globalsecurity.org/military/agency/army/1sfg.htm.

22. The term "10th Special Forces Demolition/Sabotage Committee" was provided by Colt. It could not be verified.

23. Colt's military documents do not include any reference to this schooling. It was conducted under secrecy, which may explain the absence from his set of orders.

24. Letter dated July 27, 1955, to Curtis D. Terry by order of Colonel Ekman, signed by Robert L. Brunner, CWO, USA, Asst. Adj., military records, in Colt's possession.

25. None of the military records provided by Colt mention his role with FA-56. He participated in several field-training exercises while stationed in West Germany. As an example we discuss Exercise 54-2, conducted in 1955, for which he received a written commendation signed by Lieutenant Colonel Ewald and Maj. O. A. Suchier. Military records, in Colt's possession. See also "10th Speical Forces Group (Abm)," http://usarmygermany.com/Units/HqUSAREUR/USAREUR_10th%20SF%20Gp%20ABN.htm.

26. B-29s were relatively small aircraft and not normally used for troop transport or parachute drops. But B-29s were used to drop Special Forces teams and were operated for the CIA by the U.S. Air Force Air Resupply and Communications Service (ARCS). "Teams were dropped from 500 feet in the dead of night." See "Air Resupply and Communications Service," http://home.earthlink.net/~dale_robinson/airresupply.htm. SA-16s were used to pick up the teams after their mission and fly them back to Molesworth, England.

27. According to Colt, the only reason he was not charged and given a Bad Conduct Discharge was because the trooper admitted that he was drunk and had hit Colt in the face first. Colt did not press charges against the soldier for striking an officer, and the incident was dropped.

28. The six hundred pounds would have represented explosives (C-3) and tamping material, sand and gravel used to weigh down the explosives and concentrate its force, according to Colt. With the sixty simulated guerillas and Colt's team of twelve, this weight would average about eight pounds per man.

29. According to Colt, the men had to survive on food they could obtain locally for the first five days, then, as one of their training exercises, Colt's team taught the simulated guerillas how to set up a drop zone and establish security so that a B-29 dispatched from Tripoli could airdrop C-rations to them. After that they cooked C-rations themselves. During such exercises there was, as Colt put it, "No laundry, no shaving, no bathing, and no sex." For toilets his team had the guerillas dig slit trenches.

30. The name of the lieutenant colonel is based on Colt's recollection; her name may have been spelled "Shimkiss" or another name altogether. We were unable to identify this

officer through air force historical sources. Given that the exercise was six weeks in length, her report, if it could be located, may have been issued in 1956.

31. Colt was originally scheduled to rotate back to the United States on October 10, 1956. But in a military document dated December 27, 1955, Capt. Marshall C. Byasse requests that Colt's rotation be adjusted to July 10, 1956. Based on copies of later orders, including one dated June 9, 1956, assigning Colt to Flight Training School effective August 13, apparently Colt returned earlier than his adjusted rotation.

CHAPTER 5

1. Military records, in Colt's possession. He was learning to fly an airplane called a "Grasshopper." The altercation was not in the documentation but involved Colt losing his temper, punching an instructor, and knocking him over the tail of the airplane after he had called Colt a "stupid son of a bitch" for pulling out of a dive too abruptly, which had caused the instructor to black out. The air force colonel in charge of the training told Colt: "We are sending you back to where you can punch anyone you want. We don't do that sort of thing in the air force." Colt was lucky that he did not get court-martialed.

2. The author was unable to locate documentation for the Ogden exercise.

3. Vans were manufactured as early as 1923. See "James Crabb of Sydling St. Nicholas," http://www.taubman.org.uk/family/crabbbus.html.

4. Military records, in Colt's possession. Documents show that he was "cleared for access to classified information and material to include degree indicated by 2nd Lt. AGC J. J. Colucci." His training included underwater demolition using Self-Contained Underwater Breathing Apparatus (SCUBA) gear. Colt would receive a letter of commendation from LCDR J. C. Roe for "setting an example for the entire group, . . . an excellent officer."

5. While there is no corroboration of such a strenuous swim, assuming that they had floatation support (inflatable vest), there is no reason to not believe it possible.

6. The author once dove in water fifteen feet deep in Burnham Harbor in Chicago on a bright sunny July day and found that at a depth of only three feet below the surface, all sunlight was filtered out due to the sediment and pollution in the water. It is entirely feasible that they had no light at all in harbor water below a large ship.

7. Capt. Robert W. Nollenberger to [Colt], Apr. 3, 1957; Maj. Steve P. Himic Special Orders, May 7, 1957; and 1st Lt. Gerald J. Yourman (for Capt. William T. Rachut, Adj.) Special Orders, Apr. 18, 1958, military records, in Colt's possession. Colt had not received any special training for this duty, only the standard officer training on the Uniform Code of Military Justice.

8. Attendance at the Armed Forces Day air show has been reported in recent years to be around 275,000. "Hundreds of Thousands Attend Air Show One Day Draws 275,000," News, http://www.nbc4.com/news/1468192/detail.html. In earlier days the crowds would have probably been smaller but still quite large.

9. Some people do not understand how Colt could release himself from his harness without losing his parachute and plunging from the sky. According to Colt, this procedure started with pulling out the safety fork from the release mechanism, turning the re-

lease a quarter turn (so that the red marker showed and a simple tap would have dropped him from the parachute entirely), and then bringing his elbows in tight to hold the straps under his arms. He would then hit the release with his right fist, hugging the shoulder straps very tightly under his arms, and pull the leg straps out of the release and let them drop. He would then grasp the left shoulder strap with his right hand while still holding both straps under his arms. With his left hand he would remove the left strap from the re-lease and then grasp his right shoulder strap, still hugging the straps, and with this right hand pull the right strap from the release. He would then drop down, hand by hand, to grasp the saddle, then the hanging leg straps.

10. Colt's records did not reflect his hospitalization, but the timeline of the documents do include a gap consistent with this time period. Military records, in Colt's possession.

11. Colt was released from this assignment on August 22, 1958, coinciding with his promotion to captain. Chief Warrant Officer L. Edelstein, asst. adj. (for Lt. Col. Walter F. Colbert, inf. adj.), Special Orders, Aug. 22, 1958, military records, in Colt's possession.

12. Gen. Maxwell D. Taylor Special Orders, Aug. 26, 1958, military records, in Colt's possession.

13. Colt distinctly remembers the clicking on the ground of both the guard's heels—he heard them when he and Heidi were still twenty yards away—and hearing his own heels, which had brass taps on them to reduce wear, as he walked the post. The tomb has had a pad across which the guard walks since at least 1947, though. Colt could not explain this inconsistency.

14. It is the author's belief that Colt would never consider what he did to be any-thing other than showing the highest respect to his fallen comrades in arms and would never have even gone there that night if he would have known how negatively it would be later viewed by most of those who, in their military career, were guards of the tomb and members of that detachment.

15. Maj. M. L. Hammond, asst. adj. gen., to [Colt], May 20, 1959, military records, in Colt's possession. The secret training was the forerunner to putting teams into Czecho-slovakia and other communist countries.

16. Chris Pacheco, a resource conservationist with USDA, Natural Resources Con-servation Service, at he National Water and Climate Center in Portland, Oregon, states that at Ben Lomond Peak, a "mid-elevation" site in the Ogden area, the average snow depth has been 96 inches (nine feet) and the maximum 154 inches (twelve feet) over the last thirty-nine years. "It would not be unreasonable to expect deeper snow packs at higher elevations." Pacheco, e-mail to author, Mar. 18, 2004.

CHAPTER 6

1. Colt's records indicate a one-day leave on February 8, 1960; the next document chronologically is a letter of commendation from Sen. Henry M. Jackson of the Senate Armed Services Committee dated December 29, 1962, after visiting Colt at Buon Enao, Vietnam. Military records, in Colt's possession.

2. HALO jumps are usually made to avoid radar detection of the aircraft and the jumpers. For further information, see "Special Forces," Equipment, http://www.goarmy .com/special_forces/equipment.jsp; and "Military Freefall Parachutist," http://www .specialtactics.com/halo.shtml. Colt did not teach HALO jumping but did make them as part of his own training. He said that during HALO missions, the aircraft had an oxygen console down its center to which all the troopers were connected until they were ready to jump, when they would then unhook from it and hook into the bottle each wore on his chest.

3. For additional information on the Vietnam War, see the bibliography. For more complete listings, see "Vietnam War Bibliography," http://people.clemson.edu/ ~eemoise/bibliography.html;"SpecialOperations/Forces,"www.ibiblio.org/pub/academic/ history/marshall/military/mil_hist_inst/s/specops.asc; and "Vietnam War Literature," http://www.lopezbooks.com/download.php?file=vncat.pdf. The last provides an extensive bibliography of personal accounts and published works on Vietnam.

4. Nungs are ethnic Chinese who worked with U.S. Special Forces in classified operations during the war. See "Help Us Save the Nungs," http://teamhouse.tni.net/nungs. htm. They have also been described as a Vietnamese minority group of ethnic Chinese descent. See "Special Forces Association, Chapter LXXVII," http://www.specialforces78 .com/special-forces-nungs-1.html.

5. For additional information on Marchand, see "Bio," www.pownetwork.org/ bios/m/m198.htm; on Gabriel, see "Bio," http://www.pownetwork.org/bios/g/g109.htm; on Groom, see "Bio," www.pownetwork.org/bios/g/g090.htm; and on Quinn, see "Bio," www.pownetwork.org/bios/q/q003.htm. See also the Vietnam Veteran's Memorial Wall page, http://thewall-usa.com. Doyle Caton flew with Marchand and Gabriel on their way to Okinawa before they went to Vietnam. He concurs that they were the first two Green Berets killed in Vietnam, though James Davis had been killed earlier and is considered by some to be the first American killed there. Caton, e-mail to author, May 1, 2004.

6. For further evidence that Special Forces operated under the direction of the CIA, see "Military Experiences Part III: 1961–1963," www.ratical.org/ratville/JFK/USO/chp1_ p3.html; "The Pentagon Papers," Gravel Edition, vol. 2, pp. 643–49, www.mtholyoke. edu/acad/intrel/pentagon2/doc100.htm; and "U.S. Army Special Forces Vietnam Provisional," www.groups.sfahq.com/adv_rvn_61_63.htm.

CHAPTER 7

1. The date is approximate, based on that of Cpl. Terry Cordell's death. Cordell was the man Colt replaced. See "Buon Enau Project," http://www.glanmore.org/buon- enao/buonenao.html. Colt says that his assignment to Vietnam was not a standard reassignment in army terms but rather TDY (temporary duty) to the CIA for six months.

2. For the CIA's role in Buon Enao as a "project" to arm the Rhade tribesmen to defend their villages against the VC, see "Air Commando Aircraft Down," http://home .earthlink.net/~aircommando1/CADown.htm.

In Vietnam the CIA called itself the Combined Study Division (CSD). Colt's recollection of this was independently verified. See "Table 5—U.S. Special Forces CIDG," http://www.army.mil/cmh-pg/books/Vietnam/90-23/tab5.htm. "They were under the operational control of MACV, except for 2 members allotted to the Combined Studies Division (CSD) under control of the United States Mission. CSD was the cover name of a paramilitary wing of the CIA," according to "Australian and New Zealand Forces," http://www.gruntonline.com/Order%20of%20Battle/ANZACs/anzac6.htm. We refer to the CSD throughout as the CIA for clarity.

3. "The H-21 Shawnee was the fourth in a line of tandem-rotor helicopters designed by Piasecki. The Boeing Vertol (formerly Piasecki) H-21, commonly called the "flying banana," was a multimission aircraft. The CH-21B assault helicopter could carry twenty-two fully equipped troops, or twelve stretchers and two medical attendants in its medevac role. The CH-21B was first deployed to Vietnam in December, 1961, and was the workhorse there until 1964. It could be armed with 7.62-mm or 12.7-mm door guns. The CH-21B was relatively slow, and its cables and fuel lines were vulnerable to small-arms fire; it was even rumored that a VC spear had downed a CH-21," according to "H-21 Shawnee," http://www.rotorhead.org/military/h21.asp. Truman Foy, who served in Vietnam in 1962, confirms the following story about "Mississippi" Woods flying out in his H-21 to pick up S.Sgt. Donald Jones, who had been shot in both arms. He also recalls that Jones returned to the fighting. For another reference to Woods, see "Air Commando Aircraft Down," http://home.earthlink.net/~aircommando1/CADown.htm.

4. Around this time Colt received two commendation letters. The first resulted from a visit in late 1962 by Sen. Henry M. Jackson, who wrote letters to General Harkins and to Col. George C. Morton, commending Capt. Curtis D. Terry, Detachment A-334 at Buon Enao, along with two other Special Forces officers, Lt. Harold E. Johnson, Detachment A-331 in the Serignac Valley, and Capt. Stanley Hyrowski, Detachment A-16 at Plai Yet, stating that they "[personify] all that is finest in our armed services, and it was a privilege to have had an opportunity to meet them." The second was from Maj. Gen. W. B. Rosson, saying in part that he was impressed to see "the highly professional manner in which you and your detachment are carrying out your mission. I was especially pleased with your own splendid performance." Military records, in Colt's possession.

5. For the spelling of "DIANA one-time pads," see "Communications Security," http://home.earthlink.net/~specforces/spdiana.htm; "For the Radio Operators, Special Forces Headquarters Was Work," http://home.earthlink.net/~specforces/spitsajob.htm.

6. We found no records regarding the incident with Bennefield. But Phillip D. Wilson, who served with Colt at the time, confirmed the blow up and that Harold Haney was the person present. Wilson thought Dave Nettles was the one involved rather than Bennefield, but Colt said that he was certain it was Bennefield and that Nettles was around earlier. Phone interview, Mar. 3, 2002.

7. This incident is included because Colt wants the truth to be told. He is well aware that in relating this story, the reader would be disturbed and might accuse him and the other men of abusing and killing prisoners. In response, he says that unless one was there, it is impossible to understand the "edge" that he and his men lived on, the constant stress from danger and living the life they led, like a vicious animal in the jungle. As John Laurence writes: "The same wild jungle ... attacked them [American soldiers] without

mercy. It gave them heatstroke, malaria, jungle rot, insect bites, heat rash, blisters, dysentery, foot sores, sprains, broken bones, fatigue, and all manner of bacterial infections, until the troops were dead on their feet." Laurence, *The Cat from Hué: A Vietnam War Story*, 370–71. To this litany the author would add the constant danger from booby traps, ambushes, snipers, surprise attacks, shelling, Agent Orange, and much more. On one patrol Colt was severely stricken with cramps and diarrhea, so bad that he could not go on. He asked his men to leave him behind in a thorn tree, but they refused, staying with him in the jungle until he could recover. The team's medic, Sgt. Fred Funk, treated Colt until he recovered enough strength to be carried. (See chapter 9 for a fuller account of this patrol.) Funk, who served in Vietnam in 1961, 1963–65, 1966, 1968, and 1969 (fourteen years with Special Forces of a thirty-year army career), clearly recalls helping him on this occasion: "Colt had Dengue fever [not malaria, as one historian has suggested]. We had a lot of that then. Dengue fever was like mononucleosis, but with a fever." He remembers really liking Colt, who also got him out of trouble a couple of times, and that he worked very hard at keeping himself and his men in shape. Sergeant Funk also confirms flying assault helicopters, landing choppers in Cambodia as well as in Laos and North Vietnam, his rank of chief warrant officer, and his time with the 5th Special Forces. Fred Funk, interview with author, Mar. 3, 3003.

8. See "Vietnam Studies, U.S. Army Special Forces, 1961–1971," http://www.army .mil/cmh-pg/books/Vietnam/90-23/90-23C.htm. This source also confirms that A-teams were split in half.

9. Montagnards were indigenous mountain natives of the highlands of Vietnam. The name comes from the French, meaning "mountain people." See "Montagnards— Their History and Culture," the People, http://151.200.230.122/Montagnards/VPEOP. html. At the beginning of the war, the Montagnards numbered between 1 and 1.5 million. Many thousands died during the conflict. For the estimated number of remaining Montagnards—now far less than a million—see "Save the Montagnards," http://www .montagnards.org. The tribesmen were recruited and trained by Special Forces to fight the VC and NVA.

CHAPTER 8

1. The names of the men at Ishigaki were obtained from a copy of Colt's orders.

2. For the speed of detonating cord, see "Terminology," D, http://www.hydrocut .com/Terms/D.html.

3. Maj. Gen. W. B. Rosson, special assistant to the chief of staff, to Captain Terry, Apr. 10, 1963, military records, in Colt's possession. Colt's documents do not include confirmation of the date he was promoted to major, but he recalls that it was June, 1963.

4. Twenty years later Col. Lucien E. Conien (ret.), who had been Colt's commanding officer at Fort Bragg, appeared in a nationally televised interview and revealed that the CIA was involved in the coup. Tapes released from the John F. Kennedy Library in 1998 also reveal that Kennedy approved a wired message on a Saturday in early August, 1963, that encouraged the CIA station chief in Saigon "along a line that he was already

inclined"—i.e., supporting the coup. See John F. Kennedy Library, http://www.cs.umb
.edu/jfklibrary/.

5. Lt. Col. J. J. McHugh, adj. gen. (for Col. Charles E. Oglesby, GS, chief of staff),
General Orders, October 5, 1964, military records, in Colt's possession.

CHAPTER 9

1. The author was unable to confirm this date independently, but Colt attests that
he has a certificate hanging on the wall of his home from the 5th Special Forces Group
(Airborne) verifying his last tour with the ARVN. Colt asserts that he was reassigned
from the 9th Battalion, 2d Infantry, at Fort Jackson to the 5th Special Forces Group (Airborne).

2. Sources on the South Vietnamese Special Forces and their relationship with
the CIDGs include Special Operations Research Office, "History and Role of the Special Forces in Their Relationship with the Montagnards" (American University, n.d.)
SORO-CINFAC-R-0445; Lance R. Booth, "Gypsies of the Battlefield: The CIDG Program in Vietnam and Its Evolutionary Impact" (student paper, Army War College, 1992);
and Edmund Sprague, "No Greater Loyalty," *Vietnam* (Dec., 1991): 42–48. For these
and other references, see "Special Forces/Operations: A Working Bibliography of MHI
Sources," www.ibiblio.org/pub/academic/history/marshall/military/mil_hist_inst/s/spec
ops.asc. See also http://www.army.mil/cmh-pg/books/vietnam/90-23/90-233.htm.

3. The opening of B-51 at Dong Ba Thin was April, 1964. www.militaryunits.com/
SpecialOps_project.htm.

4. Colt was awarded a Purple Heart for this "wounds received in connection with
military operations against a hostile force," on February 15, 1965. Document signed by 1st
Lt. Charles O. Walts, asst. adj. gen. (for Col. Jack D. Smith, chief of staff), Feb. 23, 1965,
military records, in Colt's possession. Colt also says that he received another Purple Heart
from when he jumped from a helicopter directly into a punji-stick trap. The wind from
the helicopter blades had blown the elephant grass down flat so that he could not see the
trap. He returned on the same chopper for treatment. Colt also recalls that he received a
third Purple Heart, thinking it may have been for a wound to his ribs when a small piece
of shrapnel penetrated his jacket when he was with the 187th Regimental Combat Team.
He does not think highly of this last award since it was for minor wounds, whereas other
recipients received much more serious injuries and deserved much more honor.

5. Document signed by 1st Lt. Charles O. Walts, asst. adj. gen. (for Col. John D.
McLaughlin, chief of staff), June 16, 1965, military records, in Colt's possession.

CHAPTER 10

1. See "C-2 (Company B)," Work-in-Progress, http://www.greenberet.net/books/
CoB.htm.

2. Col. Jerry Dodd (ret.), who at the time led an A-team as a captain under Colo-

nel Patch when Colt was XO, described Colt as "The best XO we ever had." He also said, "He's a fine man. Major Terry would probably never admit it, but he got me my A-team [command]." Jerry Dodd, telephone interview with the author, Apr. 29, 2004.

3. Dates determined from the following sources: "Vietnam, Table 5—U.S. Special Forces CIDG, Camps Established in Vietnam, July 1961–October 1964," http://www .army.mil/cmh-pg/books/Vietnam/90-23/tab5.htm (presence of Special Forces camp at Duc Co); and ibid., "Table 8," http://www.army.mil/cmh-pg/books/vietnam/90-23/tab8 .htm (camp at Duc Co converted to South Vietnamese Army Ranger and CIDG control). For Duc Co being called Chu Dron, see ibid., "Table 2—Ethnic Background of Strike Forces at U.S. Special Forces CIDG Camps, October 1964," www.army.mil/cmh-pg/ books/Vietnam/90-23/tab2.htm.

4. For confirmation that the OV-1 Mohawk observation aircraft, armed with rocket and gun pods for duty in Vietnam, could carry a pilot and an observer and had ejection seats, see "AMS Strike Photos," Strike!, http://www.geocities.com/air_mech_ strike/strikephotos.htm.

5. Martha Raye traveled to Vietnam to entertain the troops annually from about 1964 through 1973. Jerry Dodd confirms that Martha Raye was at the C-team camp in Pleiku in mid-1965. Dodd, telephone interview, Apr. 29, 2004. On one of her later visits to Vietnam, she apparently used the nursing skills of her earlier life to tirelessly help wounded when the camp she was visiting was attacked and nearly overrun. Martha Raye was brave as well as selfless. See "Story of Raye," http://www.vietnamexp.com/morestories/ MarthaRaye.htm; and "Year 1966—Vietnam War Photographs and History Guide ... The History Beat," http://history.searchbeat.com/vietnamwar/vietnam1966.htm.

CHAPTER 11

1. Number of helicopters lost is based on Colt's recollections.

2. Based on Colt's recollection, Lieutenant Caravalho had been an NCO on an A-team during his first tour to Vietnam. After that tour, he earned his commission at Officer Candidate School and returned to Vietnam as a Special Forces officer.

3. This Robert Taylor is no relation to Robert E. Taylor, mentioned earlier in Colt's career.

4. Air force captain Earl Van Inwegen provided his recollections of the events in Duc Co in an undated two-page document sent to Colt Terry in 2002. In it he confirms that he, Maj. Gerry Fritz, S.Sgt. Robert Taylor (flight engineer), and Airman First Class Ray Satterfield made the flight, landed on a foamed runway at the Tan Son Nhut Base near Saigon, and all received the Distinguished Flying Cross and a Letter of Commendation from the Vietnamese Defense Ministry.

5. Sario J. Caravalho, who served in Vietnam in 1964–65, 1967–68, and 1972–73, remembers Colt and is still in contact with him from time to time. They were in many situations together, and Caravalho knew that he could always count on Colt. Caravalho is a third-generation Puerto Rican born and raised in Hawaii. He trained with Colt in

Key West. He confirmed that he was in Duc Co and called Colt for help. Caravalho also verified the substance of the Duc Co story, including the C-123 and the .50-caliber machine gun at the end of the runway, and said that Schwarzkopf was in the camp before the attack but not during it. Sario Caravalho, telephone interview with the author, Mar. 3, 2002.

CHAPTER 12

1. Gen. Vinh Loc gives the spelling as "Pleime." Vinh Loc, *Why Pleime?* (Pleiku, Vietnam: N.p., 1966). We use the spelling most common among U.S. military sources, "Plei Me."

2. Colt and the author attempted to confirm his story with any of the team members who were in the camp at the time, but we could locate only one, and he did not recall Colt bringing beer and mail. The event is described in a letter Colt wrote at the time to his wife, a copy of which is in the author's possession. Letter, Curt Terry to Jane Maeda, Nov. 5, 1965.

3. After writing the section about Colt's trip to Plei Me, the author confirmed Colt's description of the camp based on a photograph obtained independently. Colt later wondered why the camp was built where it could be fired down upon and where a patrol was required whenever water was needed—its lone water source, a river, was far away at the bottom of the hill.

4. In A-team camps, according to Colt, Claymores were sometimes aimed toward the middle of the post to use should it be overrun. If that happened, the defenders would hide in bunkers just before setting off the mines. Anyone not in a bunker would be killed.

5. One historian disagrees with Colt as to who the men were that met him at Plei Me, but Colt is unwavering and adamant in his recollection that they were Capt. Harold Moore, Lt. Robert Berry Jr., and M.Sgt. Everett Hamby. S. Vaughn "Sol" Binzer of The Plei Me Society (2021 Clays Mill Road, Lexington, Ky. 40503) later confirmed that these three were the officers present at the time. Binzer, e-mail to author, Apr. 4, 2004. See also Letter, Curt Terry to Jane Maeda, Nov. 5, 1965, copy in author's possession.

6. The current equivalent of Project Delta, the 1st Special Forces Operational Detachment–Delta (SFOD-D) at Fort Bragg, known simply as "Delta Force," traces its lineage back to such Vietnam-era operations as this. See "WEB Hosting Talk Forums," Jeff Rambo, http://www.webhostingtalk.com/showthread.php?threadid=9987 For additional information on ARVN Rangers, see "SUA Sponte.com—Army Ranger History, Store, Wannabies, and War Stories, http://www.suasponte.com/history/vietnam/units/2.shtml; and http://mcel.pacificu.edu/as/students/arvn/critbib1.html.

7. Beckwith confirms Bennett's and Patch's roles, the death of the Vietnamese lieutenant as well as the death of a newspaper reporter who had snuck aboard one of his helicopters, Captain Moore being the CO at Plei Me, Major Thompson's involvement, the two enemy NVA soldiers chained to their guns, and the name of his helicopter pi-

lot, Khoi. He also describes having flown out with McKean in the morning looking for a LZ and having seen another helicopter lose a rotor and crash. Charlie A. Beckwith and Donald Knox, *Delta Force,* 53–66. Colt states that he was in the command helicopter with McKean, that Beckwith was not there, and that he was the first to see the rotor come off. He and McKean had to lie down on the floor so that they could look out the door opening without falling out to see what was happening. He also says that the scene was surreal because the chopper crashed and burst into flames before the still-spinning rotor that had come off hit the ground.

8. One historian does not believe that two enemy soldiers were shackled to their gun, but Colt personally saw the photographs taken by Charlie Beckwith. This scene was also described in Beckwith and Knox, *Delta Force,* 63. Joe Gallagher, a renowned war journalist, in a very reputable personal account reports the same scene, which he too personally viewed. Gallagher also identifies the reporter as a UPI Television stringer. "A Reporter's Journal from Hell by Joe Galloway," Part III, "Feet on the Ground," see http://www .digitaljournalist.org/issue0204/galloway2.htm.

9. Vinh Loc, *Why Pleime?* Vinh Loc commanded South Vietnam's II Corps tactical zone, where all of this action took place. It is interesting how people see the same event in different ways. In his account Gen. Vinh Loc hardly mentions the American Special Forces or how Beckwith and his Delta Project reinforced and helped hold the camp until the ARVN could organize its offensive and arrive with their tanks and armored personnel carriers.

10. They probably had a small toaster oven or hotplate onboard since microwave ovens were just emerging commercially. The first countertop microwave went on sale in 1967. See "The History of the Microwave Oven," http://www.gallawa.com/microtech/ history.html.

11. John Wayne was called "Duke" by his family because when he was young his constant companion was a dog named Duke. The neighbors soon began to refer to John as "Big Duke" to distinguish him from his dog, which they called "Little Duke." See "Actor John Wayne," http://users.orac.net.au/~mhumphry/wayne.html.

12. The date is approximate. Colt was at Pleiku from June, 1965, until sometime in early 1966, when he was assigned to Detachment C-5. Col. Jerry Dodd (ret.) recalls that he (Dodd) served with an A-team near Pleiku from August, 1965, to July, 1966. Dodd, telephone interview, Apr. 29, 2004. The overlapping months when John Wayne would have been in Vietnam would therefore have been between August, 1965, and whenever Colt left for C-5, which was about February, 1966. But Dodd is quoted in an earlier publication that Wayne was said to have been in Vietnam in 1966. Maurice Zolotow, *Shooting Star: A Biography of John Wayne* (New York: Simon & Schuster, 1974), 385. We are not certain as to the exact date in 1966 when Jerry Dodd, John Wayne, and Colt Terry were all in Pleiku.

13. The legend, according to Colt, is that Wayne never took off the bracelet, wore it in all his movies thereafter, and took it to the grave with him. The bracelet also is depicted on the right wrist of a memorial statue of the actor at the John Wayne Airport in Orange County, California. For Wayne receiving the bracelet, see "John Wayne in the News," The Bracelet, www.jwplace.com/news.html.

CHAPTER 13

1. The date is approximate. According to Colt, Col. Bennett left the 5th Special Forces Group (Airborne) Headquarters before Colt did and before Colonel Kelly arrived in June, 1966, to replace the 5th's CO, McKean. For details on cross-border combat operations into Cambodia, see "Chronology of Cambodian History," Telegram, Commander in Chief, MACV (Westmoreland) to Commander in Chief, Pacific (Sharp), Dec. 9, 1965, www.geocities.com/khmerchronology/tele120965.htm. See also prior correspondence www.geocities.com/khmerchronology/memo111265.htm; www.geocities.com/khmerchronology/tele112065.htm; www.geocities.com/khmerchronology/note112165.htm; and www.geocities.com/khmerchronology/memo120365.htm. See also subsequent correspondence www.geocities.com/khmerchronology/tele121165.htm; www.geocities.com/khmerchronology/letter122965.htm; www.geocities.com/khmerchronology/letter011766.htm; and www.geocities.com/khmerchronology/memo100567.htm.

2. Undated document, military records, in Colt's possession, confirms his assignment to Detachment B-57. Flying Horse apparently was Detachment B-57.

3. There were dozens of different ethnic groups and political affiliations within the Khmer indigenous who lived in Cambodia along the border with Vietnam. The Khmer Serei were considered right wing, whereas the Khmer Rouge, which emerged about this time or possibly later, were considered left wing. After extensive research, it is still unclear with which group Colt met, so the simple term "Khmer" is used herein. But the best guess is that they may have been the Khmer Serei based on the advice of one historian and other sources. Nick Carter writes that Khmer Rouge operated in the region during 1964 and 1965 "because both Steve and I received the same information about them from our separate intelligence nets. Col. Sherwood J. "Nick" Carter to the author, Oct. 17, 2002. Colt says that Steve Mayfield was a CIA man and the guy from whom Colt got his Israeli Uzi.

4. Ibid. See also note 1 above.

5. Jerry "Tiger" Walters, who served in Vietnam during 1964 and 1965–71, said that he and others went into Cambodia on foot regularly and said that choppers did go in. He recalls that Project Flying Horse had black B-model Hueys with the 240 rotor-head system and that they flew into Cambodia. Walters received a Bronze Star for jumping out of a helicopter in Cambodia to help some Montagnards who were in trouble; they had to walk about 2–2.5 miles back to return to Vietnam. Jerry R. Walters, telephone interview with author, Mar. 3, 2002; Jerry R. Walters letter to the author, Sept. 18, 2002. As Colt asked rhetorically when challenged about whether or not these helicopters flew into Cambodia, "Why would the helicopters have been painted black with no markings if they were landing in Vietnam?"

6. Howard Stevens, who served in Vietnam from 1961 to 1969, recalls Colt only a little but does remember that it was Curtis who recruited him into Special Operations, due to his involvement with Special Forces in Cambodia. He operated into Cambodia on foot but not with helicopters and trained Montagnards to use a camera to take pictures of roads and trails being built in Cambodia by the NVA to link to the Ho Chi Min Trail. Stevens confirms the use of black, unmarked helicopters and that he did use them within

two or three miles of Cambodia to drop off agents, who then went in on foot. Howard Stevens, telephone interview with the author, mar. 3, 2002; and confirmed in writing Sept. 25, 2003. Nick Carter confirms that Colt was conducting intelligence-gathering operations in Cambodia, and recounts a conversation he had with John Speers, who was in Nick's fraternity at New Mexico A&M, in which Speers told him about Colt's exploits. He also mentions that he ran a special project called 009, which "had seven or eight intelligence nets in Vietnam and Cambodia in 1964-65." Carter to author, Oct. 17, 2002.

7. Colt recalls that the helicopters went to Project Omega. For the location and dates for Project Omega, see "Special Operations.com," http://www.specialoperations.com/MACVSOG/Project_Omega.htm. For information on the Special Operations projects and detachment histories for B50-56, see "SFD B-50 Project Omega," http://www.diddybop.demon.co.uk/sfdB51.htm; and "SFD B-56 Project Sigma," http://www.diddybop.demon.co.uk/sfdB52.htm.

8. Howard Stevens has said that he never saw any evidence of Chinese in Cambodia, though he heard rumors about them being there. Stevens, telephone interview, Mar. 3, 2002.

9. Harry Ching, who served two terms in Vietnam, the second in 1966-67 as major and intelligence officer at 5th Special Forces Group (Airborne) Headquarters, does not recall (or is reluctant to discuss) Baxter being in Cambodia. He does recall that Kelly was a very politically sensitive guy, especially wanting to please General Waters at APAC (Army Pacific Headquarters in Hawaii). He recalls Colt as having a long background in Special Forces and that he had been in the same group with Keane and Bennett. Harry Ching, telephone interview with the author, Mar. 3. 2002; and confirmed in writing, Oct. 3, 2003.

10. This is not to say that the NVA and VC did not operate within Cambodia, for it has been shown that they did. This only means that Colt and his team did not locate any NVA or VC fixed bases of operation within that country.

11. The CIA, under the Freedom of Information Act and appeals thereof, claimed in 1999 that they had no knowledge of a secret operation under the name Flying Horse, even though Colt still has copies of his orders assigning him to the operation, and others who were present at the time, including Jerry Walters, have confirmed its existence.

12. The $3.2 million amount may have been $3.5 million and had broader intentions on how it was to be used, based on declassified (February 4, 1993) documents dated April 7 and May 8, 1966, obtained from the Air Force Historical Agency by Stephen Sherman, military historian, Houston, Tex., and provided to Colt on February 22, 2002. Charles M. Simpson states that normal record keeping and accounting procedures were not applicable in Vietnam: "This meant that control of materials, supplies and, above all, funds (to include CIDG pay for the Strikers) remained in the hands of U.S. Special Forces until the time they were issued to the ultimate users." Simpson, *Inside the Green Berets,* 156-57.

13. Jerry Walters confirms Colt's recollections about heisting the small aircraft and also about Walters taking Wood's jeep. He worked for Colt and said that he would have done whatever Colt asked of him. Walters, telephone interview, Walters letter to author, Sept. 18, 2002.

14. "Borrowing" equipment was a sort of tradition within Special Forces. Green Berets were committed to completing their mission, doing whatever was required. Charlie Beckwith admits to "borrowing" new jeeps from other corps. He said, "Of course, we had to change the bumper markings and things like that." Beckwith and Knox, *Delta Force*, 68–69.

CHAPTER 14

1. According to Colt, no formal orders were issued. He believes that due to the temporary nature of his filling in as CO until the replacement arrived, it was handled by an exchange of radio transmissions. Dates are approximate but close. Information on the dates that Bennett departed his command, McKean left, and Kelly arrived was derived from Colt's recollections and from "Who's Who from 5th SGF(A) Command Section (Draft)," www.greenberet.net/books/Command.htm. We were not able to confirm Bennett's assignment(s) with the 82d Airborne Division. Colt recalls that Bennett was promoted to colonel when he was first assigned and then was later promoted to one-star and, he thinks, two-star general while there. Bennett's last assignment before retiring, according to Colt, was when he became CO at Fort Carson, and he may have been a three-star general there.

2. Jack Warren was DCO July 1–October 19, 1966, consistent with Colt's recollection. "Who's Who from 5th SGF(A) Command Section (Draft)," www.greenberet.net/books/Command.htm.

3. Colt's recollection is that the reconnaissance force numbered between sixty-five and seventy men. Most were Montagnards. While this is a large number of soldiers for a patrol, he says there were good reasons for this. Operating out of an A-team camp, they did not have the luxury of calling for backup or support. If they got into a fight or ambush, they would be saved only by their immediate "action drill" and "fire power." He could have called for "slicks and gunships," but it would have taken time for them to arrive. "Slicks" refers to troop-carrying helicopters.

4. For the date the 1st Cavalry arrived in Vietnam, see "A Place to Hang Our Hat," http://www.flying-circus.org/history/places/palces.htm. They began withdrawing in March, 1971.

5. The old joke was this: The Lone Ranger and Tonto are surrounded by Indians who are about to attack them, so the Lone Ranger turns to Tonto and asks, "What are we going to do?" Tonto responds, "What do you mean 'we,' paleface?"

6. For information on the working of the Claymore mine, see "Claymore Mine," Wikipedia, http://en.wikipedia.org/wiki/Claymore_mine.

7. Bata boots were of Canadian manufacture and favored by the NVA as military footwear.

8. Howard Stevens spent sixteen to seventeen months at Duc Co. He has acknowledged his relationship with Westmoreland and that Kelly pulled him back to C-team headquarters to know more about what the general was learning. "I had first met West-

moreland when I returned from being a prisoner of war in Korea. We liked each other right off. He would meet privately with me in my small quarters to hear intelligence reports firsthand." Stevens, telephone interview, Mar. 3, 2002..

9. Alpha and Omega Projects, according to Colt's recollections.

10. NVA troops and VC traveled into Cambodia, moved along its border with Vietnam, attacked from Cambodia into Vietnam, and retreated back across the border. Others did find established NVA operational bases farther north or in Laos, but Colt's team did not. See Ed Johnson, "Did the U.S. Knowingly Kill P.O.W.s in 1970?" http://ojc.org/powforum/editor/killpw.htm.

11. The date of Wood's arrival is approximate and based only on Colt's recollections.

12. Jerry "Tiger" Walters admits to both taking Wood's jeep and going into Cambodia (accompanied by a bodyguard) to free the police chief's daughter. Walters, telephone interview, Mar. 3, 2002.

CHAPTER 15

1. The date is approximate. The names in this section have been changed to protect men who Colt believes were only following orders.

2. Ordering the assassination of a double agent was very dangerous for Colt to do. Gen. Creighton B. Abrams later brought up Special Forces officers on murder charges for a similar order, though they were acquitted when the CIA refused to release classified information. See "1969 Vietnam: CIA Assured Immunity for U.S. War Criminals," http://www.safran-arts.com/42day/history/h4sep/h4sep29.html; and Ralph McGehee, "CIA and Operation Phoenix in Vietnam," http://www.serendipity.li/cia/operation_phoenix.htm.

3. The U.S. Agency for International Development, a federal government organization, was formed in 1961 to implement America's foreign economic- and humanitarian-assistance programs.

4. Jerry Walters recalls hearing from Colt about the missing money back when it happened. He confirms stopping by the suspect's apartment while taking him to the airport and about finding the man burning papers. Telephone interview with author, Mar. 3, 2002.

5. The author was unable to locate a record of the charge sheets or any of the discipline hearings or proceedings.

6. This is total speculation on Colt's part.

7. Colt never found the answers to these questions. Inquiries and appealed inquiries by the author to the CIA under the Freedom of Information Act yielded no information about Flying Horse.

8. See "The Amazing World of Elephants," http://www.wildlywise.com/ele_text.htm.

9. Colt was awarded the Bronze Star for meritorious service in connection with military operations against a hostile force, by the direction of the president and presented

by Brig. Gen. Frank D. Miller, on March 17, 1967. The award shows Colt as being in Detachment B-57.

CHAPTER 16

1. Gen. Harold K. Johnson, chief of staff, promoted Colt to lieutenant colonel on June 22, 1967.

2. Gary Weir of the Naval Historical Center affirms that Naval Operations was not constrained from shelling even if they knew that Special Operations forces were in an area. Weir, telephone interview with the author, Mar., 2004. Dr. Ed Marolda, the Naval Historical Center's Vietnam expert, confirmed that the possibility of shelling Special Operations teams on patrol within twenty miles of the coast was a very distinct possibility. "Fire control was done out of Nha Trang and often went awry with the amount of 'Harassment and Interdiction' done in free-fire zones." Ed Marolda, telephone interview with author, March 2004. See "Korean War: Chronology of U.S. Pacific Fleet Operations, May–August 1952," http://www.history.navy.mil/wars/korea/chron52b.htm#may.

3. Colt has no records documenting this assignment. Nick Carter confirms both of Colt's assignments. Carter to author, Oct. 17, 2002.

4. The author chose to include this anecdote about Colt because the story demonstrates the affection he felt for the NCOs with whom he served and because the praise of this NCO was the only thanks Colt received for what he did at Duc Co.

5. While assisting in the research for this book, Colt learned that Bell, the Canadian he thought had died in the graveyard in Korea, though severely wounded, had survived.

6. Beckwith and Knox, *Delta Force*, 62.

7. See "Charles E. Hosking Jr.," www.sfalx.com/moh/hosking_charles_SF.htm. For Special Forces recipients of the Medal of Honor in the Vietnam War, see http://www.army.mil/cmh-pg/books/vietnam/90-23/90-23c.htm.

8. For a description of Baxter's death and the recovery of his remains, see "Sgt. Larry Wayne Maysey," www.scally.com/mia/maysey.html. Baxter's assignment to B-57 is confirmed in a document provided by Colt.

9. See "Vietnam War Recipients of the Distinguished Service Cross," http://www.homeofheroes.com/verify/0_DSC/dsc_rvn_list.html.

10. Comments about how Colt handled his experiences after the war are not intended to diminish any other soldier's experiences in combat. Colt recognizes that war affects different people in different ways.

CHAPTER 17

1. See chap. 15, note 4.

2. The author was able to confirm the existence of the letter to General Bennett and

the burglary in Las Vegas with a second independent source, who requested to remain anonymous.

3. For Bennett's role with Alexander Haig, President Nixon, and the Watergate tapes, see "Watergate Mystery," http://www.tompaine.com/feature2.cfm/ID/2530. See also "The Early Years of Chester Comstock's Career," www.artsales.com/ARTstudio/comstock/early_years.html.

4. After thirty-four years, Colt no longer has the receipt. The "breaking and entering" report was filed in 1970.

5. After extensive searching, the author was unable to find any record of General Bennett after he left the White House. Howard Stevens also recalls hearing that Bennett died in an airplane crash and that some people thought it had happened under suspicious circumstances.

6. Carter to author, Oct. 17, 2002.

Bibliography

PUBLISHED SOURCES

Adler, Bill, ed. *Letters from Vietnam*. Novato, Calif.: Presidio, 2003.

Beckwith, Charlie A., and Donald Knox. *Delta Force*. New York: Harcourt Brace Jovanovich, 1983.

Black, Robert W. *A Ranger Born: A Memoir of Combat and Valor from Korea to Vietnam*. New York: Ballantine, 2002.

Flanagan, E. M. *The Rakkasans: The Combat History of the 187th Airborne Infantry*. Novato, Calif.: Presidio, 1997.

Goldstein, Donald M., Katherine V. Dillon, and J. Michael Wenger. *The Vietnam War: The Story and Photographs*. Washington, D.C.: Brassey's, 1999.

Graham, Don. *No Name on the Bullet*. New York: Viking Penguin, 1989.

Harris, David. *Our War*. New York: Times Books, 1996.

Kelley, Mike. "1st Cav. Recon in the La Drang." *Vietnam* 12, no. 3 (October, 1999): 38–44.

Kimball, Jeffery. *The Vietnam War Files: Uncovering the Secret History of Nixon-Era Strategy*. Lawrence: University Press of Kansas, 2004.

Laurence, John. *The Cat from Hué: A Vietnam War Story*. New York: PublicAffairs, 2002.

Levine, Alan J. *The United States and the Struggle for Southeast Asia, 1945–1975*. Westport, Conn.: Praeger, 1995.

O'Ballance, Edgar. *The Wars in Vietnam: 1954–1980*. New York: Hippocrene, 1981.

Rokus, Josef W. *The Professionals: History of the Phu Lam, Vietnam, U.S. Army Communications Base*. Philadelphia: Xlibris, 2002.

Schwarzkopf, H. Norman. *It Doesn't Take a Hero: General H. Norman Schwarzkopf, the Autobiography*. New York: Bantam, 1993.

Simpson, Charles M., III. *Inside the Green Berets, the First Thirty Years: A History of the U.S. Army Special Forces*. Novato, Calif.: Presidio, 1983.

Taylor, Richard. *Prodigals: A Vietnam Story*. Havertown, Penn.: Casemate, 2003.

Vinh Loc, Maj. Gen. *Why Pleime?* Pleiku, Vietnam: N.p., 1966.

INTERNET SOURCES

"Death Tolls for the Major Wars and Atrocities of the Twentieth Century." Twentieth Century Atlas. http://users.erols.com/mwhite28/warstat2.htm.

Department of the Army. "CMH Publication 90-23," 1973. See "Vietnam Studies, U.S.

Army Special Forces, 1961–1971." http://www.army.mil/cmh-pg/books/vietnam/90-23/90-23c.htm.

"The Events: A Chronology of U.S. Involvement in the Vietnam War." History Central.com. http://www.multied.com/Vietnam/events.html.

Liberation and the Korean War. http://myhome.shinbiro.com/~mssi/preface.html.

Rotter, Andrew J. "The Causes of the Vietnam War." From *The Oxford Companion to American Military History*, ed. John Whiteclay Chambers II, 1999. http://www.english.uiuc.edu/maps/vietnam/causes.htm.

Schnabel, James F. *United States Army in the Korean War, Policy and Direction: The First Year.* 1972; Washington, D.C.: U.S. Army Center of Military History, 1992. http://www.army.mil/cmh-pg/books/P&d.htm.

"United States Army: Articles and Resources." http://usmilitary.about.com/careers/usmilitary/msub2.htm.

Index

Photos are indicated with *italic* type.